THE ORWELLIAN WORLD
OF JEHOVAH'S WITNESSES

HEATHER & GARY BOTTING

The Orwellian World of Jehovah's Witnesses

UNIVERSITY OF TORONTO PRESS
Toronto Buffalo London

© University of Toronto Press 1984
Toronto Buffalo London
Printed in Canada

ISBN 0-8020-2537-4 (cloth)
ISBN 0-8020-6545-7 (paper)

Canadian Cataloguing in Publication Data

Botting, Gary, 1943-
The Orwellian world of Jehovah's Witnesses
Bibliography: p.
Includes index.
ISBN 0-8020-2537-4 (bound). - ISBN 0-8020-6545-7 (pbk.)
1. Jehovah's Witnesses. 2. Orwell, George, 1903-1950.
Nineteen eighty-four. I. Botting, Heather Denise
Harden. II. Title.
BX8526.B67 1984   289.9′2   C84-098402-2

EXCERPTS FROM *NINETEEN EIGHTY-FOUR* BY GEORGE ORWELL ARE REPRINTED BY
PERMISSION OF HARCOURT BRACE JOVANOVICH, INC.; COPYRIGHT 1949 BY HARCOURT
BRACE JOVANOVICH, INC., RENEWED IN 1977 BY SONIA BROWNELL ORWELL.
GRATEFUL ACKNOWLEDGMENT IS ALSO MADE TO THE ESTATE OF THE LATE SONIA
BROWNELL ORWELL AND SECKER & WARBURG LTD FOR PERMISSION TO REPRODUCE
THESE EXCERPTS.

Publication of this work has been assisted under the block grant program
of the Ontario Arts Council.

There are certain people ... whom one cannot answer. You just have to go on saying your say regardless of them, and then the extraordinary thing is that they may start listening.

George Orwell, on his deathbed, to Stephen Spender, January 1950

Contents

The millenarian convert faces a potentially devastating contradiction. He has made a profound psychic investment in a set of beliefs ... at the price of abandoning whatever satisfactions might still have been obtainable from his old life. Yet he is now prey to an environment which may at any moment render those beliefs false and absurd.

Michael Barkun *Disaster and the Millennium*

The world of to-day is a bare, hungry, dilapidated place compared with the world that existed before 1914, and still more so if compared with the imaginary future to which the people of that period looked forward ... The idea of an earthly paradise in which men should live together in a state of brotherhood ... had haunted the human imagination for thousands of years.

George Orwell *Nineteen Eighty-Four*

'And YOU will know the truth, and the truth will set YOU free.'

Jesus Christ John 8:32 (*NWT*)

Preface

The greater the understanding, the greater the delusion. (*1984*, 216)

At the age of five, I placed my first *Watchtower* magazine with a Cambridge-shire housewife who had been won over by my tears. Never before had I delivered an oral speech in public to a complete stranger; in fact, my very first outing as a publisher or lay minister for Jehovah's Witnesses had come as a complete surprise. Usually, young children went along from house to house with adult Witnesses without saying a word. On this particular occasion, though, we were short of adults, and my sister, two years my senior, reluctantly agreed to drag me along with her. We went to the first door. To help her out, I knocked loudly on the door panel.

'Shhh! Not so loud!' whispered my sister

But it was too late. The door opened.

'Yes?' said the housewife.

I gazed up at the woman in awe. Then I glanced across at my sister who, to my utter consternation, was staring back at me.

'It's your turn,' she muttered.

'No. It's yours.'

'*You* knocked.'

'What do you want?' demanded the woman.

'Will you get on with it?' my sister hissed.

And so I stammered my way through an impromptu and very inadequate presentation of *The Watchtower* and *Awake!*

'I'm not interested,' snapped the woman when I had finished my pitiful pitch; and she shut the door decisively in our faces. We retreated down the walkway to the road.

'That was really mean!' I protested to my sister loudly. She walked on towards the next house. More from anger than anything else, my tears began to flow. 'That was really, really mean!' I cried.

My sister paused outside the next house. 'Are you coming?' she asked casually. 'This one's mine.'

But I was too upset. I stood beside the roadway watching her as, ever so softly, she knocked on the outside of the stucco-bolstered door-frame. Nobody answered. She waited a full two minutes and knocked again, slightly louder. No response. She breathed a sigh of relief. But as she left the house, the woman from next door, now dressed in a raincoat and carrying an empty shopping bag, approached us briskly, a slight frown on her face. She glared down at me. I flinched away.

'How old are you?' she asked.

'He's five. I'm seven,' my sister volunteered.

'Five!' The woman crouched down before me. 'And how much are your magazines?' she asked, looking me full in the face.

'S-sixpence,' I managed.

Incredibly, the woman fished into her purse and produced two threepenny bits. She pressed them into my left hand and took the magazines from my right. I beamed up at her through eyes still awash with tears. The lady gently wiped a tear from my cheek with her thumb and then marched off primly down the road towards Castle Street with never a look behind.

From that moment on, I became a regular publisher for Jehovah's Witnesses, meeting my quota of ten hours and twelve magazine placements per month, every month. Within a year, the time came for me to give my first talk in the Theocratic Ministry School at the Cambridgeshire Labour Hall, which at that time doubled as a Kingdom Hall. Standing before the makeshift podium, I fixed my eye on an overlooked cobweb in the extreme top left-hand corner of the huge, echoey room and delivered by rote a six-minute sermon called 'Knorr-and-the-Ark,' in which I recited Watch Tower Society speculations on the size of the ship and the number of representative specimens of every kind of beast and bird and butterfly ('seven clean, two unclean') that God had gathered together to escape the flood. It was not until several years later that I was able to distinguish between Noah, the patriarch of old, and Nathan H. Knorr, the president of the Watch Tower Bible and Tract Society; to my uncritical, six-year-old mind they were one and the same man.

In July 1953, my mother attended the international convention of Jehovah's Witnesses in New York and was so impressed by Canada (she had visited her aunt in Ontario) that she decided to immigrate right away (my father, an RAF navigator with the Dambusters, had been killed in action over Germany in 1943 when I was barely a month old; my mother had become a Jehovah's Witness in 1948). Mother soon became fast friends with the Canadian Jehovah's Witness establishment: with Brother Laurier Saumur, the district servant who had been persecuted in Quebec by the Duplessis regime; with Brother Percy Chapman, the branch Servant; with Brother Glen How, the Watch Tower Society's lawyer; with Brother Don Mills, now a member of the Canadian Branch Committee; with Brother Leo Greenlees and Brother Carey Barbour, now both members of the Governing Body of the Watch Tower Bible and Tract Society in Brooklyn. We helped build the Kingdom Hall in Peterborough, published regularly, and spent every summer 'vacation pioneering' – distributing literature for at least a hundred hours per month.

Immediately after my twelfth uncelebrated birthday, in July 1955, I was 'baptized' at a major district convention in New York. There for the first time I heard in person the mystical Brother Knorr give a series of rousing addresses (although I could not remember what they were about). I wanted to talk to him – to tell him what a privilege it was to be aboard his ship – and to tell him about my childish confusion, half a lifetime before, when I had mistaken the patriarch of Jehovah's Witnesses for the patriarch of the Jews. But he was inaccessible, I was told by the convention's administration office. Especially, apparently, to twelve-year-olds, however freshly baptized.

A young black friend from Brooklyn who seemed to be in the know told me that he had seen Knorr arriving earlier that day in a brand new Cadillac which was now parked at the far end of Yankee Stadium. We found the car and stood guard within earshot of the packed stadium; at last – after a three-hour wait – Brother Knorr emerged from the end door of the stadium near the bleachers. He was accompanied by a swarthy-looking gentleman dressed in a black suit. Ecstatically, I rushed up to them.

'Brother Noah! Brother Noah!' I called, unwittingly adopting the accent of my new-found friend.

Brother Knorr glanced cursorily my way over his rimless glasses as he slid sideways onto the passenger seat. As I approached the limousine, he slammed the door in my face, and then stared stonily ahead, ignoring me. The gentleman in black snarled, pointing at me with a crooked finger.

'Get back!'

The 'gentleman' got into the car beside Brother Knorr and drove away, leaving me in a state of shock in the parking lot.

I tried to interview Brother Knorr on four other occasions subsequent to the 1955 episode – three times for the Convention News Service (in New York in 1958, Ottawa in 1959, and London, England, in 1961) and once for an independent newspaper, the *South China Morning Post* (in Hong Kong in 1963). Each time, I was brushed aside, on two occasions physically, by individuals who for all the world appeared to be bodyguards.

By contrast, I found Frederick Franz, then vice-president of the Watch Tower Society (and now the president), not only approachable but downright jovial and jocular. During the 1961 convention at Wembley Stadium in London, Franz invited pioneer members of the News Service, including myself, to share a Chinese dinner, and he was the life of the party, incessantly cracking jokes and recounting anecdotes that reinforced for everyone there the notion that the man was witty as well as wise. Whereas Brother Knorr left me cold, Brother Franz was an inspiration and, owing largely to his incentive, I resolved to go pioneering overseas, beginning with a most difficult and dangerous assignment: smuggling banned anti-Franco Watch Tower Society literature – mostly tracts – into Spain. Several of our fellow-smugglers were arrested and got up to two years in jail.

Even before my first timorous steps as a witness of Jehovah, I had started collecting moths. There I started with a bang rather than a whimper: my first moth, found on a roadside in the English village of Radley when I was four years old, was a rare and portentous Death's-Head Hawk (*Acherontia atropos*), named for the prominent skull-and-crossbones design on its huge, furry thorax. It flapped feebly at the side of the narrow road, having been hit by a car, I suppose. I gathered the trembling creature into my hands and hurried home on my tricycle. My mother recognized it for what it was, and we became instant celebrities: post-war England seemed to take an uncanny interest in peaceful pursuits such as collecting butterflies and moths.

Subsequent to our move to Cambridge in 1948, I collected moths with increasing eagerness, and eventually built breeding cages to house caterpillars. We traded back and forth at school, and my collection grew. After immigrating to Canada in 1954, I collected Canadian moths, including the largest on record – a Cecropia moth (*Hyalophora cecropia*) measuring eight inches across.

I raised larvae from eggs laid by captive females and later imported many live specimens from around the world and reared them in the attic. With the onset of adolescence, I found myself more and more engrossed in the possibility of hybridizing exotic species.

Jehovah's Witnesses believe that all terrestrial animals – including insects – descended from archetypal generic 'kinds' that survived the flood. The message of 'Knorr-and-the-Ark' may have been lost on the vast majority of witnesses in the Cambridge Congregation, but it had certainly not been lost on me. I wanted to prove that all silk moths (for example) could have descended from a pair of archetypal silk moths that had docked with Noah on Mount Ararat a scant four millennia before. Systematically I imported moths from east and west of Mount Ararat – including silk moths of the *Philosamia* genus from India and Japan to the east, and Malta and Italy to the west of the fabulous mountain. I hybridized them in every possible combination, ending up with insects that approximated those closest to the posited point of origin. Then I went farther afield, genetically speaking, crossing European with North American species, and eventually hybridizing moths of different genera. My experiments left the classification system of lepidoptera in a shambles, and entomologists have since reclassified the entire order.

My experiments were conducted at home without the knowledge of school or congregation, for I had been brought up to believe that sex was 'dirty,' and what I was doing to my bugs to get them to mate involved some pretty nifty surgery, entailing modification of genitalia and transplanting of female scent organs, that would be deemed unconventional even by today's standards. The results of the experiments were eventually exhibited at the Ontario Science Fairs of 1960 and 1961. On both occasions my exhibits (the first on the *Philosamia* genus, and the second on intergeneric hybridization) won top prize. I also placed first in biology and 'pest control' in the two U.S. National Science Fairs of 1960 and 1961, held at Indianapolis and Kansas City. After winning in Indianapolis, I travelled first around America and then around the world, sponsored by the American Institute of Biological Sciences and the U.S. National Academy of Sciences, hobnobbing with well-known biologists as I uttered Witness creationist theories and reiterated with increasing complexity my sermon about 'Knorr-and-the Ark.' One of the American scientists who followed my early theories with a certain amount of dismay offered me a $10,000 scholarship to study biology for three years at the University of Arkansas. I spent the summer of 1960 in Arkansas, collecting butterflies, moths, and snakes, but most of my time was spent in preaching from house to house with Jehovah's Witnesses. The herpetologist who had befriended me was not impressed with my beliefs, and stipulated in the scholarship offer that I should no longer associate with Jehovah's Witnesses. When I would not agree to this stipulation, he wrote 'VOID' in big letters across the document. This Faustian temptation had been far too blatant to be a threat to faith, even for a boy of sixteen; in fact, it rather reinforced my faith by providing a sweet foretaste of 'persecution.'

In January 1961, while touring India with my exhibit, I met Professor J.B.S. Haldane, a prominent British scientist who had become a naturalized Indian citizen and who ran the Indian Statistical Institute in Calcutta. It happened that he and his wife, Dr Helen Spurway, had been experimenting with silk moths, some of which were of the same species as those I had hybridized. He volunteered to read over a 1,000-page manuscript I had written about my experiments.

We struck up a friendship, and after several hours of chatting generally about moths and what could be done with them to get them to co-operate in the hybridizing process I enunciated my theories regarding the origin of species, realizing that Haldane was a confirmed Lamarckian evolutionist. The butterflies and moths had all branched out from the archetypal pairs that had landed on Ararat, I explained quite seriously, and had diversified and speciated from basic 'kinds' as they went. The same was true of all the other species of animal life – the various birds and terrestrial reptiles, not to mention donkeys, monkeys, cats, and cows ...

'... kangaroos?' he said.

'And kangaroos.'

'And platypuses?'

'Uh – they're aquatic.'

'I see.'

'Look at the emu of Australia, the ostrich of South Africa, and the rhea of Argentina,' I continued brightly. 'Look at the snow leopard of China and the jaguar of Brazil. Look at the anteater and the aardvark and the armadillo. Look at –'

'I get your drift,' said Haldane. He rolled forward in his wheelchair (he had fallen down a mineshaft in Ceylon two weeks before and had broken several ribs and his left leg, so under his saffron pajamas he wore a cumbersome body cast that seemed to extend on one side down to his toes). 'I want you to meet me at the Calcutta Zoo at five a.m. sharp on Saturday morning,' he added.

'Here, I'll write it on your itinerary so you won't forget. Think you can do that?'

'Five a.m.? But why?'

'I want to show you something. Something very important.'

And so at five the following Saturday we met outside the zoo. It was still dark; the place was silent. I strolled beside Haldane as he wheeled his chair down the asphalt sidewalk past the big cats (leopards and jaguars, I noticed) and an assortment of edentates (anteaters and aardvarks). But we did not stop.

'We don't want to be late!' he said.

We made our way beneath snaking banyans to the edge of the park where a rainbow-arched footbridge spanned a tiny tributary of the Ganges. There, Haldane parked his wheelchair and stood up beside me on the bridge, silhouetted by the faint glow of the pre-dawn sky. I could make out his bulky torso; he was still dressed in his favourite saffron pajamas. He cocked his huge bald head with its bushy walrus moustache and stood there, waiting for I knew not what.

'There!' he said at length.

'What?'

'That's the first of them. Now shhh!'

I hadn't seen or heard a thing.

A full minute passed. Then close overhead a bevy of sandpipers whistled by.

'*Hydrophasianus chirurgus,*' Haldane murmured. It sounded like an invocation.

'What?'

'Pheasant-tailed jacanas,' he said. 'Shhh!'

Birds stitched the sky, at first in broad and arbitrary patterns and then in tight swooping formations moving at different speeds, in different directions and, mercifully, at different heights. Haldane knew them all, from sarus cranes to florikens, from chukors to bee-eaters, from barbets to sunbirds, from drongos to shrikes. Some, such as the terns and ibises, sounded familiar. Others, like the rusty-cheeked scimitar-babblers and the red-billed leiothrixes, sounded like a put-on, but when I challenged him on his identification of a flock of blossom-headed parakeets, he merely intoned in Latin, '*Psitticula cyanocephala bengalensis,*' with enough flair and flourish to allay any doubts.

'Linnaeus?' I asked feebly.

'Linnaeus,' he replied.

Lucky guess.

There were hundreds of species, tiered – even before the sunlight broke over the horizon – to a height of perhaps a mile, zipping endlessly back and forth, a living tapestry of moving warp and woof, swooping at random across the limitless expanse of gradually lightening blue. And then the uppermost birds caught the sun, glinting and flashing back irridescent hues of every colour. There were Indian swifts and turtle doves, sheldrakes and paddybirds, kingfishers, coppersmiths, bulbuls, and mynas – and even farther aloft, fishing-eagles and harriers and kestrels and kites – an endless assortment of birds, birds, birds, birds, birds, each species flying its particular flight path with unique beat of wing, spiralling upwards higher and higher to greet the rising winter sun. And when finally it dawned, all the birds seemed for an instant frozen in time and space, layer upon layer upon layer in a timeless daguerrotype of Being.

'Three hundred and ten species,' Haldane murmured reverently.

'Here?'

'In all of India. Representing two hundred and thirty-eight genera, sixty-two families, nineteen different orders – '

We stood there for perhaps another half-hour in absolute silence, until the sun rose over the trees and the birds dissipated, drifting off in various directions to busy themselves for another day. The marvel I had seen on the bridge – the Eternal Now of the moment of dawn – remained indelibly impressed on my brain like an after-image. It remains still.

'All of them on the ark,' Haldane was saying. 'And this is only India, and only the birds –'

'Some of them,' I replied lamely, 'were aquatic.'

Haldane's guffaw seemed to be a violation of the peace and holiness of the place, and I was relieved when he suggested returning to the cars.

Haldane had scheduled a dinner party for me and Susan Brown, a Texan student with whom I was travelling – herself a winner of the physical sciences division of the 1960 National Science Fair. But the American cultural attaché, Duncan Emery, felt that we had had quite enough exposure to J.B.S. Haldane, who had made his reputation in India partly because of his socialist sympathies. Haldane had, after all, done a considerable amount of research in Russia, including the successful transplant of the head of a dog, and there were some who thought his methods were unsound. I thought about my own sexual mutilations of hapless moths and kept resolutely quiet.

We were not to dine with Haldane, we were told. Instead, we should go to the Indo-American Society's headquarters, where IAS president Pushpa Sehney would be expecting us.

I telephoned Haldane's secretary, Mr Krishna, to cancel our engagement, but he did not convey the message; instead he took us out for a lunch of Tundory goat and tried to persuade us to disobey our 'orders' from Mr Emery. We explained that our prolonged stay with Haldane on the first visit had caused us to miss an engagement with the Indo-American Society, an engagement that had been rescheduled for the evening of Haldane's dinner party. Despite our excuses and explanations, when we arrived back at the Oberoi Grand Hotel to change prior to the rescheduled IAS function, Professor Haldane was sitting large as life in an armchair in my hotel room, his encased leg resting on the coffee table. He was reading my manuscript, making notes in the margins. Dr Spurway and Mr Krishna sat on the bed. Haldane looked up as I entered.

'Good stuff!' he said, tapping the manuscript. 'A trifle repetitious in places, but –' He noticed my consternation. 'Well? Are you ready?'

'But we told Mr Krishna on at least two occasions – Didn't he tell you? We have another engagement. We can't come!'

'What?' shouted Haldane.

'What?' shrieked Helen Spurway.

'What?' squeaked Krishna.

And then the shouting began. The roaring. The out-and-out frenetic tantrum of a man who is used to having his way. He had invited many guests, he raged. They were coming from all over India and Ceylon. How could he face them? How dare we insult him so! How dare we insult *them*!

Susan had escaped into the hallway to phone Duncan Emery, and so I withstood the broadside of expostulations and remonstrations alone. After a few minutes she interrupted.

'Excuse me, Professor Haldane. Gary, Mr Emery wants to talk to you on the telephone.' Her politeness helped to defuse the situation. I went to the phone, leaving Susan, visibly nervous, in the room with the Haldanes and their ineffectual secretary.

'Gary,' said Mr Emery, 'I want you and Susan to take a cab directly over to Pushpa Sehney's place.' He gave me the address, 'And I want you to tell Haldane that you'll be back in an hour. Got that? Phone me as soon as you get to Pushpa's, but get out of there *now*, because Sue is kind of upset. OK?'

'OK.'

I returned to the room and told Haldane our plan. Back in an hour, I promised.

'All right,' he said. 'We'll be waiting. But if you're not back in an hour, I'm going on a hunger strike in the hotel lobby to protest this outrageous insult!'

As it turned out, there *was* no Indo-American Society meeting. Pushpa and her brother were as puzzled as we were. I phoned Duncan Emery.

'Now listen carefully,' he said. 'You are not to go back to the hotel. We'll show him he can't just horn in here!'

'But I told him I'd be back in an hour!'

'I know. But Haldane's a troublemaker. Wait for an hour, and then phone him at the hotel and tell him you won't be coming.'

'That's not fair!'

'Just do as I say. We don't want an incident.'

I hung up and conferred with Susan and Pushpa. They agreed that we should go along with whatever Emery suggested.

That hour seemed one of the longest in my life. Finally I phoned the hotel. Was Professor Haldane still there?

'Professor Haldane!' said an excited Indian voice. 'Yes, yes! He's here now in the hotel lobby! He says he is not leaving. Oh what shall I do? He says it is a sit-down strike!'

'May I speak to him, please?'

'Certainly, certainly.'

Haldane came on the line. I apologized for not being able to keep our appointment; we would not be going back to the hotel to meet him. There was an explosion on the telephone, more talk of hunger strikes and sit-down strikes and the press and Americans and 'impudent young scoundrels' like myself. But I couldn't listen. This was not the Professor J.B.S. Haldane who had shared a sacred secret with me on the bridge at the Calcutta Zoo. I felt tears stinging my eyes as I apologized once again. He continued to shout into the receiver for several more minutes before, heavy-hearted, I hung up.

He went on his well-publicized hunger strike that evening. Susan and I flew to Bombay that night, a day ahead of schedule and, by next morning, news of the hunger strike had followed us across the subcontinent. Most reports sympathized with Haldane, and most reporters gave us short shrift.

Susan and I continued our tour of India, and later flew to Ankara, Teheran, Istanbul, Athens, Rome, Paris, London, and New York, taking our time, travelling first class at the expense of the United States. Even in London, reports of Haldane's hunger strike had preceded us. Eventually, after visiting Washington, DC, Beltsville, MD, and Cornell University at Ithaca, NY (I had intended to visit the Watch Tower Bible School of Gilead there, but got side-tracked by Cornell's Department of Entomology), I flew back to Canada.

Soon I was back into the routine of my technical school training, taking courses in machine shop, drafting, auto mechanics, remedial English, and chemistry – the prescribed program for a Witness who wishes eventually to pioneer. I was bored stiff within a month, and in the chemistry lab performed experiments on my own. I blew up the brand new lab by accident and was promptly expelled from Grade Twelve. I never did matriculate; I went off to Europe and eventually back to Asia instead.

By the end of 1961, I had become established as a pioneer in Hong Kong and at eighteen had taken charge of the English-speaking congregation there. At first, I lived at the Bethel branch office on Prince Edward Road, where I received a curious initial assignment – spying on the two Chinese translators, both of whom were graduates of the Watch Tower Society's missionary school of Gilead. They were suspected of 'dabbling in psychology.' Ken Gannaway, then the assistant branch servant, was adamant that I should make a list of all the books I saw them reading; but the only suspicious title I could come up with was Dostoevsky's *Crime and Punishment*, which in my naïveté I took to be a book on prison reform. One of the translators, Daniel Ng, was repri-manded for having such 'worldly' books in his possession.

Jehovah's Witnesses are not encouraged to read widely; Watch Tower Soci-ety literature – including the regularly published *Watchtower* and *Awake!* – is deemed to be sufficient fodder for any active mind. Accordingly, it was not until 1964 – when I was twenty-one years old – that I read my first serious work of fiction: George Orwell's *Nineteen Eighty-Four* (1949). The title had a familiar ring to it. As early as 1958, my Grade Nine English teacher – knowing full well that I was a Jehovah's Witness who refused to stand for the national anthem, refused to vote in class elections, refused to attend school assemblies, or join cadets, or celebrate Christmas or birthdays or St Valen-tine's Day or Hallowe'en – had asked my class what religious group believed that the end of the world was going to come in 1984. All of us were mystified.

'Botting, stand up!'

I stood.

'What religious group believes the world will come to an end in 1984?' he repeated.

'I don't know, Sir,' I replied quite honestly.

'Don't know!' he bellowed. 'Don't know! Here you are, claiming to be a Jehovah's Witness, getting out of school assemblies and cadets, and yet you *don't know* that Jehovah's Witnesses believe the end of the world is coming in 1984?'

'I've never heard that one before, Sir.'

'Don't smart-mouth me, Botting! Get to the office.'

When I got home, I asked my mother if she had ever heard of such a thing.

'It's not our place to speculate,' she said, 'but Armageddon *has* to come *long* before 1984. "This generation *will by no means pass away*,"' she cited, alluding to the Watch Tower belief that the generation of baptized Witnesses alive in 1914 would not die before the End. 'A generation is seventy years. So it should come *long* before 1984. That would be the absolute latest.'

I asked Arnold Johnston, then the Peterborough congregation overseer, the same question. He just scoffed.

'Armageddon's just around the corner, you know that. Why, it could be here next *week*! Tell your teacher he's wrong. *Dead* wrong!'

I did, and my teacher didn't thank me for it. Nor did he ever explain where he had heard the allegedly spurious 'Doctrine of Nineteen Eighty-Four.'

When, six years later, I sat down to read Orwell's last novel, it was not just the title that seemed startlingly familiar. I had been here before. For me, there was little satirical about the book; it was starkly real. I identified totally with Winston Smith. I saw O'Brien in the very mannerisms of Brother Franz on the far side of a Peking duck, the jovial confidant *cum* confessor, wise and yet somehow sinister in his wisdom. But even closer than individual Witnesses to specific characters in the novel was the world of Jehovah's Witnesses to that of Ingsoc – a world in which everyone conformed, to the letter, to the shifting published proclamations of a collective oligarchy ruling in God's name. All my world lacked, in fact, was a Julia.

Heather and I had first met at a Witness wedding reception in March 1964 and subsequently saw each other at assemblies and conventions. Just as I had taken technical courses in high school, so she had enrolled in a special commercial program that would prepare her for stenographic work and leave her free to pioneer; her family's involvement with the Witnesses went back to the 1930s. She vacation pioneered in 1964 and 1965 before becoming a legal secretary in Toronto. I, too, was interested in law, and entered Trent University, intending to study law and eventually to article for Glen How, the Watch Tower Society's lawyer.

Heather and I were married in a private ceremony in 1967, following which Heather too returned to school, and eventually to university, where she majored in anthropology. In 1975, I received my doctorate in English literature from the University of Alberta, having focused my research on Orwell and another modern British novelist – 1983 Nobel laureate William Golding. Heather continued her postgraduate studies in religious anthropology.

The raw research data used in this book was collected over a ten-year period, beginning in 1973; but it was not formulated and systematized until 1980, when Heather wrote the first draft of her doctoral dissertation 'The Power and the Glory: The Symbolic Vision and Social Dynamic of Jehovah's Witnesses.' Her thesis, primarily an analysis of the power relations operative within the Jehovah's Witness movement, focused on a specific 'microsociety' of individuals within the movement, showing the levels of involvement, commitment, and status achieved within the sect by each person in the microsociety. The more general background material used in her dissertation – including the outline of Witness history, beliefs, and social imperatives – has been incorporated into this book.

Gary Botting
Red Deer, 4 April 1984

Acknowledgments

Our sincere thanks are extended to the many individuals who have been supportive of this project – including many Jehovah's Witnesses who, for reasons that shall become clear, must remain anonymous. Perhaps it will suffice to thank the corporation that purports to represent them, the Watch Tower Bible and Tract Society, from whose publications we have drawn a composite of Witness doctrine as it has unfolded over the years. On the other hand, we are indebted to several persons whose insights have led them to part with Jehovah's Witnesses. In particular, we wish to thank Dr James Penton of the University of Lethbridge and his wife, Marilyn, for their initial encouragement of the idea of writing a book based on Heather's research, and their totally unselfish recommendations regarding publishing such a work. Raymond V. Franz, formerly of the Governing Body of Jehovah's Witnesses, read over certain sections of the manuscript and made recommendations that undoubtedly strengthened the veracity of the text; we were impressed by his insistence on both fairness and frankness with respect to representing the views of the Watch Tower Society. We also wish to thank Mr and Mrs Mike Zebroski, who, despite personal trials, have been most supportive of our project.

On the editorial side, we wish primarily to thank Virgil Duff, of the University of Toronto Press, whose energy and enthusiasm are contagious; not only did he provide us with office space and 'instant feedback,' but he and his wife, Janet, opened up their home to us during a critical developmental phase of the manuscript. We were fortunate too to benefit from the extraordinary editorial skills of B. Beetham-Endersby. Dr David Bai, Dr David Young, Dr Regna Darnell, and Dr Mamie Young of the Department of Anthropology, and Dr Earl Waugh of the Department of Religious Studies of the University of Alberta all provided advice with respect to the direction of the initial research. Dr Birk Sproxton and Professor Bill Meilen reviewed key sections of the text. Substantial financial support for the early research was received from the Killam Foundation in the form of scholarships.

On a more personal note, we wish to thank our good friends Mrs Doris Windrim, Miss Susan Archibald, and Miss Elizabeth Craig for their ongoing moral support and monitoring of crucial developments at the periphery of the sect. Finally, we must thank our four children, Michelle, Trent, T.K., and Tara, for their patience and forbearance, if not their understanding, as we developed the manuscript year by year.

H.D.H.B.
G.N.A.B.

Abbreviations

1984	George Orwell. *Nineteen Eighty-Four*. New York: Harcourt, Brace and World 1949
ABU	*Aid to Bible Understanding* [1969] 1971
BGHF	*'Babylon the Great Has Fallen!' God's Kingdom Rules* 1963
CEJL	Sonia Orwell and Ian Angus, eds. *The Collected Essays, Journalism and Letters of George Orwell* (4 vols). Harmondsworth: Penguin 1970
DMGHE	*Did Man Get Here by Evolution or by Creation?* 1967
ELEF	*Enjoy Life on Earth Forever* 1982
GKTY	*God's Kingdom of a Thousand Years Has Approached* 1973
IBRWG	*Is the Bible Really the Word of God?* 1969
IGWC	*Is There a God Who Cares?* 1975
JWDP	*Jehovah's Witnesses in the Divine Purpose* 1959
JWTC	*Jehovah's Witnesses in the Twentieth Century* 1978
LEFSG	*Life Everlasting in Freedom of the Sons of God* 1966
MBBS	*My Book of Bible Stories* 1978
MSAT	*'Make Sure of All Things'* 1953
MSWD	*Man's Salvation out of World Distress at Hand!* 1975
NWT	*New World Translation of the Holy Scriptures* 1981
OAOM	*Organized to Accomplish Our Ministry* 1983
OKPD	*Organization for Kingdom-Preaching and Disciple-Making* 1972
PLPR	*From Paradise Lost to Paradise Regained* 1958
PRMT	*Paradise Restored to Mankind – By Theocracy!* 1972

Introduction

It was a sort of hymn to the wisdom and majesty of Big Brother ... (*1984*, 18)

As Jehovah's Witnesses, we have both had an obvious subjective immersion into the Witnesses' corpus of belief. But, in researching this book, we have sought to examine Jehovah's Witnesses from a more objective perspective in order to come to understand the dynamics of attraction to, as well as defection from, the Witnesses' world. Such an examination has become imperative, for the denomination is becoming increasingly regimented as it perceives the 'last days' of this world drawing near. Since 1982, the Watch Tower Bible and Tract Society has focused pointedly on 'unity at all costs' – emphasizing the need to close ranks on dissidence or 'independent thinking' that might challenge the mainstay of Witness doctrine, even going so far as to say that 'there cannot even be coexistent tendencies or schools of thought within the Christian congregation' (*WT* 15 September 1983, 18).

In order to appreciate how the Watch Tower Bible and Tract Society has been able to command the absolute obedience of the majority of Jehovah's Witnesses, it is necessary to understand the fundamental symbols which contain and express meaning within the Witnesses' belief system. These symbols will have a certain familiarity for readers of George Orwell, for the symbolic and organizational structure of Jehovah's Witnesses can best be explained in terms of oligarchical collectivism, as defined and elucidated in *Nineteen Eighty-Four*. This should not be too surprising since Orwell emerged from the same

Protestant tradition as the Witnesses, experienced the unfolding of secular history through some of its most critical times, and came to similar conclusions as Jehovah's Witnesses regarding the importance of 1914 as a landmark of the loss of human innocence. The war of 1914–18 is alluded to again and again in Orwell's writings as being the turning-point of human history. Furthermore, he saw a need for the establishment of the kingdom of heaven on earth: 'The Kingdom of Heaven has somehow got to be brought to the surface of the earth. We have got to be the children of God, even though the God of the Prayer Book no longer exists' (*CEJL* 2: 33). Whereas 'a normal human being does not want the Kingdom of Heaven: he wants life on earth to continue,' the 'chosen' Christian, 'if he were offered the chance of everlasting life on this earth would refuse it' (*CEJL* 2:159; 4:344). Orwell had reached these conclusions independently of any formal religion or creed, but they are strikingly familiar stances to those taken by Jehovah's Witnesses, as we shall see.

but it is not in the *theological* perspectives of the witnesses that they most resemble orwell. the resemblance comes closest when we examine their ideas regarding theocracy. *nineteen eighty-four* depicts an attempt by a superstate to adopt and impose a theocratic system on the populace – in effect, to create a 'kingdomof heaven on earth.' orwell was not trying to be a prophet when he wrote his final novel; nor was he being flippantly satirical. Rather, *Nineteen Eighty-Four*, like *Animal Farm* before it, is a moral fable. As Orwell stated in 'Why I Write' (1947):

What I have most wanted to do throughout the past ten years is to make political writing into an art. My starting point is always a feeling of partisanship, a sense of injustice. When I sit down to write a book, I do not say to myself, 'I am going to produce a work of art.' I write it because there is some lie that I want to expose, some fact to which I want to draw attention, and my initial concern is to get a hearing. (*Decline of the English Murder and Other Essays*, 186)

The novel was intended as a serious warning as to what could happen if certain totalitarian trends that Orwell saw developing during and shortly after the Second World War were allowed free rein. From the vantage-point of 1947, he could see 'three possibilities ahead of us': 1 / that the Americans would bomb Russia before the USSR had nuclear capability ('this is, I think, the least likely outcome of the three, because a preventive war is a crime not easily committed by a country that retains any traces of democracy'); 2 / that the Cold War would continue until the USSR and other countries had nuclear capability and would use it to destroy civilization ('retaining no more of the culture of the past than a knowledge of how to smelt metals. Conceivably this is a desirable outcome'); and 3 / that fear of the Bomb would become so great that nobody would use it:

This seems to me the worst possibility of all. It would mean the division of the world among two or three vast super-states, unable to conquer one another and unable to be overthrown by any internal rebellion. In all probability their structure would be hierarchic, with a semi-divine caste at the top and outright slavery at the bottom, and the crushing out of liberty would exceed anything that the world has yet seen. Within each state the necessary psychological atmosphere would be kept up by complete severance from the outer world, and by a continuous phony war against rival states. Civilizations of this type might remain static for thousands of years. ('Towards European Unity,' *CEJL* 4:424)

Since Orwell wrote this, no nation has used nuclear bombs aggressively, and it would seem that the third possibility – 'the worst possibility' – is becoming a reality. The world has become divided into 'two or three vast super-states,' and within these super-states, internal rebellion has been unsuccessful; rather, the crushing out of liberty and the imposition of a 'semi-divine' ruling class has become a reality in substantial portions of the modern world.

Nineteen Eighty-Four is a fictional exploration of the possible outcome of allowing the third alternative to run rampant. As Winston Smith comes to understand, such an eventuality would depend on a secret weapon bar none: God. Winston must discover for himself the nature of 'the central secret,' the 'never-questioned instinct' that man in every age has deferred to: the instinct to worship. The central secret of the Party that sets it apart from totalitarianism is the focusing of this instinct on a specifically named God that has been decreed to *exist*. The original motive of the Party is to affirm this fact by giving the abstraction-that-is-God a concrete reality, and then presenting this reality to the people as a godhead, the central focus of the theocracy: Big Brother.

Big Brother is infallible, all-powerful, and immortal – in other words, he is identical in potential and in personality to the Hebrew Jehovah, after whom he is modelled. He is at once a vengeful God and a God of love; 'all knowledge, all wisdom, all happiness, all virtue, are held to issue directly from his leadership and inspiration' (*1984*, 209). Despite representations of Big Brother on the telescreen and on ubiquitous posters which proclaim 'BIG

BROTHER IS WATCHING YOU,' he is invisible: 'Nobody has ever seen Big Brother.' Although he is ubiquitous, he is not omnipresent. From the objective, heretical view of the Party given in *the book*, 'Big Brother is the guise in which the Party chooses to exhibit itself to the world. His function is to act as a focusing point for love, fear, and reverence, emotions which are more easily felt towards an individual than towards an organization' (209). All members of the Party must love Big Brother. The central 'Truth' of the Party is that God is power incarnate, that he is the sovereign ruler of the universe against whom no man can stand, and that he demands exclusive devotion: 'And remember that it is for ever' (266–71, 280, 293).

The identification of Big Brother with Jehovah is made very early on in the novel, as is the association of Emmanuel Goldstein with the fallen Lucifer. During the 'Two Minutes Hate' the image of Goldstein, 'the hostile figure,' dissolves into the image of Big Brother, 'full of power and mysterious calm, and so vast that it almost filled up the screen' (17). Even after the face of God fades, the faithful remain ecstatic:

The little sandy-haired woman had flung herself forward over the back of the chair in front of her. With a tremulous murmur that sounded like 'My Saviour!' she extended her arms towards the screen. Then she buried her face in her hands. It was apparent she was uttering a prayer.

At this moment the entire group of people broke into a deep, slow, rhythmical chant of 'B-B! ... B-B! ... B-B!' – over and over again, very slowly, with a long pause between the first 'B' and the second – a heavy, murmurous sound, somehow curiously savage ... Partly it was a sort of hymn to the wisdom and majesty of Big Brother ... (17–18)

What the Party faithful are chanting is an affirmation of existence – 'BE! BE! ... BE! BE! ... BE! BE!' – but, more importantly, an affirmation of the existence of Big Brother himself. 'B-B' is an affectionate name for Big Brother, and links directly to the reference to God's name in the Bible at Exodus 3:13, 14:

Then Moses said to God, 'Indeed, when I come to the children of Israel and say to them, "The God of your fathers has sent me to you," and they say to me, "What is His name?" what shall I say to them?'

And God said to Moses, 'I AM WHO I AM.' And He said, 'Thus you shall say to the children of Israel, "I AM has sent me to you."' (New King James Version)

The Authorized King James, Douay, and American Standard versions all render the 'name' in capitals – 'I AM THAT I AM' – and a footnote to the American Standard Version states alternative renderings: 'Or, I AM, BECAUSE I AM Or, I AM WHO AM Or, I WILL BE THAT I WILL BE.' The *New World Translation* of the Watch Tower Bible and Tract Society renders it, 'I SHALL PROVE TO BE WHAT I SHALL PROVE TO BE.' No matter what the rendering, it is generally believed by Bible scholars that this Scripture, with its curious use of forms of the verb 'to be,' is the source of the name 'Jehovah':

Apparently this utterance is the source of the word *Yahweh*, the proper personal name of the God of Israel. It is commonly explained in reference to God as the absolute and necessary Being. It may be understood of God as the Source of all created beings ... The word 'Jehovah' arose from a false reading of this name as it is written in the current Hebrew text. (The New American Bible 1971, 43 fn)

Jehovah's Witnesses believe that the name 'Yahweh' was known before Moses asked his question but concur that 'certainty of pronunciation is not now attainable' and that there were variable spellings in both Hebrew and Greek: 'Greek transliterations of the name by early Christian writers point in a somewhat similar direction with spellings such as *I.a.be* and *I.a.ou.e*, which, as pronounced in Greek, resemble Yahweh' (*ABU*, 885). Orwell has given Big Brother not only all the attributes of Jehovah, but his name as well.

Although we can point to any number of totalitarian states that use some of the methodology of terror described in *Nineteen Eighty-Four*, these remain merely totalitarian; they can be explained in terms of Orwellian power politics but not in terms of Orwellian theocracy. Although many churches claim to be 'theocracies' in the sense that they acknowledge the supremacy of God, few actually present themselves in such a way as to embed God into their organizational structure 'at the apex of the pyramid' (*1984*, 209). Jehovah's Witnesses regard Jehovah in exactly this position and have even incorporated him into organizational charts (see chapter 3). The message that Jehovah's Witnesses proclaim is that their God, Jehovah, set up his kingdom in heaven in 1914 and will within 'a generation' of 1914 extend his kingdom to the planet Earth; but before he sets up his kingdom on earth, the planet must be purged of all who oppose the kingdom, including whole nations of people who place their faith in other sovereign states, and all those who place their faith in any religion other than Jehovah's Witnesses. All these people – more than four billion men, women, and children – will be destroyed in the Battle of Armageddon, which many Witnesses believe is already overdue.

Each one of Jehovah's Witnesses defines himself and embues his personal life with meaning through his total commitment to the Watch Tower Bible and Tract Society, which is controlled by the eighteen-man Governing Body of Jehovah's Witnesses. The Governing Body in turn is recognized as the 'authoritative spokesman' of Jehovah God. Watch Tower Society publications give constant advice and counsel to Jehovah's Witnesses with a view to assisting them to achieve the goal of everlasting life in a future earthly paradise, promised as a reward for their obedience (*WT* 15 December 1981, 21–6 and 15 April 1981, 13–23).

Belief alone holds no promise of future life-everlasting, however. A strict code of ethics for social conduct is imposed upon each individual by the society. And because Jehovah's Witnesses believe that 'faith without works is dead' (James 2:26), they are moved to apply a rigid code of ethics to their lives and to engage in preaching and literature distribution so that they will not be judged unworthy in the final days of 'the Time of the End.' Not only must they lead unblemished lives, but they must be industrious in the 'publishing,' 'proclaiming,' or 'preaching' work, which entails the distribution of literature for an optimal ten hours a month; full-time distributors, called 'pioneers,' must put in at least ninety hours a month. All of this work is voluntary, but publishers receive a 40-per-cent discount and pioneers an 80-per-cent discount on the literature they purchase at the Kingdom Halls. Missionaries, circuit overseers, district overseers, special pioneers, and branch-office workers receive small allowances each month.

Not every faithful Jehovah's Witness expects to live forever in paradise on earth. A small group, including the leadership, expects to go to heaven to rule with Christ. The total number of this special class of potential rulers is 144,000 (Rev. 7:4); it includes the apostles and many of the disciples of Christ's day, and other faithful Christians who became 'Jehovah's Witnesses' prior to 1935. Virtually all Jehovah's Witnesses to adopt the faith since 1935 belong to the 'Earthly' (rather than 'Heavenly') Class.* Only about 9,300 of the 'Heavenly' Class – called the Remnant – survive on earth, but today most of them are

---

* Other names for the 'Heavenly' Class are the 'Little Flock' Class, the 'Kingdom' Class, the 'Bride' Class, the 'Anointed' Class, the 'Faithful and Discreet Slave' Class, the 'Watchman' Class (*WT* 1 January 1984, 15), and the 'Joint Heirs of Christ' Class – all of which refer to the same select group. The 'Earthly' Class is also referred to as the 'Other Sheep' Class and the 'Great Crowd.'

very, very old. Indeed, the president of the Watch Tower Bible and Tract Society, F.W. Franz – who is the leading ideological light of Jehovah's Witnesses – is well into his nineties.

In the current organization of Jehovah's Witnesses, then, there are two main groups: the 9,300 who are the 'elect' (chosen by God to serve him in his 'administration' in heaven beginning at the moment of their death), from the ranks of whom an 'earthly administration' has been chosen to carry out the 'preaching' work in these last days; and the millions of Witnesses who are 'not of this flock' (the 'Other Sheep' who do the bulk of the preaching work), from whose ranks are appointed the middle and lower levels of administration, including local congregational servants and elders. Since there are more than 46,000 congregations around the world, and since the bulk of the 'elect' are Americans clustered around New York and Pennsylvania, the average congregation is not privileged to have a member of the Remnant in its midst. Members of the Remnant are the only ones who may partake of the bread and the wine, representing Christ's body and blood, at the annual Memorial of Christ's Death (attended in 1983 by 6.8 million people world wide). Accordingly the bread and wine are passed in most congregations without anyone taking a bite or a sip.

The initial focus of our study of Jehovah's Witnesses reflected the disciplines we represent; our personal academic backgrounds are those of the symbolic anthropologist interested in the power dynamic of religious institutions, and the literary critic interested in mythic and religious motifs in modern and contemporary literature. The initial study consisted of an ethnographic analysis of a specific congregation of Jehovah's Witnesses studied over a fifteen-year period from 1965 to 1980, and a detailed literary analysis, article by article and book by book, of all Watch Tower literature published during that period. Clear correlations between the ethnographic data and literary analysis emerged, indicating that the congregation tended to follow national and international patterns of growth and attrition. Many factors, both internal and external, could account for the fluctuations in membership between 1965 and 1980, but it is our contention that the single most important factor was the varying doctrinal and social imperatives expressed in Witness literature. How could a body of literature influence so many people so profoundly? What is its power? How is that power manifested both verbally and visually? These were the questions that most interested us, and as anthropologist and literary critic, we sought the answers primarily within the Witness literature itself.

In effect, we have applied a methodology of literary analysis to an anthropological topic. Our reason for doing this is linked to the nature of the Jehovah's Witness sect itself. Its primary focus is its publication work; indeed, its adherents call each other 'publishers' and preaching consists primarily of placing publications with members of the public. It must be remembered that with printing runs in excess of ten million copies an issue, *The Watchtower* is one of the most widely circulated magazines of any kind in existence. One Witness publication – *The Truth that Leads to Eternal Life* – has had a circulation of 115 million copies. The entire life of each Jehovah's Witness is tied inextricably to these and other Watch Tower publications, which are studied at least five times per week in formal meetings and usually every morning and every evening by devoted Witnesses. The importance of Watch Tower literature to the success of the sect – and particularly to the power dynamic working within it – cannot be underestimated.

Most of the time, Witness literature carefully avoids admitting anything that hints at internal crisis. None the less, a careful analysis of the raw data contained in Watch Tower publications from year to year reveals that, although the number of baptisms in a given year is invariably high, the increase in the number of publishers recorded for the same year will invariably be considerably lower. Newly baptized Witnesses are usually enthusiastic publishers; having found 'the Truth,' they tend to be anxious to tell others about it. The discrepancy in the figures provided each year in the *Yearbook* and *The Watchtower* is explicable only if one assumes that publishers of longer standing have become inactive, thus reducing the net increase in a given year. By using the data presented in the *Yearbook* and *The Watchtower* each January, one can easily calculate that each year thousands forsake the sect, even as a comparatively larger number of new converts embrace it. Compounded over the last twenty years, the discrepancy between the number of newly baptized ones and the increase in publishers would indicate that there has been a total attrition in excess of a million people. Although a significant portion of this attrition can be explained in terms of physical death, it remains that, according to the data provided by the Witnesses themselves, the rate of disaffection and disassociation from the sect is much higher than is immediately obvious. This book examines the phenomena both of attraction to and defection from the Jehovah's Witness movement.

THE ORWELLIAN WORLD
OF JEHOVAH'S WITNESSES

CHAPTER ONE

The World View of Jehovah's Witnesses

Whatever the Party holds to be the truth, *is* truth. (*1984*, 252)

Each year over the past two decades, literally hundreds of thousands of individual 'seekers after Truth' have opted for Jehovah's Witnesses as being the
religious society offering symbols of significance most consonant with their
individual aspirations and visions of man's purpose and destiny. Each year,
tens of thousands of Jehovah's Witnesses forsake the religion which they once
actively embraced to search for other alternative realities of significance. In
1983, the 2.5 million active Jehovah's Witnesses in 46,235 congregations
located in 205 countries, preaching in almost as many different languages,
spent close to 436,721,000 hours distributing more than a billion pieces of
literature and conducting regular Bible studies with 1,797,112 potential converts and unbaptized Witness children, all of whom are themselves brought
under pressure either to 'preach the good news' or to declare themselves unin-
terested in the vision (*WT* 1 January 1984, 23). More than 200,000 of the
Witnesses are full-time preachers or pioneers.

The concept of the imminent End of the World is central to the assumptions and activities of Jehovah's Witnesses, who believe that most major Bible
prophecies are being fulfilled in the twentieth century. We are now living in
what Jehovah's Witnesses call 'the Time of the End' – a period of unparalleled
decadence that began in 1914 and that has seen technological advances that
could for the first time in history wipe man off the face of the earth. In
particular, the Soviet Union and the United States are armed and bristling,

and can be expected to push each other to the brink of global war. The Witnesses point particularly to the prophecy of Daniel, which says that in the 'time of the end' the king of the south (the United States, represented by the eagle) will engage 'in a pushing' with the king of the north (the Soviet Union, represented by the bear – Dan. 11:40): 'Soviet reactions to the tough line recently adopted by the "king of the south" show that the "king of the north" does not intend to be ridden over roughshod. Since World War II, the Soviet Union has been "thrusting out his hand" to grab control over various "lands" and "hidden treasures," including oil' (*WT* 15 July 1981, 6). The prophecy describes major invasions and the deployment of armies and ships. The official Watch Tower position holds that the prophecy of Daniel applies totally to these modern nations, and 'the present fulfillment of these prophecies shows that we are now living at the "time of the end"' (*WT* 15 July 1981: 6–7). Neither the USSR nor the U.S. will win the conflict, however, because Jesus Christ will step in at the last minute to 'bring to ruin those ruining the earth.'

The scenario for the ultimate End Game is plotted out by the Witnesses with reference to other scriptures. In particular, they quote Matthew 24, where the disciples ask Christ, 'What shall be the sign of thy coming, and of the end of the world?' (Authorized King James Version). The list of expectations included wars, famines, pestilences, earthquakes, hatred, deception, betrayal, iniquity, world-wide preaching by false prophets, and finally, 'He that shall endure unto the end, the same shall be saved. And this gospel of the kingdom shall be preached in all the world for a witness unto all nations; and then shall the end come' (Matt. 24:13,14).

So central is this scripture to Witness theology that in 1983 the Watch Tower Bible and Tract Society devoted several issues of *The Watchtower* to discussion of the 'Signs of the End,' starting on 1 April ('WARS: A Sign of What?') and continuing to 15 July ('FEAR: A Sign of the End?'). The culminating issue of the series showed an atom bomb explosion on the front cover. Never have Jehovah's Witnesses been quite so blatant in their warnings of the world's end.

Who are Jehovah's Witnesses? The definition given by the Witnesses themselves is illuminating:

Servants of Jehovah, the Almighty God, and active witnesses to his sovereign supremacy. Since the time of Christ Jesus they are Christian ministers, doing the will of God by following the course exemplified by Christ their Leader. The name Jehovah meaning 'The Purposer', his witnesses declare him as the only true God, who is now working out his purpose of vindicating his name and sovereignty and blessing all faithful mankind through his kingdom. Not a sect or cult that follows or adulates human leaders or rites and ceremonies. (*MSAT*, 193)

According to Witness literature, Jesus Christ is the 'Chief Witness of Jehovah,' but Abel was 'the first of an unbroken line of Jehovah's Witnesses on Earth' (195–7). The appellation 'Christian' rightfully belongs *only* to Jehovah's Witnesses, according to their beliefs, for the 'Christian congregation under Christ *is* the present-day "Nation" of Jehovah's Witnesses.' They do not consider themselves to be a part of this world and therefore are apolitical, but they are required to preach because 'active service, not ritual, comprises their worship.' By definition each Witness is considered to be a minister, for 'one not preaching is not one of Jehovah's Witnesses' (195–7). The Witnesses believe that only 144,000 followers of Christ will go to heaven, but that other Witnesses have hopes of everlasting life on earth. These other Witnesses, in a different class from the 144,000 members of the 'Little Flock' Class, are called the 'Other Sheep': 'Members of the "Other Sheep" Class are also properly called Jehovah's Witnesses because of their work, in harmony with the Heavenly Class' (196).

Watch Tower publications distinguish between individual 'Jehovah's Witnesses' and the 'Organization of Jehovah's Witnesses' (199). Within this 'Theocratic Organization' or Theocracy, Jehovah and Christ are considered to be 'their superior authorities and lawmakers, judges,' and 'their Constitution is the Bible' (199). The surviving members of the 'Little Flock' Class receive counsel on theocratic organization from God and Christ through representative members of their class who constitute a 'Visible Governing Body' (200). The Governing Body's responsibilities and duties as listed in *Make Sure of All Things*, include 'taking the lead in actual preaching work ..., making decisions, issuing counsel on doctrinal matters, reproving, correcting, settling disputes on organizational matters, directing conduct of [the] organization, making appointments to special service positions in congregations, dividing territory, making territory and missionary assignments, directing defense of the good news before courts and legal bodies, directing relief work to benefit the needy among the entire Christian congregation, supervising cleanness of the organization' (200–3). To facilitate the co-ordination of all activities under the Governing Body's auspices, a carefully kept record of work done by each minister ensures that 'preaching may be properly directed and individuals aided' (206). In this way, too, the Organization of Jehovah's Witnesses, other-

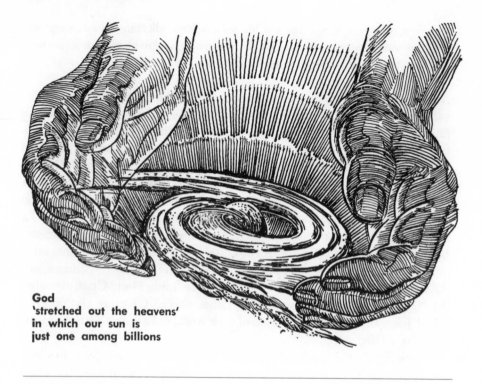

God
'stretched out the heavens'
in which our sun is
just one among billions

Figure 1 *WT* 15 January 1978, 4

wise known as 'The Society,' is able to consolidate its membership and justify its own critical role within the general scheme of things (cf *OAOM*: 'Appendix,' passim, 173–218).

The key to the success of the Organization of Jehovah's Witnesses lies in the central symbols of the denomination that are used as the focus of power in defining reality and providing the meaning behind that reality for the Witnesses. Paramount among these symbols is that of Jehovah himself who is seen as an omniscient, omnipotent universal force – the ultimate power as well as the ultimate concern of the universe – whose absence is inconceivable: without Jehovah, nothing would exist (*WT* 1 February 1980, 3–5; *Awake!* 22 February 1981, 12). He is at once loving and vindictive, concerned and dispassionate (*WT* 15 January 1981, 1–10; 1 November 1980, 114); yet Jehovah is not a God of contradiction. Only one thing is truly known about him: it is impossible for him to lie. No one has ever seen Jehovah's face because 'no man

Figure 2 *Awake!* 22 February 1981, 12

may see me and yet live' (Exod. 33:20; cf *1984*, 209). Until very recently, Jehovah was never portrayed in Witness literature in images other than of an anonymous right hand or pair of hands coming down from heaven (see figures 1 and 2); but in 1983 the society departed from tradition by depicting him metaphorically as the 'Great Shepherd' (see figure 3). As well as being the source of all energy and creator of the universe, Jehovah has detailed knowledge of every personality:

Surely, the resurrection is an outstanding example of Jehovah's concern for the individual. Why so? Because it shows that He has kept a record, down to the most minute detail, of the personality of those who are to be restored to life. The Supreme Controller of the universe, with its millions of galaxies and stars, is undaunted by the need to recall all that personality data and to imprint it in a recreated brain and heart. (*WT* 1 January 1983, 7; cf *1984*, 268–9)

**The Great Shepherd lovingly cares
for all his "sheep"**

Figure 3 *WT* 1 January 1983, 7

Since Jehovah is a person, in whose image man was created, he has a finite form. He is, therefore, neither pantheistic nor omnipresent, 'for he is spoken of as having a location' (*ABU*, 665) and he has a body (*YCLF*, 37). Like Big Brother of *Nineteen Eighty-Four*, he is 'from everlasting to everlasting' and is 'Almighty' (cf *1984*, 209, 263). The Witnesses define Jehovah as the 'Greatest Personality in the universe, distinguished by that exclusive name. The Great Theocrat, the Unfailing Purposer, the True and Living God, Creator and Supreme Sovereign of the universe' (*MSAT*, 188). Jehovah is not a triune god (the doctrine of the Trinity 'would deny his Almighty Supremacy') but is One Person with an 'incorruptible body' and 'with qualities of sight, hearing, etc.' It is impossible 'to make likeness or comparison to Him' (189). Although he is not omnipresent, his 'Power extends everywhere' (191).

The second key symbol is that of Jesus Christ as a completely separate personage from God. According to the Witnesses,

Figure 4 *WT* 15 November 1982, 9

Jesus, the Christ, a created individual, is the second greatest Personage of the universe. Jehovah God and Jesus together constitute the Superior Authorities (Rom. 13:1, *NW*) toward all creation. He was formed countless millenniums ago as the first and the only direct creation by his Father, Jehovah, and, because of his proved, faultless integrity, was appointed by Jehovah as his Vindicator and the Chief Agent of life toward mankind. (*MSAT*, 207)

Within the Witness literature, Christ is portrayed as an archetypal man – a perfect being sent to earth in human form by God specifically to provide redemption for mankind for the sins of Adam, in the process giving up his prestigious status as the Archangel Michael. Once he had finished his 'earthly course' at age 33½, he gave up his life in a 'perfect sacrifice' and returned to heaven to be at the right hand of God in anticipation of ruling as King of God's Kingdom (*WT* 15 January 1978, 6; see figures 4 and 5). All created things in the universe were created *through* Christ and *for* Christ as God's first-born heir; however, 'the Son's share in the creative works ... did not make him a co-Creator with his Father. The power for creation came from God

Figure 5 *WT* 15 January 1978, 6

through his holy spirit or active force' (*ABU*, 918); Christ was merely the 'agent or instrumentality' through whom God worked. Christ came to earth through a process of genetic transfer:

Since actual conception took place, it appears that Jehovah God caused an ovum or egg cell in Mary's womb to become fertile, accomplishing this by trans- ferral of the life of his firstborn Son from the spirit realm to earth. (Gal. 4:4) Only in this way could the child eventually born have retained identity as the same *person* who had resided in heaven as the Word ... While modern geneticists have learned much about laws of heredity and about dominant and recessive characteristics, they have had no experience in learning the results of uniting perfection with imperfection, as was the case with Jesus' conception. From the

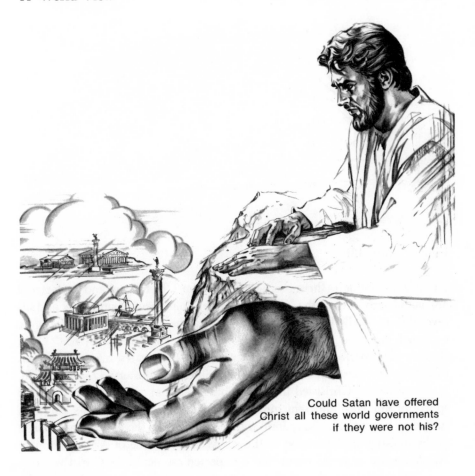

Could Satan have offered
Christ all these world governments
if they were not his?

Figure 6 *YCLF*, 17

results revealed in the Bible, it would appear that the perfect male life force
(causing the conception) canceled out any imperfection existent in Mary's ovum,
thereby producing a genetic pattern (and embryonic development) that was perfect from its start. (920)

The Witnesses believe that Christ was born on or about 2 October 2 BC, was
baptized 'about the same time of the year in 29 C.E., and died about 3 p.m. on
Friday, the fourteenth day of the spring month of Nisan (March–April), 33

Figure 7 *PLPR*, 131

C.E.' (920). Although Christ is not God, he is the 'Chief Agent and Perfecter of our faith,' according to the Witnesses. 'By his fulfillment of prophecy and his revelation of God's future purposes, by what he said and did and was, he provided the most solid foundation on which true faith must rest' (933). Because of his perfection, he is considered to be 'the greatest man ever to walk this earth, the most outstanding figure of all human history' (*Yearbook* 1983, 3). The crowned Christ led the purge in heaven that ousted Satan from that sphere of influence and sent him to earth in 1914, when Christ's kingdom started in heaven. The 'kingdom' will be extended to the earth after Satan is finally defeated and confined in the 'abyss' at the Battle of Armageddon or Har-Magedon, a global event that is expected momentarily. Christ will rule over the earth for a thousand years before handing over 'the keys to the Kingdom' to his father, Jehovah (*WT* 15 January 1979, 15; 1 December 1981, 4–8; and 1 January 1983, 13).

A third key symbol is Satan the Devil. He has been described as 'a mighty spirit creature' (*WT* 1 January 1983, 14), and only since 1982 have any anthropomorphic representations of Satan been published in Witness literature. Whereas Jehovah is depicted as a *right* hand, Satan's *left* hand has been shown tempting Christ (see figure 6). In earlier representations of the Temptation, Satan is absent (cf in particular figure 7). More often, Satan is shown in Witness literature in the various forms he is wont to take (see figures 8, 9, and 10), including the snake of Eden, the dragon of Revelation, and a 'falling angel.' Satan the Devil inhabits the Witnesses' imaginations in anthropomorphic form as a savage and evil personage who is aware of every human action,

Figure 8 *TIGL*, 158

but is not omniscient, is not able to read innermost thoughts, and is not as powerful as either Jehovah God or the enthroned Christ, who is predestined to defeat Satan at Armageddon (*WT* 15 April 1966, 229–42). Satan is currently 'misleading the entire inhabited earth' – especially since 1914 – but he does so in very subtle ways: 'Sadly, each year some are overcome by Satan's methods. They leave Jehovah. Many of them, in fact, must be disfellowshipped from the Christian congregation for their ungodly conduct. (1 Corinthians 5:13) Others become, as it were, "prisoners of war" by getting caught up in the Devil's system' (*WT* 15 January 1983, 18–19).

The Devil is shrewd, cunning, crafty, a master of deception, and so operates by using lures, such as materialism, spiritism, sexual temptation, 'independent thinking,' and even 'suggestive music,' to draw people away from God (*WT*, 19–27). Satan himself is 'god of this system of things' or 'god of this world' (*YCLF*, 18; cf *1984*, 13–14). Orwell's description of 'Emmanuel Goldstein, the Enemy of the People' is an interesting comparison: 'It was a lean Jewish face, with a great fuzzy aureole of white hair ... a clever face, and yet somehow inherently despicable, with a kind of senile silliness in the long thin nose' (*1984*, 13; see *YCLF*, 21). Satan's literal 'demons' influence most of mankind.

Figure 9 *BGHF* (1963), 551

The fourth key symbol is the Bride of Christ herself, the 'Bride Class' consisting of 144,000 men and women to be resurrected to heavenly glory to rule with Christ after his Second Coming or *parousia* ('presence') in 1914. The 144,000 are traditionally conceived of as wearing white robes and standing row on row before Jehovah; no single person stands alone. The selection of the 144,000 joint heirs began with Christ's choosing his apostles in the first century and 'it seems evident that the heavenly calling in general was completed by about the year 1935 C.E. ... Does this mean that none are now being called by God for heavenly life? Until the final sealing is done, it is possible that some few who have that hope may prove unfaithful, and others will have to be chosen to take their place. But it seems reasonable to us that this would be a rare occurrence' (*UWTG*, 112; cf *WT* 1 February 1975, 84). Those whose 'minds and hearts become set on the prospect of being joint heirs with Christ' (*UWTG*, 113) and who have not yet been transformed to their heavenly destiny constitute 'the Remnant,' members of which remain on earth as spiritual leaders of Jehovah's Witnesses in the 'happy hope' of heavenly resurrection,

Figure 10   *WT* 15 March 1982, 16

joining Christ and the rest of the 144,000 'in the twinkling of an eye' at the
moment of death. The number of the Remnant remained around the 10,000
mark for several years, but by 1983 fewer than 9,300 were partaking of the
'emblems' of the bread and wine (representing Christ's body and blood) at the
annual Memorial of Christ's Death held on 14 Nisan of the Jewish calendar.
Members of the Remnant are the *only* Witnesses who partake (*WT* 1 January
1984, 23; *UWTG*, 114).

All fourteen members of the Governing Body of the Watch Tower Bible
and Tract Society claim to be members of the Remnant of the Bride Class;
thus the society claims that since its activities on Earth are directed by the

Figure 11 *WT* 15 January 1979, 20

'Bride of Christ,' it is an approved, 'perfect' agency of Jehovah, operating a 'spiritual paradise' under the direction of the Kingdom of Christ which has been established in heaven: 'If you have conformed to Jehovah's righteous ways, then you are no doubt already beginning to enjoy the promised condi-

Figure 12 *WT* 15 January 1980, 10

tions that have appropriately been termed a spiritual paradise' (*UWTG*, 107; *WT* 1 January 1984, 10). The Remnant will also direct the initial reconstruction of the earthly paradise after Armageddon (*GKTY*, 29). In many ways, the 'Little Flock' corresponds to Orwell's Inner Party, which is described as 'a nation of warriors ... marching forward in perfect unity ... all with the same face' (*1984*, 74). The concept of the supposed perfection of the 'Little Flock' was explored for the first time in *United in Worship of the Only True God* (1983):

[Christ's] shed blood serves a twofold purpose – cleansing from sin those humans who exercise faith in it, also making operative the new covenant between God and the congregation of spiritual Israel, which is composed of spirit-anointed Christians ... It is these precious provisions that make it possible for members of the 'little flock' to be declared righteous by God, actually having human perfection credited to them. (115)

The Watch Tower Bible and Tract Society also regards itself as the 'Mother Organization,' the 'Mother' being represented in the traditional imagery of Revelation 12 (see figure 12). Here, she is 'adorned with the sun, standing on the moon, and with the twelve stars on her head' (*WT* 15 January 1980, 10). The child that she protects from Satan is the offspring of Christ – God's Kingdom, which Christ will rule for 1,000 years before giving it to Jehovah (*WT* 15 January 1980, 9–15; see also *BGHF*, 552 and *PLPR*, 176–7).

A fifth key symbol is Armageddon or Har-Magedon – the battle in which Christ will purge the earth of Satan's influence. During this pitched battle, the world as we know it will be destroyed; only Jehovah's people will survive (*WT* 1 July 1977, 394 and 1 January 1983, 14). According to the Witnesses, Armageddon is the 'battle of Jehovah God Almighty in which his executive officer Christ Jesus leads invisible forces of righteousness to destroy Satan and his demonic and human organization, eliminating wickedness from the universe and vindicating Jehovah's universal sovereignty' (*MSAT*, 24). Although it is Jehovah's battle, his Witnesses are kept constantly in a state of preparedness, and the parallel with Oceania is clear:

Meanwhile no Inner Party member wavers for an instant in his mystical belief that the war *is* real, and that it is bound to end victoriously, with Oceania the undisputed master of the entire world.

All members of the Inner Party believe in this coming conquest as an article of faith. (*1984*, 193–4)

Figure 13 *WT* 15 October 1980, cover

Figure 14 *WT* 15 January 1981, cover

The Witnesses believe that the nations of the world will have a chance to try out their nuclear weapons in actual warfare but that God will intervene to direct the Battle of Armageddon in such a way as to protect his 'chosen ones.' Furthermore, they believe that world religion must be the first to fall – before the institutions of politics and big business. They also believe that before the end the 'King of the North' (the Soviet Union) will have acquired control over most of the world's mineral resources. Armageddon must come within the generation of mankind living at the time of Christ's Second Coming in 1914 (Matt. 24:34; Prov. 90:10); so it is expected very shortly indeed (see *UWTG*, 182–3).

The sixth key symbol is 'the Great Crowd' of faithful Witnesses who expect to survive the battle of Armageddon and inhabit the paradise on earth to be established during the millennial reign of Christ – a crowd parallel to Orwell's Outer Party (see figure 14). Their hoped-for everlasting life in paradise on earth will be physical existence; theirs will be the task of preparing the earth for the eventual resurrection of most of dead humanity. The Witnesses do not believe in the immortality of the soul; the 'soul' for them is not synonymous with 'spirit' but is simply the living human body – hence, 'human soul = body + breath of life from God' (wssD, 23). 'Spirit' means simply 'breath of life from God' or 'life force,' not a separate existence after death; for the Witnesses 'the dead are dead and there is no survival after death' (wssD, 82):

The human soul is the living, intelligent creature himself, the material, visible, tangible person, and not an invisible, untouchable, ethereal something inside the human body ... The soul is, therefore, not something separate and distinct from the human body that can leave the body in dreams and at death or that can transmigrate or pass at death into another body, to be thus reborn at death into another body. (wssD, 25–6; cf 1984, 276)

Thus the 'Great Crowd' Class consists of souls or living persons who work, now and after Armageddon, to fulfil God's purposes under the direction of the Bride Class. Any who die faithful will be remembered by God, and at the time of resurrection will be given 'an independent human body as it pleases Him ... They will have the same personalities that they had when they died and so will be recognizable by acquaintances,' (wssD, 83) but they will have no memory of death. This symbol speaks with particular force to all Witnesses other than the 9,300 or so who consider themselves to be of the Remnant. The role of the 'Great Crowd of Other Sheep' is carefully defined by the organization, for despite their earthly destiny, the Great Crowd must show no less a degree of loyalty to the kingdom of Jehovah and Christ (wT 15 March 1982, 19). Today, the Great Crowd is responsible for the bulk of the preaching work of Jehovah's Witnesses world wide (wT 1 January 1984, 14–24; cf 1984, 210; see figures 15, 16).

The seventh symbol is the millennial 'new order of things' on earth – also called 'the earthly realm of the Kingdom,' 'the Paradise realm of the Heavenly Kingdom,' and 'the Millennial Judgement Day' (wT 1 January 1983, 14; GKTY, 139–46; and YCLF, 181; cf 1984, 205). This 'new world' is the immediate reward that the Great Crowd will earn by proving loyal to Jehovah and his organization through preaching activity. The 'new order of things' will allow paradise to be restored on earth through the hard work of those surviving Armageddon. Note how carefully the symbol of paradise (proleptically depicted in figure 17) follows the description in Isaiah 11: 6, 8 (NWT):

Today the "little flock" and the "other sheep" form "one flock," one organization of Jehovah's loyal witnesses

Figure 15 *WT* 1 May 1981, 25

And the wolf will actually reside for a while with the male lamb, and with the kid the leopard itself will lie down, and the calf and the maned young lion and the well-fed animal all together; and a mere little boy will be leader over them ...

And the sucking child will certainly play upon the hole of the cobra ...

The Great Crowd will be responsible for the initial clean-up after Armageddon in preparation for the return of the multitudinous dead anticipated to share with them the pleasures of paradise.

The eighth key symbol is the earthly resurrection in which it is believed that billions of the dead will be raised from the grave after Armageddon to live up to a thousand years prior to being tested a final time. Virtually all of mankind not destroyed by Armageddon itself will have the opportunity of an earthly resurrection, according to Witness eschatology, including 'the dead faithful men of old' and the 'young ones killed by Herod!' (see figure 18). The revivification of loved ones is a critical tenet of belief and hope for the Witnesses, who look forward to being reunited with those friends and relatives who await the call to come forth from 'the memorial tombs' (*IGWC*, 27). By the time the masses of the dead begin to be resurrected, the earth will be well on its way to becoming the paradise God intended it to be when he first created Eden. Over the next five hundred years or so, billions of

Jehovah's Arrangement for His "Sheep"

(1) The "fine shepherd": Jesus Christ, who surrenders his soul for the "sheep"
(2) "The doorkeeper": John the Baptizer, who introduces the "shepherd" to the "sheep"
(3) "The sheepfold": The Kingdom fold of the Abrahamic Covenant arrangement
(4) The "sheep" in this fold: The "little flock," from Jews and Gentiles
(5) "The door of the sheep": Jesus
(6) The "stranger," "thief," "the hired man": Apostates and false shepherds
(7) The "other sheep": The "great crowd" and others who inherit the Kingdom's earthly realm

Figure 16 *WT* 15 July 1980, 26

people will have been resurrected. All humanity will gradually become one race as they attain perfection, and all mankind will speak one language – antedeluvian Hebrew:

In harmony with His original purpose, God will bring mankind as a whole back to the one family language, the language with which He endowed mankind's first human father, only with embellishments from other languages that God invented at the Tower of Babel.

For those who lived prior to the Flood, including the eight human survivors of that Noachian deluge, this will present no great problem at their resurrection from the dead to life on earth under God's Millennial kingdom. But for the vast

During the millennium
God will reverse
desolated conditions on earth,
eliminate disease and bring about
peaceful balance in the animal kingdom

Figure 17 *WT* 15 October 1979, 9

majority of the rest of mankind, it will mean learning a new language, the language God purposes for all humankind. In view of good language instructors used by the Kingdom, there should be no great problem on this account. Even resurrected babies can be taught the new language from infancy. (*GKTY*, 50)

The fringe benefits of this speculative blessing ('What a unifying effect this will have on the human family! Think of their all being able to read the inspired Hebrew Scriptures, each one for himself!' [*GKTY*, 50]) are tempered with a footnote:

This does not mean, however, that the one universal language of God's new order of things will be printed and written in the present-day square style Hebrew alphabetic letters. Even today there are extant Hebrew publications

Imagine the joy of welcoming back from the dead faithful men of old, and the happiness of mothers receiving back their young ones killed by Herod!

Figure 18 *WT* 15 June 1979, 17

that are spelled out in the Latin style alphabetic letters used in the English language. (*GKTY*, 50 fn)

Even after mankind has attained perfection and paradise has been restored, Armageddon survivors and the resurrected ones will not be considered to be 'living' in God's eyes until they are tested a final time (*GKTY*, 36; cf *1984*, 177, 222, and *WT* 1 December 1982, 31). Those proving worthy by their resistance to Satan's wiles will go on living forever, whereas those who succumb to temptation will be obliterated.

Witnesses are critical and often bitingly satirical of the heavenly hope proferred by most Christian religions. Referring to 'the life for man that Jehovah God originally purposed,' the 1 June 1981 *Watchtower* asked rhetorically: 'And what is that? Bliss in heaven sprawled out on a billowy cloud, twanging a harp as you float along in space and eternity? No! It is not that vain and useless existence that idle dreamers have conjured up as heavenly life' (6). And yet the earthly hope of everlasting life in the post-millennial paradise is ultimately not far off this description:

With melodious voices and all their musical skills that they have developed they will gratefully praise Him. They will forever join the heavenly throngs in responding to the enthusiastic call of the last one of the inspired Psalms:
   'Praise Jah, you people! ... Praise him with the blowing of the horn. Praise him with the stringed instrument and the harp. Praise him with the tambourine and the circle dance. Praise him with strings and the pipe. Praise him with the cymbals of melodious sound. Praise him with the clashing cymbals ...' (*GKTY*, 162)

Other symbols venerated by the Witnesses largely consist of theological niceties shared with the rest of Christendom, with minor variations. The instrument of Christ's death, the Witnesses avow, was the straight torture stake, not the cross (*ABU* 1971, 1608–9; *WT* 15 November 1979, 24; see figure 19). The cross and church steeples are held to be signs of decadent pagan influence and are regarded as being phallic symbols. Although Witnesses regard the cross as being a carry-over of pagan sex-worship and a representation of the vagina, they do not regard the straight torture stake as being in any way phallic; nor do they regard their own watchtower symbol as in any way resembling a church steeple. They would certainly not admit to any connection with the classical use of the watchtowers of the East, South, West, and North in several occult traditions. Most Witnesses have no knowledge of the world view of Freud; however, when it comes to concrete symbols, they are very Freudian in outlook, making a major issue of the decadent sexual symbology of Christendom. The Roman Catholic Church is seen to be at the forefront of organized religion, and Satan, disguising himself as the Angel of Light he

Figure 19 *WT* 15 November 1982, 8

once was, inspires all 'false religion,' which, as 'Babylon the Great,' is depicted as a prostitute (see figure 20).

Besides these variations in theological symbology, the Witnesses have adopted certain specific doctrines and beliefs that distinguish them in the second half of the twentieth century and that have given them considerable publicity, some of it adverse. Their organization of assemblies is legendary, as are the mass baptisms by total immersion in water. Their 1958 international assembly, for which they rented both Yankee Stadium and the adjacent Polo Grounds, attracted more than a quarter of a million people and led New York City Council to introduce a by-law prohibiting such large gatherings. Nevertheless, the packed stadiums remain an important Witness motif. In 1981 the 'Kingdom Loyalty' district conventions drew a total attendance of 4,147,256 'with 44,357 new Witnesses being baptized,' and in 1982 the 'Kingdom Truth' district assemblies drew 1,108,022 in the United States alone (*WT* 1 January 1983, 23–4).

Babylon the Great rides the scarlet-colored wild beast

Figure 20 *BGHF*, 577

The Witnesses' non-political stance includes conscientious objection to military service of any kind; furthermore they do not show patriotism in the form of standing for national anthems or saluting flags. They do not join in public prayer delivered by non-Jehovah's Witnesses – including the recitation of the Lord's Prayer, which they argue was given by Christ merely as a model for genuine extemporaneous prayer. Nor do the Witnesses celebrate festivals of pagan origin such as Christmas, Easter, or Hallowe'en. They argue that Christ was born in October (shepherds, they point out, would not be watching their flocks by night in late December – even in the vicinity of Bethlehem), and besides, the Bible does not condone the celebration of birthdays of any kind (*YCLF*, 213–16).

Perhaps the most conspicuous practice of Jehovah's Witnesses is the preaching activity in which they engage. The preaching work is performed by every active Witness, each of whom must record a minimum of an hour a month as a 'publisher' engaging in public house-to-house service; the monthly 'quota' that all good Witnesses are expected to meet in field service is ten hours. The full-time 'pioneers' are now expected to preach for ninety hours per month and 'special pioneers' for 140 hours per month. The preaching of the 'good news of the Kingdom' is an essential task to the Witnesses as it is an obligation proclaimed by both Christ and Paul (Matt. 24:14; Luke 9:2; 2 Tim. 4:2). Most Witness literature is geared to this preaching activity and is designed for public consumption as well as for the elucidation of the membership. Every *Watchtower* bears the subtitle *Announcing Jehovah's Kingdom*.

Yet another high-profile Witness tenet is their position on the use of blood: since it is sacred, it should not be used for any purpose – not even for fertilizer:

Consider, for instance, the use of blood as fertilizer. When an Israelite hunter poured an animal's blood out on the ground it was not in order to fertilize the soil. He was pouring it on the earth out of respect for blood's sacredness. So, would a Christian with a similar appreciation of the significance of blood deliberately collect it from slaughtered animals so that he could use it as fertilizer? Hardly, for such commercialization of blood would not be in accord with deep respect for the life-representing value of blood. (*WT* 15 October 1981, 31)

Given Paul's admonition to 'abstain from blood' (Acts 15:19), the Witnesses have applied the scriptural principal to blood transfusions, causing concern in the medical and legal professions, since infants born with the RH factor or other blood deficiencies or Witnesses severely injured in accidents would necessarily die without transfusions. The Witnesses are as opposed to transfusions of blood as they are to eating improperly bled meat; there is no difference in their eyes between the outright eating of blood and the taking of it into the system intravenously. Recently invented blood substitutes such as Fluosol, which was developed by Japanese physicians specifically with the Witnesses in mind, have eased the plight of Witnesses who otherwise would choose death rather than have a transfusion (McKinley 1982, 44); still, 'We do not desperately try to keep ourselves or our loved ones alive for a few more days or years by violating God's law, as if this life were everything ... With our whole heart we believe that faithful servants of God – even those who die – will be rewarded with eternal life' (*UWTG*, 160).

That the Bible is the inspired word of God is a central assumption upon which Jehovah's Witness doctrine rests. The world, the Witnesses believe, was created in six creative periods of 7,000 years each. The order of creation given in the first chapter of Genesis is regarded as literally true. Thus, while all forms of vegetable life were created by God in the third creative period, the sun did not appear until the fourth, and insects were not created until the fifth – some 14,000 years after plants. God used some other means of triggering photosynthesis in 'grass, vegetation bearing seed according to its kind and trees yielding fruit,' prior to the appearance of the sun, and he used mechanical means such as wind or water or even self-pollination to tide vegetation over until the invention of the bee: 'Why should we doubt that the One who created the vegetation in all its amazing diversity could also see to it that, before the appearance of insects, the plants were pollinated in one of the above ways or in still other ways that men have not yet discovered?' (*IBRWG*, 23–5). Mammals (including Adam and Eve) were created in the sixth creative period. The Witnesses believe that all extant kinds of terrestrial animals survived the global flood by the providence of Noah and the ark. The global flood was total, they believe, and mountain chains such as the Rockies, the Alps, and the Himalayas did not exist before the flood in 2370 BC (*IBRWG*, 38). Although the Witnesses do not believe in evolution, they do believe that all extant species of terrestrial animals 'descended' from the animals that survived the flood by seeking refuge on Noah's ark:

For example, there are many 'species' in the cat family, such as tigers, panthers, leopards, and so forth. But many of these could have descended from an original cat 'kind.' So, too, with the various types of dogs in the dog family. Thus, not all of today's animal varieties needed to be in the ark. Only representative numbers of each 'kind' would be required. When the facts are analyzed, it becomes plain that the ark's capacity was sufficient to hold them all. (*IBRWG* 43)

TABLE 1
What Jehovah's Witnesses Believe

Belief	Scriptural reason
Bible is God's Word and is truth	2 Tim. 3:16, 17; 2 Pet. 1:20, 21; John 17:17
Bible is more reliable than tradition	Matt. 15:3; Col. 2:8
God's name is Jehovah	Ps. 83:18; Isa. 26:4; 42:8, AS; Ex. 6:3
Christ is God's Son and is inferior to him	Matt. 3:17; John 8:42; 14:28; 20:17; 1 Cor. 11:3; 15:28
Christ was first of God's creations	Col. 1:15; Rev. 3:14
Christ died on a stake, not a cross	Gal. 3:13; Acts 5:30
Christ's human life was paid as a ransom for obedient humans	Matt. 20:28; 1 Tim. 2:5, 6; Titus 2:14; 1 Pet. 2:24
Christ's one sacrifice was sufficient	Rom. 6:10; Heb. 9:25–8
Christ was raised from the dead as an immortal spirit person	1 Pet. 3:18; Rom. 6:9; Rev. 1:17, 18
Christ's presence is in spirit	John 14:19; Matt. 24:3; 2 Cor. 5:16; Ps. 110:1, 2
Kingdom under Christ will rule earth in righteousness and peace	Isa. 9:6, 7; 11:1–5; Dan. 7:13, 14; Matt. 6:10
Kingdom brings ideal living conditions to earth	Ps. 72:1-4; Rev. 7:9, 10, 13–17; 21:3, 4
Earth will never be destroyed or depopulated	Eccl. 1:4; Isa. 45:18; Ps. 78:69
God will destroy present system of things in the battle at Har-Magedon	Rev. 16:14, 16; Zeph. 3:8; Dan. 2:44; Isa. 34:2
Wicked will be eternally destroyed	Matt. 25:41–6; 2 Thess. 1:6–9
People God approves will receive eternal life	John 3:16; 10:27, 28; 17:3; Mark 10:29, 30
There is only one road to life	Matt. 7:13, 14; Eph. 4:4, 5
We are now in the 'time of the end'	Matt. 24:3–14; 2 Tim. 3:1–5; Luke 17:26–30
Human death is due to Adam's sin	Rom. 5:12; 6:23
The human soul ceases to exist at death	Ezek. 18:4; Eccl. 9:10; Ps. 6:5; 146:4; John 11:11–14
Hell is mankind's common grave	Job 14:13, Dy; Rev. 20:13, 14, AV (margin)
Hope for dead is resurrection	1 Cor. 15:20–2; John 5:28, 29; 11:25, 26
Adamic death will cease	1 Cor. 15:16; Rev. 21:4; Isa. 25:8; 1 Cor. 15:54
Only a little flock of 144,000 go to heaven and rule with Christ	Luke 12:32; Rev. 14:1, 3; 1 Cor. 15:40–53; Rev. 5:9, 10

Belief	Scriptural reason
The 144,000 are born again as spiritual sons of God	1 Pet. 1:23; John 3:3; Rev. 7:3, 4
New covenant made with spiritual Israel	Jer. 31:31; Heb. 8:10–13
Christ's congregation is built upon himself	Eph. 2:20; Isa. 28:16; Matt. 21:42
Prayers must be directed only to Jehovah through Christ	John 14:6, 13, 14; 1 Tim. 2:5
Images must not be used in worship	Ex. 20:4, 5; Lev. 26:1; 1 Cor. 10:14; Ps. 115:4–8
Spiritism must be shunned	Deut. 18:10–12; Gal. 5:19–21; Lev. 19:31
Satan is invisible ruler of world	1 John 5:19; 2 Cor. 4:4; John 12:31
A Christian must have no part in inter-faith movements	2 Cor. 6:14–17; 11:13–15; Gal. 5:9; Deut. 7:1–5
A Christian must keep separate from world	Jas. 4:4; 1 John 2:15; John 15:19; 17:16
All human laws that do not conflict with God's laws should be obeyed	Matt. 22:20, 21; 1 Pet. 2:12; 4:15
Taking blood into body through mouth or veins violates God's laws	Gen. 9:3, 4; Lev. 17:14; Acts 15:28, 29
Bible's laws on morals must be obeyed	1 Cor. 6:9, 10; Heb. 13:4; 1 Tim. 3:2; Prov. 5:1–23
Sabbath observance was given only to the Jews and ended with Mosaic law	Deut. 5:15; Ex. 31:13; Rom. 10:4; Gal. 4:9, 10; Col. 2:16, 17
A clergy class and special titles are improper	Matt. 23:8–12; 20:25–7; Job 32:21, 22
Man did not evolve but was created	Isa. 45:12; Gen. 1:27
Christ set example that must be followed in serving God	1 Pet. 2:21; Heb. 10:7; John 4:34; 6:38
Baptism by complete immersion symbolizes dedication	Mark 1:9, 10; John 3:23; Acts 19:4, 5
Christians must give public testimony to Scriptural truth	Rom. 10:10; Heb. 13:15; Isa. 43:10–12

The official position of the Watch Tower Society is that those who reject the Genesis account of creation 'reject Christianity' (*IBRWG*, 34), and that those who reject the account of the flood 'put themselves not only at odds with the actual evidence but also in conflict with Jesus Christ, the Founder of Christianity' (*IBRWG*, 44; cf *1984*, 268).

Jehovah's Witnesses conform to the dictates of the Watch Tower Bible and Tract Society because they believe that the society represents God's will on earth; to rebel against the organization is to invite obliteration (*WT* 15 February 1975: 109–11). In order to gain eternal life, one must not waste time and energy pursuing materialistic pleasures in this world, but must sacrifice time and energy to Jehovah by preaching the news of his kingdom. Once baptized, Witnesses must conform to the will of the society or suffer severe social censures which affect friends and relatives – and their own chances of entering paradise.

CHAPTER TWO

The Historical Development of Jehovah's Witnesses

'Who controls the past,' ran the Party slogan, 'controls the future: who controls the present controls the past.' (*1984*, 35)

The history of the Witnesses consists of four distinct phases paralleling the tenures of the four presidents who have controlled the organization from its inception in 1874 to the present (see figure 21). The Russell period is of particular interest to those seeking to understand the evolution of the organization as a formal theocracy and the contemporary criticism of it on the part of modern dissidents. Russell's theology and attitudes towards organization surprise, at times shock, those Witnesses who seek their roots by reviewing Witness publications over the last century.

Russell, born on 16 February 1852, was raised in a strict Presbyterian home by a mother who was determined to see her son become a minister, even though the family had a prosperous chain of men's clothing stores: '"Charles, I want you to know that I gave you to the Lord as Samuel's mother gave him. It is my hope and prayer that in God's providence you may become a minister of the Gospel"' (White 1968, 14). From an early age Russell shared his mother's dream. However, what he could not accept was the predestination doctrine of his native religion which offered the relegation to eternal torment as the prerogative of God. The Calvinist proposition that salvation was in effect determined before birth was repugnant to Russell. He could not reconcile biblical descriptions of the love, justice, wisdom, and power of God with the rapt, ad hoc randomness attributed to God by the Presbyterians (Roger-

Charles T. Russell
1874–1916

Joseph F. Rutherford
1916–1942

Nathan H. Knorr
1942–1977

Frederick W. Franz
1977–Present

Figure 21 *WT* 15 October 1977, 633

son 1969, 5). He turned briefly to the Congregational Church, but that involvement was also unsatisfactory. At the age of seventeen Russell became involved in a discussion of his own doubts with an 'infidel,' and found himself unable to pursue the search for meaning within the confines of established Christianity. According to White,

he spent his spare time in the next few years studying the claimed divine revelations of Oriental religions. He rejected each in turn as unsatisfactory. He became torn between agnosticism, skepticism, and the conflicting claims of all the religions he had studied. To a devout youth like Charles, reared to reverence and feel close to God, this experience can be most disturbing. He longed for his former spiritual peace of mind, but was unable to find anything that satisfied his intellect. Russell's ideals were gentleness and love of fellow man, and he could not respect a God who was any the less. (White 1968, 14–16)

In 1870 he attended a public address by Second Adventist speaker Jonas Wendell, and this proved to be a major turning point in his private life that had implications for the numbers who would join him, first in his private studies, and later in the development of a major sectarian movement which he could not foresee, and of which he in all probability would not have approved had such foresight been granted him (Rogerson 1969, 6; *Yearbook* 1975, 34).

He began to study Bible chronology, a popular topic among the growing millennarian movements of his time, and an exercise essential to his quest to resolve apparent contradictions in the Bible. He initiated and sustained a lengthy examination of the prophecies of William Miller who had predicted that the return of Christ would occur in 1944. Russell was convinced that Miller had erred only in the calculation of the dates, and from this contact with Miller's work came Russell's life-long interest in the computation of historical dates as set out in the Bible with particular reference to their prophetic nature in relation to current events. In 1875 Russell made a trip to Philadelphia and during his stay read a copy of *Herald of the Morning*, a magazine in which the editor, N.H. Barbour, declared that Christ had returned invisibly in the preceding year. Russell began a lengthy correspondence with Barbour and eventually they formed a partnership, with Russell contributing heavily to both the content and the financing of several published documents, not least of which was *The Divine Plan of the Ages*. In this document, Russell, the sole author, published his 'history of the world' with reference to both current events *and* 'apparent contradictions' within the Bible.

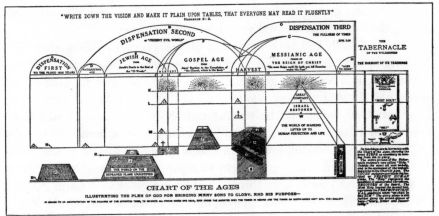

"CHART OF THE AGES," AN INSERT IN "STUDIES IN THE SCRIPTURES," VOL. I, "THE PLAN OF THE AGES"

Figure 22 *JWPD*, 67

Within the pages of *The Divine Plan of the Ages* – the first volume of *Studies in the Scriptures* – Russell dealt with the entire 'history' of mankind from 6,000 years in the past to 1,000 years in the future. The first age covered the period from the fall of Adam to the time of Noah. During this period, Russell had speculated, God left man in the care of the angels who ran afoul of the divine scheme of things by 'mixing' with human beings genetically to produce the gigantic 'nephilim.' God expressed his displeasure with this situation by producing the flood, which only eight human beings survived: Noah, his wife, their three sons, and their wives. In the second epoch, the 'Age of the Patriarchs,' which began immediately after the flood and lasted until the death of Jacob, God dealt directly with specific family leaders, such as Abraham, Isaac, Jacob, Joseph, and Job. The third phase was the 'Jewish Age' in which God expanded his sphere of concern from that of the individual to that of the 'nation' – Israel. This period did not end until Jesus expired on 14 Nisan 33 CE. The 'Gospel Age', which Christ's death ushered in, would end in 1914 as the 'Millennial Age' (or 'Messianic Age') dawned (see figure 22).

The vision of the ushering in of this last great phase, during which man (according to his own choice, based on an acceptance of the ransom of Christ) could attain perfection, was tempered by the intellectual milieu of the world in which Russell lived. He correlated apocalyptic visions of transformation in the

Bible with the groundswell of revolution fomenting in the Western world during the late nineteenth and early twentieth centuries.

Once the earth had been made safe from organized religion, commerce, banking systems, mercantilism, capitalism, industrial organizations, political institutions, and society in general, the way would be open for God to take over (*The Watch Tower and Herald of Christ's Presence* 1 March 1916, 71–2). However, God would not be starting entirely from scratch. Russell firmly believed that the natural Jews would be returned to their homeland in Palestine; he had even encouraged this in a secular way by writing to the barons Rothschild and Hirsch urging them to make property acquisitions in the Holy Land, and shortly after this Rothschild did purchase land in Palestine (White 1968, 51–2). The Jews living in this one protected area would then be converted to Christianity and, from Palestine, the Christianization and perfection of the human race would begin:

Thereafter he would make with them [the Jews] the New Covenant, bringing the sincere and devoted among them to human perfection. They would live throughout the thousand years and evermore without dying or even becoming ill. The Gentiles or non-Jews, later on in the Millennium would become Jews and come under this covenant. If they made progress in developing a righteous character they too would be blessed with life. (White 1968, 68)

The 'new age' or 'new world' for Russell would be one of universal salvation for mankind as a whole.

Universal salvation through grace and the perfection of man would require a universal church. That select group of 144,000 described in Revelation 20 as arrayed in white garments and standing before the throne of God would constitute the 'church' of the Millennial Age and would be chosen from among the most spiritual Christians of the Gospel Age. However, the church of the dawning age would have no earthly existence. Russell was fully aware of the potential for his own loosely knit 'ecclesias' to take on the form of a church over time if he were not careful to prevent such an undesirable turn of events. It was essential to him that his followers not be counted among all the other religions he envisioned going down at Armageddon. The International Bible Students Association, as the Organization of Jehovah's Witnesses was then called, and the subsidiary corporation which was demanded by law for the production of the Watch Tower publications *had* to remain separate from the governance of the church, as stipulated in Russell's Last Will and Testament. The legal corporation was to continue publishing *The Watch Tower*, and only *The Watch Tower*, under the auspices of an editorial committee of five. The legal publishing firm was in no way to be confused with the religious body. Russell wrote in *The Watch Tower* of February 1884: 'We belong to NO *earthly organization*; hence, if you should name the entire list of sects, we should answer, No, to each and to all.' In view of Russell's stance, an objective observer may ask how the group became so exclusivist and sectarian to the extent that they stated in 1983: 'Jehovah's *earthly organization* stands out as separate and distinct from all other organizations' (*Yearbook* 1983, 257; italics added; cf Franz 1983, 52–4, 356–7).

On 31 October 1916, Charles Taze Russell died, and the legal publishing company and religious ecclesias came under the presidency of Joseph ('The Judge') Rutherford. Many challenged his self-assumed authority (*JWPD*, 69). Rutherford's most powerful opponent was P.S.L. Johnson, who believed himself to be the legitimate successor to Russell. The conflict came to a head with the release of the seventh volume of *Studies in the Scriptures* entitled *The Finished Mystery*, supposedly written by Russell before his death. At noon on 17 July 1917, Rutherford released the book in the Bethel dining room, giving each member of the Bethel family a copy. A five-hour debate ensued, during which Johnson and several members of the resident Bethel factory staff verbally sparred with Rutherford, claiming that the book had not been written or authorized by Russell: 'All voiced their grievances in the open before the entire headquarters staff. This controversy showed a number of the Bethel family were in sympathy with this opposition to the Society's administration under Brother Rutherford. If allowed to continue, it would disrupt the entire operation of Bethel; so Brother Rutherford took steps to correct it' (*JWDP*, 71). In all, about 4,000 members – about 20 per cent of the total membership – left the organization in the wake of a major letter-writing campaign organized by Johnson and his associates (*JWDP*, 73). During this time, Rutherford dismissed the editorial committee, took control of *The Watch Tower** personally, and began to publish a second magazine, *The Golden Age*, which eventually became *Awake!*

The Finished Mystery, with its predictions of the imminent end of the world, created controversy not only in the Brooklyn Bethel but also in governments around the world – especially those formally at war. On 12 February 1918,

---

* *The Watch Tower* became *The Watchtower* in 1931; the corporation retains the original spelling – hence, 'Watch Tower Bible and Tract Society.' New affiliate companies use the combined form, however – hence 'Watchtower Farms' and 'Watchtower Construction.'

the Government of Canada declared a ban on certain books, including *The Finished Mystery*:

The Secretary of State, under the press censorship regulations, has issued warrants forbidding the possession in Canada of a number of publications, amongst which is the book published by the International Bible Students Association, entitled 'STUDIES IN THE SCRIPTURES – The Finished Mystery,' generally known as the posthumous publication of Pastor Russell. 'The Bible Students Monthly,' also published by this Association at its office in Brooklyn, New York, is also prohibited circulation in Canada. The possession of any prohibited books lays the possessor open to a fine not exceeding $5,000 and five years in prison. (*WT* 1 March 1918, 77)

On 7 May the United States District Court for the Eastern District of New York issued warrants for the arrest of Watch Tower officials, including J.F. Rutherford, W.E. Van Amburgh, A.H. Macmillan, R.J. Martin, C.J. Woodworth, C.H. Fisher, F.H. Robison, and G. DeCecca. Allegedly, they

unlawfully and feloniously did conspire, combine, confederate and agree together, and with divers other persons to the said Grand Jurors unknown, to commit a certain offense against the United States of America, to wit: the offense of unlawfully, feloniously and wilfully causing insubordination, disloyalty and refusal of duty in the military and naval forces of the United States of America when the United States was at war ... by personal solicitations, letters, public speeches, distributing and publicly circulating throughout the United States of America a certain book called 'Volume VII. Bible Studies. The Finished Mystery,' and distributing and publicly circulating throughout the United States certain articles printed in pamphlets called 'Bible Student's Monthly,' 'Watch Tower,' 'Kingdom News' and other pamphlets not named. (*Rutherford* v. *United States* 14 May 1919, 258 F 855, Transcript of Record, I:12)

On 21 June 1918, seven of the eight Watch Tower officials received sentences of twenty years on each of four counts, the terms to run concurrently. DeCecca was given ten years on each of the same four counts. Subsequently, Witnesses all over the continent were beaten, whipped, tarred and feathered, imprisoned, and even blinded in mob attacks that were eventually documented in detail in *The Golden Age* (1920, 713–15).

Rutherford and the other officers of the society were denied bail and were held at Atlanta Federal Penitentiary until 26 March 1919, when they were released on bail of $10,000 each (*JWDP*, 86). On 14 May 1919, their convictions were overturned, and a year later, on 5 May 1920, they were completely exonerated by the attorney general.

After their release, Rutherford and the other officers developed a more streamlined organization to co-ordinate the increased preaching activities. At the time of Russell's death, the first president still firmly expected the earthly battle of Armageddon momentarily. It was left to Rutherford to rework Bible chronology in order to push Armageddon farther into the future, predicting it first for 1918, then for 1920, and finally for 1925, in which year the Watch Tower Society was to see a spectacular 44 per cent rise in membership, largely in response to speculation in *'Millions Now Living Will Never Die'* (1920) that 1925 was 'of necessity' the deadline for Armageddon (88–97; cf Franz 1983, 164–97).

Under Rutherford, a major goal of the Watch Tower leadership had become corporate expansion and, as we shall see, God became embedded within the Governing Body itself in a process which passed through mystification to deification. This was a critical shift in the society's historical development: from this point on the corporation seemed to focus on increased membership as much for the sake of the statistics themselves as for the sake of the persons on which they were based. According to contemporary dissidents searching for the causes of a decline into what they regard as 'oppressiveness,' when God and man became fused in the form of an authoritarian Governing Body, the simple message of Christ's Gospel got lost in the shuffle.

Although Rutherford does warrant credit for bringing political peace to the organization, he was never able to muster the kind of personal popularity the charismatic Russell had. When Rutherford died in 1942 he was quickly and quietly replaced by his former right-hand man – the more efficient but even less charismatic Nathan H. Knorr.

The most outstanding feature of Knorr's tenure was the complete transfer from individual to corporate leadership: the society became in effect a collective oligarchy. None of the society's publications since 1942 acknowledge authorship – a reflection of Knorr's insistence that all inspiration comes directly from God through the organization, led by the faceless 'Writing Committee' of the Governing Body. One is reminded of O'Brien's claim regarding *the book* in *Nineteen Eighty-Four*: '"I wrote it. That is to say, I collaborated in writing it. No book is produced individually, as you know"' (264). The Watch Tower's official rationalization for the use of religious corporations has remained consistent to this day:

It has proved to be the course of wisdom for the 'faithful slave' to organize
certain corporations that are recognized by the laws of various countries. These
religious corporations own and operate printing facilities that produce and distri-
bute Bibles and Bible literature on a worldwide basis for use in the Kingdom
ministry ... These and other legal corporations are used by the modern-day
Governing Body of Jehovah's Witnesses to facilitate preaching of the good news
worldwide. (OAOM, 26–7)

During his tenure as president, Knorr was more concerned with international promotion of the Watch Tower Bible and Tract Society than with
doctrine. He expanded printing production throughout the world and became the epitome of the organization man – especially when it came to international assemblies on the back doorstep of Brooklyn. In 1958, when the
Watch Tower Society conducted its last major international convention in
New York, a quarter of a million Witnesses from around the world packed out
both Yankee Stadium and the adjacent Polo Grounds. Knorr had a flair for
theatrical spectacle, and the mass baptisms conducted at each assembly became in themselves memorable motifs of a 'living' church.

Still, the society's publications remained paramount in the proselytizing or
'witnessing' work. Frederick W. Franz, while still vice-president of the organization under Knorr, explained the process the society used in approving
articles for publication:

The President is the mouthpiece. He pronounces the speeches that show
advancement of the understanding of the Scriptures ... They go through the
editorial committee, and I give my O.K. after Scriptural examination. Then I
pass them on to President Knorr, and President Knorr has the final O.K. ... The
editorial committee does the research work, and then it comes finally under the
review of the President of the Society, the Chairman of the Board of Directors.
He issues the final approval and sends it to press ... There is no voting upon it.
If it is published it is accepted ... There is no difference of view in the Board of
directors ... After the matter is published there is agreement ... I said that the
research work is done by the Editorial Committee. Articles are submitted and
they go through a regular procedure of being reviewed and approved, signatures
attached, and finally reach the President, and he, if he approves, sends it to
press ... I am a member of the Board of Directors as well as a member of the
Editorial Committee, and so I give my signature to an article of which I

approve, and I do so as a member of the Editorial Committee primarily, and also as a member of the Board of Directors. President Knorr does the same.*

Franz himself has long been recognized as the Witnesses' 'top ideologue' (Ostling 1982, 40) and, according to most authorities from the 'inside,' Knorr's rubber-stamping and signature was in most cases a mere formality; he tended not to involve himself deeply in the actual writing and research but concerned himself instead with promotion and production. This was especially true after 1961, when Franz, having finished his all-consuming work as chairman of the New World Bible Translation Committee, became free to examine doctrinal concerns.

Franz was author of *Life Everlasting in Freedom of the Sons of God* (1966), a book first released in Toronto on 22 June 1966 in which 1975 was first mentioned as being a likely target date for Armageddon, precipitating a major adjustment in the direction and rate of growth of the society:

In this twentieth century an independent study has been carried on that does not blindly follow some traditional chronological calculations of Christendom, and the published timetable resulting from this independent study gives the date of man's creation as 4026 B.C.E. According to this trustworthy Bible chronology six thousand years of man's creation will end in 1975, and the seventh period of a thousand years of human history will begin in the fall of 1975 C.E.

So six thousand years of man's existence on earth will soon be up, yes within this generation ... So in not many years within our own generation we are reaching what Jehovah God could view as the seventh day of man's existence.

How appropriate it would be for Jehovah God to make of this coming seventh period of a thousand years a sabbath period of rest and release, a great Jubilee sabbath for the proclaiming of liberty throughout the earth to all its inhabitants! (29–30)

This was the first indication that 1975 was to become for Jehovah's Witnesses a major 'symbol of significance.'

The application of Bible chronology to the contemporary world was to have a major impact on Jehovah's Witnesses for well over a decade; in fact,

* Transcript of Record: Pursuers Proof in the Case of Douglas Walsh *vs.* The Right Honourable James Latham Clyde, M.P., P.C., as representing the Minister of Labour and National Services [conscription case], in the Scottish Court of Sessions, November 1954, 100, 106–8. Hereinafter cited parenthetically as 'Transcript.'

TABLE 2

From 'Chart of Significant Dates'

CE	Anno mundi	
1957	5982	(October) Russia sends up first satellite; causes world to fear
1962	5987	(October 11) Pope John XXIII opens Vatican Council II
1963	5988	Pope John XXIII, at Council, publishes encyclical *'Pacem in Terris'* in which he praises United Nations Organization. June 3, he dies despite blood transfusions
1964	5989	(May) 'Spy satellites' and astronauts increase world tension
1965	5990	(October 4) Pope Paul VI visits United Nations Headquarters in New York city, endorses United Nations and confers with president of USA. December 8, he closes Ecumenical Council Vatican II
1966	5991	Threat of World War III grows more ominous as between 'king of the north' and the 'king of the south.' (Dan. 11:5–7, 40) Expansion of organizations of Jehovah's Christian witnesses continues, and international series of 'God's Sons of Liberty' District Assemblies are scheduled to begin on June 22, in Toronto, Ontario, Canada. Book *Life Everlasting – in Freedom of the Sons of God* to be released Saturday, June 25, 1966
1975	6000	End of 6th 1,000-year day of man's existence (in early autumn)
2975	7000	End of 7th 1,000-year day of man's existence (in early autumn)

LEFSG, 35

the reverberations continue to this day. The problem was that while the society wrote of 'how appropriate it would be' to apply Bible chronology to the world, individual members (naturally enough) spoke of the applications as *certainties*. *Life Everlasting in Freedom of the Sons of God*, released on 25 June 1966 in Toronto, contained an explicit chronological chart, the last three entries of which are particularly interesting. Note, for example, the self-fulfilling prophecy of the release date of the book itself and the attention given to the district assemblies, which are linked as being equally weighty material to the prospect of the Third World War and Adam's 6,000th birthday.

Of more immediate significance than 1975, however, was the timing of the original announcement. Clearly the Watch Tower Society writers believed that the sixth month of 1966 would be a date to remember, and *The Watchtower* explicitly tied 6/66 to the 666 of Revelation 13:18. One article in the 1 June 1966 issue entitled 'Can You Avoid the Mark of the Beast?' explained

The symbolic wild beast ascending out of the sea

Figure 23 *WT* 1 June 1966, 344; see also *BGHF*, 508

that the number 666 'stands for fallen man's imperfections and shortcomings. God uses six to the third (emphatic) degree in the wild beast's name (6 + 60 + 600), emphasizing powerfully the inadequacy, imperfection and deficiency of the human political organization and how foolish it is to put any hope and trust in it for man's everlasting welfare' (343). The article concluded, 'Turn NOW to God's Word. Jehovah's Witnesses, who have put into your hands this copy of *The Watchtower*, are glad to help you, free of charge, to learn of God's provision for delivering those who endure so as not to receive the mark and for saving them to everlasting life in his righteous new order' (347). The admonition was accompanied by an illustration of the 'symbolic wild beast ascending out of the sea' (see figure 23). Other articles in the issue warned against intellectual freedom ('Make no mistake. Those who insist on exercising unfettered mental freedom sooner or later find themselves in opposition to God and his Word, the Bible' – 323) and stressed the urgency of seeking refuge within the organization (325–6).

In fact, at first, the 1966 'prophecy' of the 1975 deadline had little appreciable effect on the progress of the Witness movement – the organization certainly saw nothing like the 18 per cent increase of 1950 or the 6 per cent increase of 1960. Statistics for the year ending in August 1966 had shown the smallest increase since the war – about 2.4 per cent (see table 3). By 1968, however, the prophecy had been established in the minds and imaginations of the Witnesses and reinforced by public speeches and articles in *Awake!* and *The Watchtower*. Frederick Franz asked at the assemblies in late 1966, 'What about the year 1975? What is it going to mean, dear friends? ... Does it mean that Armageddon is going to be finished, with Satan bound, by 1975? It could! It could!' (*WT* 15 October 1966, 631). The major article in the 15 August 1968 *Watchtower*, entitled 'Why Are You Looking Forward to 1975?' reiterated the arguments of the 1966 book (494–501) and speculated that 'the end of that sixth creative "day" could end within the same Gregorian calendar year of Adam's creation. It may involve only a difference of weeks or months, not years' (499). Many speakers at public talks and assemblies echoed this note of urgency. Systematic psychological pressure mounted as the decade of the seventies dawned and in 1970 and 1971 the number of active Witnesses increased by 20 per cent to 1.5 million in August 1971. The pressure continued until the eleventh hour, with the *Kingdom Ministry* declaring in May 1974: 'Reports are heard of brothers selling their homes and property and planning to finish out the rest of their days in this old system in the pioneer service. Certainly this is a fine way to spend the short time remaining before the wicked world's end' (3). Of course, the end did not come in 1975, and understandably many Witnesses – especially those who had sold their homes – became very disillusioned. But the Witnesses seemed more numbed than shocked by Armageddon's non-arrival.

Knorr died on 7 June 1977, and Frederick Franz took over the mantle of office two weeks later. Already Franz had attempted to soften the blow of the failure of the 1975 'prophecy' in another series of conventions held in 1975, reinforced by *Watchtower* articles of 1 October 1975, by suggesting that the 'seventh day' had not started until after the creation of Eve rather than of

TABLE 3
International Publishers and Pioneers

Year	Average publishers	Peak publishers	% inc.	Pioneers
1940	–	95,327	–	–
1945	127,478	141,606	–	6,700
1950	328,572	373,430	18.0	–
1955	570,694	642,929	8.5	17,011
1960	851,378	916,332	6.0	30,584
1961	884,587	965,169	3.9	29,844
1962	920,920	989,192	4.1	33,560
1963	956,648	1,040,836	3.9	38,573
1964	1,001,870	1,075,523	4.7	42,938
1965	1,034,268	1,001,870	3.2	47,853
1966	1,058,675	1,118,665	2.4	47,092
1967	1,094,280	1,160,604	3.4	53,764
1968	1,155,826	1,221,504	5.6	63,871
1969	1,256,784	1,336,112	1.7	76,515
1970	1,384,782	1,483,430	10.2	88,871
1971	1,510,245	1,590,739	9.1	95,501
1972	1,596,442	1,658,990	5.7	92,026
1973	1,656,673	1,758,429	3.8	94,604
1974	1,880,713	2,021,432	13.5	127,135
1975	2,062,449	2,179,256	9.7	130,225
1976	2,138,537	2,248,390	3.7	196,656
1977	2,117,194	2,223,538	−1.0	124,459
1978	2,086,678	2,182,341	−1.4	115,389
1979	2,097,070	2,186,075	0.5	127,558
1980	2,175,403	2,272,278	3.7	137,861
1981	2,247,486	2,361,896	3.3	151,180
1982	2,342,634	2,477,608	4.2	172,859
1983	2,501,722	2,652,323	6.8	206,098

Compiled from *Yearbooks*, 1941–84

Adam (579–84). But his rationalization did not help the statistics. Whereas 1974 and 1975 had seen great leaps forward in terms of active witnesses (the 1974 increase of 13.5 per cent was the largest annual growth in two decades), the number of publishers dropped 1 per cent from 1976 to 1977, and the number of full-time preachers dropped from an all-time peak of 196,656 in 1976 to 124,459 in 1977 and 115,389 in 1978 (see table 3).

Subsequent to 1977, Brooklyn tightened the reins of control and started a purge of 'apostates' and others who did not measure up to the new, rigid standards, or who failed to show absolute faith in the Watch Tower Bible and Tract Society as the 'voice of God.' The purge reached fever pitch in 1978 when close to 30,000 Witnesses were disfellowshipped. The 1979 *Yearbook* reported:

The Lord Jesus Christ, who knows the spiritual condition of each one who professes to be his follower, does not tolerate lukewarmness. He advises any who are in that state now to rectify their condition if they are to please him. And just as some deviated from the truth in the first century, it is not surprising that the same thing happens today. Jehovah knows those who belong to him. Warning examples of what befell the Israelites as they were about to enter the Promised Land should keep us individually from becoming overconfident. The seriousness of this matter is emphasized in the fact that 29,893 were disfellowshiped last year. There is no question that our faith is being tested today. (30–1)

As the spread of 'apostasy' continued, the Governing Body began looking inside its Brooklyn offices and found ample evidence that disaffection was growing inside the headquarters itself. Official admission of error in connection with 1975 was long in coming, and initial denials from the society that it had made an error did not endear it to its membership. The 15 July 1976 *Watchtower* suggested that any who were 'disappointed' by the non-arrival of Armageddon 'should now concentrate on adjusting his viewpoint, seeing that it was not the word of God that failed or deceived him and brought disappointment, but that his own understanding was based on wrong premises' (441). The society waited until March 1980 to make a public apology:

With the appearance of the book *Life Everlasting in Freedom of the Sons of God*, and its comments as to how appropriate it would be for the millennial reign of Christ to parallel the seventh millennium of man's existence, considerable expectation was aroused regarding the year 1975. There were statements made then, and thereafter, stressing that this was only a possibility. Unfortunately, however, along with such cautionary information, there were other statements published that implied that such realization of hopes by that year was more of a probability than a possibility. It is to be regretted that these latter statements apparently overshadowed the cautionary ones and contributed to a buildup of expectation already initiated. (*WT* 15 March 1980, 17)

Alluding to the 15 July 1976 reprimand, the 'apology' continued: 'In saying "anyone," *The Watchtower* included all disappointed ones of Jehovah's Witnesses, hence including *persons having to do with the publication of the information* that contributed to the buildup of hopes centred on that date' (17–18; italics in original). In the following month, the society began to clamp down on 'persons having to do with the publication of the information,' dismissing almost every member of the Writing Department, including its sometime chairman, Raymond V. Franz, the nephew of the president and, since 1971, himself a member of the Governing Body. Eventually, several members of the Writing Department – including Raymond Franz – were disfellowshipped. This whole episode has an uncanny resemblance to the treatment of Winston's friend Syme in *Nineteen Eighty-Four*. Syme, who works in the Research Department, is 'a philologist, a specialist in Newspeak. Indeed, he was one of the enormous team of experts now engaged in compiling the Eleventh Edition of the Newspeak Dictionary' (49). (The dismissed members of the Writing Department had all been engaged in compiling the first edition of the Bible encyclopedia *Aid to Bible Understanding* which, according to Raymond Franz, had been drawn from existing Bible concordances and encyclopedias but altered to reflect Watch Tower rather than 'Babylonish' doctrine.) When Syme predicts that 'by 2050 – earlier, probably – all real knowledge of Old-speak will have disappeared,' precipitating vast changes in the way people think ('The whole climate of thought will be different. In fact there will *be* no thought, as we understand it now. Orthodoxy means not thinking – not needing to think. Orthodoxy is unconsciousness'), Winston knows what will happen: 'One of these days, thought Winston with sudden deep conviction, Syme will be vaporized. He is too intelligent. He sees too clearly and speaks too plainly. The Party does not like such people. One day he will disappear' (53–4). Winston ponders this possibility for some time:

There was something subtly wrong with Syme. There was something that he lacked: discretion, aloofness, a sort of saving stupidity. You could not say that he was unorthodox. He believed in the principles of Ingsoc, he venerated Big Brother, he rejoiced over victories, he hated heretics, not merely with sincerity but with a sort of restless zeal, an up-to-dateness of information, which the ordinary Party member did not approach. Yet a faint air of disreputability always clung to him. He said things that would have been better unsaid, he had read too many books, he frequented the Chestnut Tree Café ... (55–6).

And sure enough, Syme vanishes: 'A morning came, and he was missing from work: a few thoughtless people commented on his absence. On the next day nobody mentioned him' (148). Eventually, Winston and Julia, who are also employed in 'writing departments,' are also 'purged.'

On 28 April 1980, the Chairman's Committee of the Governing Body of the Organization of Jehovah's Witnesses sent a memorandum to the members of the Governing Body, listing 'Wrong Teachings Being Spread About' in various congregations with the claim that they had come from within the Brooklyn headquarters. The memo acted as a catalyst for the Governing Body to conduct investigations into alleged 'apostasy,' and a good many people were interrogated and, eventually, either dismissed from their positions or 'purged.'

In a pamphlet entitled *What Happened at the World Headquarters of Jehovah's Witnesses in the Spring of 1980?* Randall Watters, who had served in Brooklyn headquarters for six years until he voluntarily left in July 1980, revealed that 'great disturbances had been in the works for years': 'In the spring of 1980 three prominent members of the Writing Department of the Watchtower Bible and Tract Society in Brooklyn, N.Y., suddenly became subject to intense interrogation. These men were responsible for writing most of their recent books. One was subsequently thrown out of the organization. Another, a member of the Governing Body of Jehovah's Witnesses, was stripped of his privileges, and the third was later encouraged to leave' (Watters 1981, 1). The surprise interrogation of Raymond Franz on 21 May 1980 remained a well-kept secret for nearly a year. *Time* magazine reported: 'Opponents [on the Governing Body] were unable to get a two-thirds majority for his disfellow-shipping on the spot, but he was forced to resign from Bethel. In all, about a dozen officials were purged, almost certainly the worst doctrinal crisis Watch Tower headquarters has ever faced' (Ostling 1982, 40). Said Franz: 'By one stroke they eliminated all my years of service ... I frankly do not believe there is another organization more insistent on 100% conformity' (Ostling 1982, 41). He was eventually disfellowshipped in December 1981.

Many Jehovah's Witnesses have already forgotten the controversy over 1975; indeed many deny that there ever *was* a controversy and refuse to believe that the society ever made *any* predictions. Faithful Witnesses have rearranged their memories, smugly, to accord with the official Party line. But many at the centre of things at the headquarters of the Watch Tower Bible and Tract Society could not so easily forget, and this, for them, was to become a liability. Raymond Franz has pointed out in his autobiography, *Crisis of Conscience* (1983), that the leadership of the organization is characterized by an almost naive ad hoc approach to unfolding history that belies the likelihood of long-term scheming or, until very recently, long-term planning.

HOUSE-TO-HOUSE RECORD

STREET .... Terr. No. ....

PUBLISHER'S NAME ....

Symbols

CA — Call Again	B — Busy	M — Man
NH — Not Home	C — Child	W — Woman

House or Apt. No.	Date	Sym-bol	Name, Placement and Remarks

S-8   10/53

Field service form

Figure 24

Despite these internal difficulties, which will be discussed in greater detail in subsequent chapters, the Watch Tower Bible and Tract Society has continued to grow; according to *The Watchtower* of 1 January 1984, by September 1983 Jehovah's Witnesses numbered some 2,652,323 active members (23), each of whom imbued his personal life with meaning through his commitment to the society as the authoritative spokesman of Jehovah God. The renewed pressure on the headquarters staff in the wake of the 1980 purge resulted in added pressure down the ladder of command, and increasingly, during hard economic times when unemployment ran high, Witnesses were urged to pioneer (see *WT* 15 November 1982, 22–3, and 1 January 1984, 18–19, 24). Indicative of the success of the increased preaching activity is the fact that by January 1984 *The Watchtower* had reached a circulation of 10,200,000 for each issue.

More than ever before, the process of field service is carefully organized to assure maximum coverage of the congregational territory. Congregations keep careful track of each individual's preaching activities and report regularly to the supervisory 'branch office' which in turn compiles statistics for submission to the Watch Tower headquarters in Brooklyn for the society's annual report. A virtual obsession with statistics stems directly from the Watch Tower Bible and Tract Society's own data-collecting system which requires that each member fill out prescribed service record forms (see, for example, the field service form in figure 24).

The information gathered on the House-to-House Record is tallied monthly by the publisher and recorded by the congregation secretary who acts as a liaison between the congregation and the circuit overseer and branch office. Every month, the figures on the individual reports are tallied and submitted to the local branch office, which publishes a monthly report for the nation in the branch-office publication *Our Kingdom Ministry*. The branch submits the various figures concerned with preaching activity, including the average number of publishers for the twelve months, and the peak number of publishers attained during the year. These figures are in turn tabulated in the *Yearbook* and in the 1 January issue of *The Watchtower* each year. When presented in annual, international form, these statistics become in themselves major symbols of success and proof positive of Jehovah's continued blessing upon his organization (see table 4). The jargon used in presenting these statistics is almost identical to that used by the citizens of Oceania in *Nineteen Eighty-Four*, when they voice 'their gratitude to Big Brother for the new, happy life which his wise leadership has bestowed upon us. Here are some of the completed figures ...' (58).

TABLE 4
1983 Service Year Report of Jehovah's Witnesses Worldwide

Country	Population	1983 peak pubs.	Ratio, one pub-lisher to:	1983 av. pubs.	% inc. over 1982	1982 av. pubs.	1983 no. bptizd.	Av. pio. pubs.	No. of congs.	Total hours	Av. Bible studies	Memorial attendance
Alaska	439,300	1,574	279	1,501	10	1,361	99	148	24	259,842	968	4,033
Algeria	19,100,000	26	734,615	20	11	18	2		3	1,431	23	80
American Samoa	32,395	84	386	80	23	65	5	9	1	21,200	109	266
Andorra	39,940	94	425	78	-7*	84	2	2	1	8,523	39	208
Anguilla	6,524	16	408	14	8	13	2	1	1	2,462	2	30
Antigua	70,794	199	356	188	-1*	190	7	18	4	34,023	120	552
Argentina	28,000,000	46,245	605	43,815	10	39,927	4,149	3,456	638	7,650,441	44,029	102,839
Aruba	67,014	295	227	280	-2*	286	12	10	5	35,291	180	927
Australia	15,376,100	37,636	409	35,982	9	33,153	2,160	2,426	582	6,066,759	16,160	72,457
Austria	7,555,338	15,108	500	14,771	5	14,052	765	811	224	2,340,307	6,944	25,638
Azores	250,700	299	838	271	-3*	278	18	25	12	52,499	227	834
Bahamas	209,505	602	348	554	8	515	57	58	11	111,513	667	2,290
Bangladesh	95,000,000	20	4,750,000	15	25	12	1	5	1	5,143	35	50
Barbados	265,000	1,425	186	1,310	10	1,196	92	84	16	193,453	990	3,543
Belau	13,000	30	433	27	-16*	32		8	1	11,878	78	146
Belgium	9,788,017	20,230	484	19,342	4	18,547	1,118	1,081	289	3,103,415	7,687	40,236
Belize	145,000	627	231	594	2	585	63	55	17	120,933	600	2,906
Benin	3,380,000	1,269	2,664	1,062	-2*	1,082		26	66	109,056	686	4,536
Bermuda	54,050	304	178	281	11	254	17	30	4	57,542	236	680
Bolivia	5,500,000	3,462	1,589	3,228	14	2,839	369	513	76	948,826	4,609	14,783
Bonaire	9,704	39	249	36	-8*	39	1	2	1	7,359	34	115
Botswana	800,000	373	2,145	342	8	318	22	28	16	64,551	348	1,217
Brazil	128,783,373	145,904	883	133,765	9	122,661	11,649	7,283	2,498	18,451,361	98,278	392,844
Britain	54,773,400	92,320	593	87,732	5	83,564	5,154	6,518	1,154	14,708,668	41,725	178,293
Brunei	190,300	18	10,572	9	-44*	16	1	2		1,361	15	62

* Percentage of decrease

Country	Population	1983 peak pubs.	Ratio, one publisher to:	1983 av. pubs.	% inc. over 1982	1982 av. pubs.	1983 no. bptizd.	Av. pio. pubs.	No. of congs.	Total hours	Av. Bible studies	Memorial attendance
Burma	31,170,000	1,214	25,675	1,103	2	1,082	49	184	70	314,752	858	3,334
Burundi	4,500,000	280	16,071	256	20	213	11	43	9	73,823	478	729
Canada	24,716,200	77,003	321	73,139	7	68,410	3,670	5,395	1,131	11,831,289	35,093	148,625
Cape Verde Rep.	301,500	155	1,945	145	17	124	9	17	6	38,640	283	563
Cayman Islands	16,821	51	330	46	18	39	4	8	1	11,372	52	118
Central Afr. Rep.	2,400,000	1,230	1,951	1,118	7	1,046	50	106	42	226,165	963	5,738
Chad	4,200,000	155	27,097	114	7	107	16	26	10	52,383	172	626
Chile	11,682,260	21,344	547	19,323	13	17,078	1,842	1,568	288	3,527,985	23,110	70,552
Colombia	28,980,000	20,779	1,395	18,827	9	17,212	1,533	1,236	289	3,248,630	20,753	80,786
Congo	1,600,000	917	1,745	845	6	795	23	28	38	113,675	759	2,924
Cook Islands	17,000	64	266	54	-4*	56	2	7	4	11,778	44	238
Costa Rica	2,403,781	7,511	320	6,946	11	6,275	690	415	148	1,156,323	6,846	20,351
Curaçao	165,011	980	168	930	10	848	66	83	11	196,283	1,194	3,152
Cyprus	500,000	1,051	476	1,033	1	1,020	72	68	13	155,402	483	2,057
Denmark	5,113,802	14,023	365	13,580	3	13,173	408	694	228	1,723,233	4,296	23,476
Djibouti	300,000	13	23,077	10	67	6	1	3	1	1,912	11	44
Dominica	70,302	209	336	198	2	194	12	19	7	39,607	153	758
Dominican Rep.	5,647,977	7,709	733	7,432	6	6,983	589	687	131	1,496,247	10,894	28,072
Ecuador	8,829,000	7,504	1,177	6,892	17	5,905	579	708	119	1,535,075	9,906	36,827
El Salvador	5,147,275	12,008	429	11,085	15	9,611	1,457	1,105	200	2,510,088	16,383	44,967
Equatorial Guinea	300,060	77	3,897	60	43	42	9	17	3	30,369	232	325
Falkland Islands	1,830	3	610	3	-40*	5		1	1	324	3	11
Faroe Islands	44,408	83	535	69	15	60		14	4	17,890	35	135
Fiji	658,000	819	803	761	3	737	61	119	24	185,528	787	3,061
Finland	4,841,481	14,365	337	14,000	3	13,620	616	1,133	255	2,202,961	6,262	23,602

Country												
France	54,257,000	77,867	697	75,209	6	71,095	4,412	3,635	1,221	11,876,440	38,807	154,103
French Guiana	73,022	283	258	268	9	245	21	19	4	57,120	400	949
Gabon	850,000	413	2,058	378	11	342	19	12	13	52,921	427	1,067
Gambia	695,886	13	53,530	12	9	11	1	4	1	7,234	38	70
Germany, F.R.	59,676,500	106,834	559	104,931	3	101,454	4,781	4,269	1,494	14,855,646	38,818	182,416
Ghana	11,649,476	23,298	500	22,082	4	21,287	1,373	2,136	482	4,386,628	26,887	84,476
Gibraltar	31,183	103	303	96	16	83	10	3	1	10,942	25	155
Greece	9,740,417	21,143	461	20,533	7	19,112	819	1,320	439	3,229,663	6,945	36,698
Greenland	51,903	72	721	68	-4*	71		5	7	11,110	38	128
Grenada	112,000	331	338	314		314	8	30	7	60,986	298	1,038
Guadeloupe	324,000	3,185	102	3,064	8	2,848	213	100	42	467,124	3,240	8,873
Guam	105,979	212	500	201	13	178	21	40	1	58,488	270	687
Guatemala	7,000,000	6,630	1,056	6,325	7	5,921	522	372	104	1,060,061	6,206	24,189
Guinea	5,143,284	199	25,846	152	-1*	154	4	41	12	63,651	258	813
Guinea-Bissau	530,000	8	66,250	6		6		1	1	772	10	20
Guyana	842,000	1,181	713	1,147	5	1,095	71	158	29	258,156	1,080	3,874
Haiti	6,000,000	3,530	1,700	3,248	6	3,077	216	233	76	617,748	4,171	18,713
Hawaii	993,700	4,953	201	4,812	6	4,558	228	671	60	1,109,396	4,497	14,151
Honduras	3,955,116	3,318	1,192	3,162	7	2,966	218	271	68	678,383	4,290	16,542
Hong Kong	5,300,000	1,120	4,732	1,077	11	972	119	239	14	386,828	1,526	2,361
Iceland	231,958	146	1,589	133	16	115	11	15	2	30,009	88	349
India	710,000,000	5,842	121,534	5,574	9	5,136	384	579	254	1,112,969	3,454	16,834
Ireland	4,907,217	2,215	2,215	2,124	5	2,021	127	313	77	554,453	1,012	4,328
Israel	5,466,000	297	18,404	281	8	261	15	21	5	50,906	170	600
Italy	56,243,935	105,709	532	102,714	9	94,648	8,338	9,920	1,489	21,718,296	65,736	233,042
Ivory Coast	9,273,167	1,710	5,423	1,640	11	1,472	91	173	47	389,263	2,344	6,284
Jamaica	2,300,000	7,176	321	6,842	4	6,588	468	421	166	1,040,470	5,213	19,256
Japan	118,601,534	82,160	1,444	77,577	15	67,730	8,932	27,399	1,504	34,247,263	113,065	198,052
Jordan	3,500,000	61	57,377	54	29	42	3	2	2	5,943	39	153
Kenya	18,000,000	3,005	5,990	2,840	10	2,583	282	518	98	943,953	4,262	8,567

* Percentage of decrease

Country	Population	1983 peak pubs.	Ratio, one publisher to:	1983 av. pubs.	% inc. over 1982	1982 av. pubs.	1983 no. bptizd.	Av. pio. pubs.	No. of congs.	Total hours	Av. Bible studies	Memorial attendance
Kiribati	60,000	12	5,000	11	57	7		3	1	4,604	17	55
Korea	40,000,000	33,171	1,206	31,044	7	28,891	2,403	5,491	562	8,002,637	26,101	71,535
Kosrae	6,005	33	182	27	13	24	3	4	1	7,087	35	111
Lebanon	3,000,000	2,014	1,490	1,865	3	1,811	104	83	48	272,910	1,141	4,211
Lesotho	1,365,910	746	1,831	657	3	635	52	67	42	141,236	539	3,212
Liberia	1,800,000	1,137	1,583	1,082	5	1,030	57	115	30	250,166	1,339	5,120
Libya	2,856,000	18	158,667	7	133	3			1	603	6	6
Liechtenstein	26,380	40	660	37	16	32		3	1	6,026	25	78
Luxembourg	435,500	1,082	402	1,048	4	1,006	72	82	20	193,279	734	2,431
Macao	375,000	12	31,250	11	22	9		6	1	8,983	20	38
Madagascar	9,483,000	1,530	6,198	1,408	21	1,159	164	102	31	260,139	2,206	6,170
Madeira	258,240	421	613	396	8	367	35	23	11	63,035	327	1,050
Malaysia	14,400,312	634	22,713	618	7	579	55	77	18	168,550	927	1,573
Mali	7,000,000	42	166,667	40	5	38	2	15	1	24,341	123	103
Malta	360,222	232	1,553	201	42	142	39	25	2	47,718	131	415
Marshall Islands	31,042	200	155	136	7	127	4	28	2	39,408	228	898
Martinique	328,566	1,429	230	1,370	10	1,245	110	58	22	215,199	1,162	3,634
Mauritania	1,700,000	2	850,000	2	New					24	1	2
Mauritius	956,914	600	1,595	549	13	486	60	55	10	114,779	534	1,464
Mayotte	53,000	9	5,889	6	500	1		2	1	3,248	17	24
Mexico	75,029,693	133,852	561	122,327	15	106,573	13,070	10,068	4,474	22,602,302	138,795	619,564
Montserrat	12,335	30	411	22	-4 *	22	2	2	1	4,484	25	111
Morocco	20,419,555	91	224,391	82		85	1	7	2	19,124	60	186
Nauru	6,000	4	1,500	2		2				217	1	20
Nepal	14,000,000	28	500,000	26	37	19		3	1	5,189	15	81

Netherlands	14,362,428	521	26,995	1	26,618	1,057	1,585	290	3,907,612	8,024	47,097
Nevis	11,230	267	29	7	27	80	6	1	10,965	34	91
New Caledonia	147,500	254	495	16	428	386	35	8	94,093	563	1,426
New Zealand	3,203,300	374	7,580	6	7,132	6	582	119	1,268142	4,304	17,523
Niger	4,990,000	64,805	67	-3*	69		17	5	27,131	86	152
Nigeria	83,728,000	774	102,356	6	96,489	3,587	5,849	2,212	15,944,359	80,435	303,994
Niue	3,232	359	8		8			1	674	4	49
Norway	4,129,610	561	7,140	5	6,824	311	226	177	787,393	2,197	14,135
Pakistan	92,000,000	416,290	207	7	193	18	46	6	72,316	324	658
Panama	2,088,585	572	3,462	4	3,321	265	267	76	627,251	3,940	12,678
Papua New Guinea	3,006,799	1,849	1,557	7	1,460	114	144	83	308,090	1,677	6,529
Paraguay	3,150,893	1,666	1,734	7	1,617	77	154	44	312,779	1,697	4,391
Peru	18,900,000	1,100	15,788	9	14,530	1,574	2,019	321	3,862,378	19,476	67,192
Philippines	50,000,000	695	64,601	7	60,098	4,381	7,116	2,236	11,762,119	30,357	203,991
Ponape	23,140	304	67	14	59	1	17	1	23,967	84	314
Portugal	9,345,000	372	23,341	9	21,447	1,861	1,283	395	3,243,527	15,397	61,479
Puerto Rico	3,300,000	179	17,991	7	16,817	1,100	1,014	244	2,840,227	13,869	53,177
Réunion	515,814	679	744	10	677	56	43	12	129,166	506	2,107
Rodrigues	34,834	1,833	17	13	15	3		1	2,349	14	47
Rota	1,274	142	6	100	3	1	3		3,034	11	18
Rwanda	5,600,000	16,000	324	14	285	60	46	15	111,144	694	1,020
St Eustatius	1,335	445	3	200	1		1		928	8	30
St Helena	6,000	65	79	-6*	84		1	2	6,956	21	196
St Kitts	35,135	308	104	5	99		11	2	21,110	94	277
St Lucia	115,000	362	275	10	249	28	34	5	55,999	291	1,066
St Martin	15,926	179	77	8	71	10	6	1	13,480	51	281
St Pierre & Miquelon	6,000	462	10	43	7		1	1	1,817	9	30
St Vincent	108,000	783	125	7	117	2	13	4	26,549	107	397
Saipan	15,519	597	21	-9*	23	1	8	1	12,951	40	67
San Marino	21,622	288	73	-3*	75		3	1	11,542	21	133

* Percentage of decrease

Country	Population	1983 peak pubs.	Ratio, one pub-lisher to:	1983 av. pubs.	% inc. over 1982	1982 av. pubs.	1983 no. bptizd.	Av. pio. pubs.	No. of congs.	Total hours	Av. Bible studies	Memorial attendance
São Tomé	80,000	17	4,706	14	75	8	4	3	1	5,622	48	115
Senegal	6,000,000	389	15,424	375	3	365	25	64	9	124,225	571	963
Seychelles	69,000	53	1,302	50	11	45	5	2	1	8,151	54	154
Sierra Leone	3,354,000	709	4,731	614	4	588	21	110	32	186,386	860	2,942
Solomon Islands	249,500	615	407	567	13	504	38	67	32	129,550	545	2,405
South Africa	30,981,999	31,744	976	30,345	10	27,587	1,822	2,393	918	5,572,819	21,271	92,350
South-West Africa	1,031,927	337	3,062	302	5	287	24	27	13	67,529	325	870
Spain	38,118,000	53,496	713	51,485	5	48,938	3,547	3,816	832	9,256,352	33,795	115,667
Sri Lanka	15,300,000	764	20,026	715	7	669	42	115	24	204,192	826	2,559
Sudan	22,000,000	147	149,660	133	19	112	14	12	3	34,023	245	367
Suriname	350,000	946	370	887	7	830	57	92	15	175,831	826	2,773
Swaziland	554,589	742	747	652	−1*	658	26	43	38	127,705	483	2,426
Sweden	8,330,700	19,101	436	18,439	4	17,781	865	1,506	315	2,898,294	8,653	32,556
Switzerland	6,467,200	11,905	543	11,582	5	11,049	600	415	238	1,650,807	6,547	22,719
Syria	9,100,000	129	70,543	63	−50*	126	1	2	7	6,052	26	305
Tahiti	157,000	538	292	492	6	462	33	41	11	84,371	447	1,289
Taiwan	18,500,000	960	19,271	932	3	909	61	168	23	261,176	951	2,926
Tanzania	20,400,000	1,910	10,681	1,837	8	1,701	124	197	83	417,851	1,536	5,372
Thailand	50,731,000	821	61,792	793	3	771	49	121	27	206,725	680	1,886
Togo	2,732,875	2,232	1,224	1,907	17	1,628		68	67	237,916	1,933	5,717
Tonga	90,128	41	2,198	35	17	30	4	8	1	13,736	55	164
Trinidad	1,106,638	3,627	305	3,367	4	3,243	266	386	44	661,292	3,253	9,750
Truk	38,650	43	899	35	9	32		10	2	15,587	89	366
Tunisia	6,535,000	49	133,367	42	−2*	43		2	1	4,473	24	86
Turkey	45,000,000	800	56,250	771	2	753	22	45	12	132,787	452	1,415

	Population	Peak Pubs.	Ratio, 1 Pub. to	Av. Pubs.	% Inc.	Av. Pubs.	No. Bptzd.	Av. Pio.	No. of Cong.	Total Hours	Bible Studies	Memorial
Turks & Caicos Is.	7,436	33	225	31	7	29	1	6	1	11,099	58	122
Tuvalu Islands	8,000	23	348	18	6	17	4	3	1	4,691	31	155
Uganda	14,500,000	279	51,971	240	13	213	42	31	11	83,296	492	848
U.S. of America	231,932,000	643,170	361	616,058	6	581,934	35,303	52,808	7,837	103,985,822	390,678	1,574,212
Upper Volta	7,318,695	201	36,411	186	11	168	22	40	8	73,394	362	786
Uruguay	2,850,000	4,799	594	4,458	6	4,186	297	432	90	887,719	5,043	14,516
Vanuatu	130,000	55	2,364	48	45	33	8	4	2	10,578	90	211
Venezuela	17,000,000	22,194	766	20,392	13	18,048	1,752	1,930	212	4,259,711	25,754	81,098
Virgin Is. (Brit.)	12,000	84	143	80	5	76	4	2	3	9,121	59	339
Virgin Is. (U.S.)	96,000	474	203	448		449	27	34	8	76,751	455	1,640
Wallis & Futuna Is.	12,500	3	4,167	2		2		1		271	3	
West Berlin	1,869,600	4,968	376	4,893	2	4,805	143	208	61	699,290	1,932	7,891
Western Samoa	160,000	161	994	136	10	124	19	18	2	35,339	126	594
Yap	9,320	51	183	46	15	40	4	12	1	18,045	84	106
Zaïre	30,000,000	28,126	1,067	26,234	6	24,648	2,593	4,591	905	7,920,238	42,908	123,718
Zambia	6,242,000	57,034	109	52,994	1	52,556	2,707	3,825	1,393	9,104,427	60,882	282,984
Zimbabwe	7,542,300	12,753	591	11,552	8	10,676	634	750	480	1,949,290	7,868	33,914
177 Countries		2,399,199		2,272,630	7.1	2,122,372	151,662	200,471	41,708	413,970,263	1,678,617	6,343,307
# 28 Other Countries		253,124		229,092	4.0	220,262	10,234	5,627	4,527	22,750,728	118,495	424,400
GRAND TOTAL (205 countries)		2,652,323		2,501,722	6.8	2,342,634	161,896	206,098	46,235	436,720,991	1,797,112	6,767,707

MEMORIAL PARTAKERS WORLDWIDE: 9,292

* Percentage of decrease
# Work banned and reports are incomplete

CHAPTER THREE

The Cyclical Movement of History and Prophecy

The cyclical movement of history was now intelligible, or appeared to be so; and if it was intelligible, then it was alterable (*1984*, 204).

As we have seen, many Jehovah's Witnesses, firmly believing that Armageddon was due to arrive by October 1975 – the postulated 6,000th anniversary of Adam's creation – sold their properties and quit their jobs, bracing themselves for the inevitable. Many could not understand why the world as we know it was not destroyed then and there. But an explanation was soon forthcoming from the society: Adam and Eve were the culmination of God's creation, and therefore were created towards the end of the sixth creative day. But how close to the end is nowhere specified. Thus, there is an indeterminate period from Adam's creation until the *end* of the sixth creative day and his fall from God's grace that now is crucial for millions of Jehovah's Witnesses who await 'the end of this system of things' (*WT* 15 July 1976, 432).

Obviously there is still a lot of leeway for interpretation here. The period of time elapsing from the creation of Adam to the next recorded chronological event, the birth of Seth, is 130 years (Gen. 5:3). During that time (in terms of the culture myth), Eve was created, Adam and Eve succumbed to temptation, they were cast from the Garden of Eden, and they gave birth to two sons, Cain and Abel, who grew old enough to farm before Cain killed his brother. Eve conceived Seth 'in place of Abel, because Cain killed him' (Gen. 4:25).

All of this points to the fact that, if one considers only the elapsed time since Adam's fall from grace in calculating the exact time of the impending Battle of Armageddon, there is a great deal of flexibility – a variable of as much as a century. To many readers there is an air of science fiction about the Witnesses' account of Adam's responsibilities and the time it might have taken for him to realize them:

Fully adult though he was, the day of his being created was still the first day he had lived. Everything he saw – every tree, flower, plant, every stream, lake, river, every creature of all the bird, animal and fish creation – he was seeing for the very first time. This was true of everything he did ... How long would he be allowed time to satisfy that curiosity before taking on added responsibility as a family head?

That Edenic home does not seem to have been some tiny plot of ground. It contained all the varieties of trees within its boundaries ... It would take time for Adam to go exploring all of this in order to become familiar with the area he was assigned to care for and cultivate. (WT 15 July 1982, 436–7)

Similarly, the Witnesses speculate that the naming of the animals would have taken Adam considerable time:

The brevity of the Genesis account surely does not require our thinking that God simply gathered all the animals and birds into a big group and then had them file past Adam while he quickly called off names for them, one by one. True, he may have had to deal only with basic family kinds rather than all the varieties of creatures that have developed out of those family kinds. But even so, we cannot rule out the possibility that God's 'bringing' these creatures to Adam may have involved their moving in sufficiently close to allow Adam to study them for a time, observing their distinctive habits and makeup, and then select a name that would be especially fitting for each. This could mean the passing of a considerable amount of time. (437)

Accordingly, 'our having advanced six thousand years from the start of human existence is one thing. Advancing six thousand years into God's seventh creative "day" is quite another' (437). Most Jehovah's Witnesses accepted this argument without question as the rationale for Armageddon's non-arrival.

Two other factors may have influenced the Governing Body in allowing the 1975 expectation to build up: First, 1977 was to be a 'Jubilee' year for Jehovah's nation – traditionally a year of triumph – and 1976 marked a traditional 'sabbatical year' under the old Hebrew law of Deuteronomy and Leviticus:

Starting with the time of entering the Promised Land, the nation of Israel was to count six years during which time the land was sown, cultivated and harvested, but the seventh year was to be a sabbath year, during which the land must lie fallow ... Seven of these seven-year periods $(7 \times 7 = 49)$ were to be counted, and the following year, the fiftieth, was to be a Jubilee year. It shared features of the sabbatical year. The land again had complete rest ... This meant that the produce of the forty-eighth year of each fifty-year cycle would be the primary source of food for that year and for a little over two years following ... Jehovah's special blessing on the sixth year resulted in a crop yield sufficient to furnish food through the sabbath year. (Lev. 25:20–2)

Similarly, God provided a bountiful and sufficient harvest in the forty-eighth year to supply the nation through the sabbath year and the Jubilee that followed, if the Jews kept his law. (ABU 971)

The Jubilee year, for the Hebrews, meant freedom from bondage and debt, for 'If the nation kept God's laws, then, as he said: "No one should come to be poor among you."' The focus on 'keeping God's laws,' here was to become an important issue in the sense that if the forty-eighth year did *not* prove to be productive, there was a built-in rationalization: the 'nation' had somehow failed to obey the strictures of God: 'When the Jubilee arrangement was properly observed, the nation was restored in the Jubilee year to the full and proper theocratic state that God purposed and established at the beginning. Government was on a sound basis ... Israel, while obedient, would enjoy the perfect government and prosperity that only the true theocracy could provide' (ABU 971).

According to the Witnesses, the first Jubilee year was celebrated in 1424 BC – the year after the Israelites entered the Promised Land. The 68th Jubilee year came in 1977. From the vantage point of the mid-sixties, it must have seemed remarkable to the Governing Body that the 'year of plenty' to tide the 'Nation' over the Sabbath and Jubilee years should fall on the same year as the 6,000th anniversary of Adam's creation. In retrospect, 1975 *can* be seen as a very fruitful year for the Witnesses in terms of their 'harvest' – more people flocked into the fold for the first time in 1974–5 than in any other year before or since. This fact is likely to become a 'symbol of significance,' as has 1925 very recently: 'A milestone was reached with the publication of *The Watch-*

tower of March 1, 1925. Its leading article, entitled "Birth of the Nation," made plain the prophecies showing that God's promised Kingdom had been born in the heavens in 1914 ...' (*WT* 1 January 1984, 10).

Another major factor in encouraging the notion that 1975 would bring Armageddon was the belief, still current, that Armageddon must come in 'this generation,' meaning in the lifespan of a man (seventy years, according to Ps. 90:10) from 1914, when Christ returned at the end of the 'Seven Gentile Times':

The years contained in each time would amount to the number of days in a pro-phetic lunar year, namely, 360 days. Each day would stand for a year, according to the way in which Gentile nations reckon time. Thus calculated, the 'Seven times' would total up to 2,520 years. (Compare Daniel 4:16, 23, 25, 32) Since they began when the Babylonians overturned the typical kingdom of God at Jerusalem in 607 B.C.E., in the latter half of that year, they were due to end in the year 1914. (*WT* 1 January 1983, 11)

As we have seen, the Witnesses believe that Christ set up his kingdom in heaven in 1914, that the Devil was cast down to the earth where he has been creating misery ever since, and that 'This generation [the one that was *at least fifteen years old* in 1914, according to the *Awake!* of 8 October 1968] would by no means pass away' before the end would come (Matt. 34:34). All of these factors seemed to point to the fact that, if Jehovah was pleased with his nation and if it kept his laws, Armageddon would come in 1975.

Interestingly, the 607 BC date has been roundly challenged from within the organization, particularly by the careful scholarship of Carl Olof Jonsson of Sweden, who has substantiated by the use of seven different secular sources that the fall of Jerusalem came, not in 607 BC but in 587–6 BC – twenty years later than the society claims. Jonsson was eventually disfellowshipped for his pains, but after three years of ignoring his calculations, the society released *'Let Your Kingdom Come'* (1981) which contained an appendix outlining Jonsson's arguments and conceding that 'if one accepted the above Neo-Babylonian chronology, the desolation of Jerusalem would have been in the year 587/6 B.C.E.' (186). It also conceded that 'major lines of evidence for this secular chronology' were Ptolemy's Canon, the Nabonidus Harran Stele (a pillar discovered in 1956 which agrees with Ptolemy's Canon), VAT 4956 (a cunei-form tablet containing information consistent with Ptolemy's Canon), and 'thousands of contemporary Neo-Babylonian cuneiform tablets ... that record simple business transactions, stating the year of the Babylonian king when the transaction occurred' (187). But rather than relying on this apparently overwhelming quantity of secular evidence, the society relies upon a prophecy at Jeremiah 29:10, and the writers say, 'We are willing to be guided primarily by God's word rather than by a chronology that is based principally on secular evidence or that disagrees with the Scriptures' (189; cf Jonsson 1983 passim).

The absolute reliance upon the literal accuracy of the Bible lies at the heart of the belief system of Jehovah's Witnesses, who use Bible chronology as an interpretative device for defining their own organizational history as well as the history of the world at large. Accordingly, Jehovah's Witnesses maintain that the most accurate chronological chart of human history can be mapped out by reference to the Bible alone. Apparent inconsistencies in timing are regarded as misunderstandings on the part of the reader, for 'the evidence already at hand convincingly demonstrates the remarkable accuracy and care that distinguished the copying of the Bible books, resulting in the preservation of their internal integrity' (*ABU*, 223). By and large, the Witnesses debunk secular histories and chronologies which do not conform to the Bible account, claiming that they 'do not qualify as the standard of accuracy by which to judge Bible chronology' (*ABU*, 333). If this assumption is challenged, the entire doctrinal framework, based on the significance of 1914, could collapse like a house of cards before the society has a chance to reformulate in an organic manner an alternative chronological explanation. A major doctrinal shift will be required if Armageddon does not materialize by the end of 1984; not only will this shift entail new leadership, but it will also involve, even now, the gradual insertion in the columns of *The Watchtower* of the groundwork for a potential alternative chronology that, down the road, can be cited in support of an anticipated doctrinal shift that will move Armageddon two decades into the future.

Interestingly, recent issues of *The Watchtower* have focused on 1935 as being a significant date. The issue of 15 December 1982, for example, indicated that that was the year in which the paradise hope was first offered to the 'Great Crowd of Other Sheep':

As lovers of the whole 'truth' of God's Word, the spiritual remnant are not envious so as to hold back anything profitable from those 'other sheep' but have lovingly published worldwide that grand earthly hope, particularly since the year 1935 ...

Down to the spring of 1935 the dedicated, baptized witnesses of Jehovah had entertained in true faith the 'one hope' that was set before them in Ephesians 4:

4–6 ... But in that memorable year of 1935, at the convention held in Washington, D.C., the 'great multitude,' as visualized at Revelation 7:9–17, was identified as being composed of the Fine Shepherd's 'other sheep' of John 10:16. The anointed remnant who still held on to their valid 'one hope' rejoiced greatly over this advancing light upon the Holy Scriptures and set themselves to act whole-heartedly in the gathering of those 'other sheep.' (19; see also *TFMG* 123–205)

In the autumn of 1979, two consecutive issues described 'Hitler's thousand-year (or, millennial) dream' of the Third Reich, 'which was born on January 30, 1933' and which began persecuting the Witnesses in 1934 (*WT* 15 October 1979, 3; see also 1 November 1979, 3–14); beside a picture of goose-stepping Nazis is the caption, 'As Jehovah protected Daniel, so he protects witnesses from modern-day "lions"': 'Though Jehovah's Witnesses may not nowadays be thrown into literal lions' pits, they live in a world where their "adversary, the Devil, walks about like a roaring lion, seeking to devour someone"' (20–1).

Some dissident Witnesses have claimed that, applying the chronology suggested by Jonsson to the Watch Tower calculation of the Gentile Times, there is ample evidence that the Second Coming of Christ occurred not in 1914, but in 1934–5, and that Satan's being cast from heaven 'to the vicinity of the earth' precipitated the rise of the Antichrist and the short-lived Nazi 'Thousand-Year Reich.' Others have suggested that the act of extending to the Great Crowd the prospect of paradise on earth in 1935 was a clear indication that the 'kingdom' established in heaven in 1914 had been extended to the earth in 1935 in the form of a 'spiritual paradise' (compare *UWTG*, 107, 112, 188). Although any such claim on the part of Jehovah's Witnesses would be considered 'apostasy,' Watch Tower literature contains the seeds of doctrinal shift, should that be considered necessary (see *GKTY*, 7–9; *PRMT*, 145).

Despite the accepted veracity of the Bible and the acknowledgement that Paul admonished the 'spiritual man' to examine 'all things' (1 Cor. 2:15), the society has of late been most adamant that the Governing Body collectively is the sole channel of communication from God to man. It has actively discouraged independent Bible study, not only among members at large, but even among members of the volunteer Bethel family: 'The Bible is an organizational book and belongs to the Christian congregation as an organization; not to individuals, regardless of how sincerely they may believe that they can interpret the Bible. For this reason the Bible cannot be properly understood without Jehovah's visible organization in mind' (*WT* 1 October 1967, 587). This was merely the rephrasing of an earlier *Watchtower* reference: 'In view of its unbreakable connection with the Christian Theocratic Organization, the Bible is organization-minded and it cannot be fully understood without our having the Theocratic organization in mind ... All the sheep in God's flock must be organization-minded, like the Bible' (15 September 1954, 528). More recently, in 1981, the same theme was reinforced in an article entitled 'Do We Need Help to Understand the Bible?' which concluded:

The record that the 'faithful and discreet slave' organization has made for the past more than 100 years forces us to the conclusion that Peter expressed when Jesus asked if his apostles also wanted to leave him, namely, 'Whom shall we go away to?' (John 6:66–69). No question about it. We all need help to understand the Bible, and we cannot find the Scriptural guidance we need outside the 'faithful and discreet slave' organization. (*WT* 15 February 1981, 19)

This 1981 article was the first external manifestation of a deep doctrinal rift occurring in the Brooklyn headquarters respecting the right of individuals to examine the Bible for themselves. On 30 April 1980, just prior to Raymond Franz's being stripped of his duties, another member of the Governing Body, Karl Klein, advised the Bethel family, 'If you have a tendency towards apostacy, get a hobby and keep yourself busy to keep your mind off it. Stay away from deep Bible study to determine meanings of the scriptures.' Yet another member of the Governing Body, A.D. Schroeder, said of those who had been studying the Bible independently, 'All the things they are teaching ignore the framework we have been developing all these many years,' echoing the disappointment of Frederick Franz himself who four days before had told the assembled Bethel family that the dissidents 'expected me to ignore the influences of world events in the light of Bible prophecy for the last 67 years, and to start over where we began 67 years ago' (Watters 1981, 3).

Despite the society's insistence that Jehovah's Witnesses follow its dictates upon pain of disfellowshipping, it does not claim infallibility. Thus, the membership is at the mercy of the society in terms of doctrinal shift. The membership must believe in the oracle, no matter how wrong it may be – and indeed Frederick Franz is considered by members of the Governing Body to have been 'our oracle for the last 67 years' (Watters 1981, 3). Franz himself admitted, under cross-examination in the Walsh hearing that from time to time 'there was a need for a review of our beliefs respecting how the prophecies would be fulfilled' (Transcript, 105):

Q So that what is published as the truth today by the Society may have to be admitted to be wrong in a few years?

A We have to wait and see.

Q And in the meantime the body of Jehovah's Witnesses have been following error?

A No. They have been following misconstructions on the Scriptures.

Q Error?

A Well, error. (Transcript, 114)

The importance of Bible chronology to the Witnesses was emphasized by Franz as the interrogation continued. Asked about the speculated date of Adam's creation, which had been 'altered three times,' Franz replied:

A The date has been corrected.

Q But once the date was published by the Society all Jehovah's Witnesses were bound to accept it as Scripturally true?

A Yes.

Q And liable to be disfellowshipped if they demurred to the date?

A If they caused trouble over it, because the Scriptures say that if anyone is a disturber inside the congregation he is hindering the growth of the congregation – and its activities and should be disfellowshipped.

Q Even though he per chance were supporting the date now taken by the Society when the Society was publishing a wrong date?

A One who may have a difference of understanding like that will wait upon Jehovah God to see if he is correct, and he will abide by what is published for the time being.

Q But if he so awaits and understands he is correct what is he to do?

A He gets blessing because of his submission and waiting upon Jehovah and not leaving it to his own understanding.

Q In this respect also, namely the date of the coming of mankind upon the earth, two errors have been published as authoritative Scripture?

A Yes, as authoritative chronological dates. The creation of man remains absolutely true. (Transcript, 119)

Franz's view was reinforced the next day by the society's lawyer, H.G. Covington, who added, 'You must understand we must have unity, we cannot have disunity with a lot of people going every way; an army is supposed to march in step.'

Q If a member of Jehovah's Witnesses took the view himself that the prophecy was wrong and said so he would be disfellowshipped?

A Yes, if he said so and kept persisting in creating troubles, because if the whole organization believes one thing, even though it be erroneous, and somebody else starts on his own trying to put his ideas across, then there is disunity and trouble, there cannot be harmony, there cannot be marching ... Our purpose is to have unity.

Q Unity at all costs?

A Unity at all costs ...

Q And unity based upon an enforced acceptance of false prophecy?

A That is conceded to be true. (Transcript, 346–7)

This testimony, given under oath in a court of law by the legal counsel of the Watch Tower Bible and Tract Society, is probably the most classic example of sincerely expressed *doublethink* that one is likely to find anywhere. *Doublethink*, as Orwell conceives it in *Nineteen Eighty-Four*, 'is a vast system of mental cheating':

Doublethink means the power of holding two contradictory beliefs in one's mind simultaneously, and accepting both of them. The Party intellectual knows in which direction his memories must be altered; he therefore knows that he is playing tricks with reality; but by the exercise of *doublethink* he also satisfies himself that reality is not violated. The process has to be conscious, or it would not be carried out with sufficient precision, but it also has to be unconscious, or it would bring with it a feeling of falsity and hence of guilt. *Doublethink* lies at the very heart of Ingsoc, since the essential act of the Party is to use conscious deception while retaining the firmness of purpose that goes with complete honesty. To tell deliberate lies while genuinely believing in them, to forget any fact that has become inconvenient, and then, when it becomes necessary again, to draw it back from oblivion for just so long as it is needed, to deny the existence of objective reality and all the while to take account of the reality which one denies – all this is indispensably necessary. (215–16)

Moreover, the acknowledged forcing of Jehovah's Witnesses to accept false prophecy can be identified as a particular *type* of Orwellian *doublethink* – *blackwhite*:

Oceanic society rests ultimately on the belief that Big Brother is omnipotent and that the Party is infallible. But since in reality Big Brother is not omnipotent and the Party is not infallible, there is need for an unwearying, moment-to-moment flexibility in the treatment of facts. The key word here is *blackwhite* ... Applied to a Party member, it means a loyal willingness to say that black is white when Party discipline demands this. But it means also the ability to *believe* that black is white, and more, to *know* that black is white, and to forget that one has ever believed the contrary. (213)

The Governing Body of the Organization of Jehovah's Witnesses claims divine right when it comes to legislating what is right or wrong in terms of the interpretation of Scripture, without the stricture of infallibility. The implications of this fact for the Witnesses at large cannot be underestimated, for relatively arbitrary interpretation of Scripture can be used, not only to create and present self-fulfilling prophecies that may well dazzle the membership with their apparent complexity, but also to legitimize a host of variable doctrines. In fact, the very power of the leadership depends upon such legitimization. The society rationalized its shifts in doctrinal direction in the *Watchtower* article 'The Path of the Righteous Does Keep Getting Brighter' (1 December 1981), which echoes the Ingsoc truism: 'No change in doctrine ... can ever be admitted' (*1984*, 214).

At times explanations given by Jehovah's visible organization have shown adjustments, seemingly to previous points of view. But this has not actually been the case. This might be compared to what is known in navigational circles as 'tacking.' By maneuvering the sails the sailors can cause a ship to go from right to left, back and forth, but all the time making progress towards their destination in spite of contrary winds. (27)

Such tacking, *The Watchtower* suggests, must be understood in terms of 'progressive understanding' (29). But David Reed asked rhetorically in his first issue of *Comments from the Friends*, published while he was still a Witness in good standing, 'Isn't this navigational maneuver something that a sailor does purposefully and intentionally? ... If the men at the helm are confused or scuffling over what course to steer, wouldn't the ship's unsteadiness be better described by the words at Ephesians 4:14, "tossed and carried hither and thither by every wind of teaching ..."?' (January 1982, 2). Reed, at that time writing under the pseudonym 'Bill Tyndale, Jr,' pointed out several examples of total directional shifts, including the issues of 'saying hello' to disfellowshipped persons ('1972: No! 1974: Yes! 1981: No!') and calling Jehovah's Witnesses 'ministers' ('1975: Yes! 1976: No! 1981: Yes!' [February 1982, 1]).

David Reed was disfellowshipped subsequent to his pointing out these inconsistencies.* H.G. Covington, the society's lawyer, was disfellowshipped subsequent to *his* legal *faux pas*. The fact is, Jehovah's Witnesses are forced to take themselves and their symbolic vision very seriously indeed. However phantasmagorical the vision may seem to the uninitiated observer, to a committed Witness, there is no sense of unreality whatsoever in their world view; indeed, as *Awake!* has stated of the Witnesses, 'They discovered that this hope is not just a delusion – something to hold on to in order to hide from reality; no this *is* reality' (22 November 1982, 19). They refer to their world view and organization as 'the Truth'; to be a Jehovah's Witness is to be 'in the Truth'; and Witnesses call their beliefs 'truths.' Eric Dardel has written, 'Our "truth" of the moment is often only a myth that does not know it is one' (Sebeok 1972, 20). However, Jehovah's Witnesses are prepared to put their total faith in their collectivized 'truth' through a permanent suspension of disbelief. As Winston Smith comes to realize, 'In a way, the world-view of the Party imposed itself most successfully on people incapable of understanding it. They could be made to accept the most flagrant violations of reality, because they never fully grasped the enormity of what was demanded of them' (*1984*, 157).

The Watch Tower Bible and Tract Society derives its legitimacy as a theocracy from the same source as the symbolic vision that it presents to the world – the Bible. This was first established as a 'truth' during Rutherford's administration; Rutherford perceived a series of prophetic parallels which refer specifically to the historical development of the society. By presenting itself as the fulfilment of Bible prophecy, the society has been able to justify its claims, to the satisfaction of its membership, and hence has come to have power over the group (*WT* 1 March 1982, 3–9). The process of legitimization of the Watch Tower Bible and Tract Society as the official spokesman of God has not changed materially since Rutherford's day. Interestingly, it was Rutherford himself who said of Pope Pius XI's declaring 1933 a 'holy year': 'The act ... is a presumptuous sin before Almighty God. No man or company of men are running Jehovah's business so as to enable them to "change times and laws"' (*The Golden Age*, 10 May 1933, 483–90).

---

* Later Reed wrote of *Nineteen Eighty-Four*: 'Some twenty years ago, while in high school, we read this classic novel about a future totalitarian society. This book's principal character, Winston Smith, is a lover of truth trying to keep his sanity under a system in which "truth" changes from day to day, according to the whim of the Party. If you have been put on trial for the way you comb and shave, or cross-examined concerning your thoughts, as we have, you may appreciate some of the parallels noted here' (*Comments from the Friends* March 1982, 3).

The persecution that befell the leaders of the Watch Tower Society during the 1914–18 war was interpreted by them as a distinct prophetic period that fulfilled Bible prophecy. Since the Watch Tower Society regarded itself as the sole legitimate agency of God through which the command to 'preach to all the nations' of Matthew 24:14 was to be realized, when the preaching activity of the society was effectively frustrated during the war years, God's will was apparently challenged. Seeking explanation from the Scriptures, the Watch Tower leadership turned to Daniel 7:25 and 12:7. Commenting on the significance of these scriptures to the modern organization and the interruption of its preaching activities, the publication *Your Will Be Done on Earth* (1958) commented: 'The Anglo-American dual world power outstandingly opposed the carrying out of that law by the holy people of Jehovah God. In doing so it fulfilled the angelic prophecy: "He ... shall wear out the saints of the Most High, ... and they shall be given into his hand for a time, two times, and a half a time"' (180). But whereas Jehovah's Witnesses interpret the 'seven times' of Daniel 4 in a figurative manner to indicate 2,520 years (rather than 2,520 days, which is derived from the 360 days in the traditional Jewish year multiplied by seven years), the 'times, two times and half a time' of Daniel 7 is interpreted as lasting for three and a half literal years – a position which they claim is supported by Revelation 11:1–3: 'And I will cause my two witnesses to prophesy a thousand two hundred and sixty days dressed in sack-cloth' (*NWT*). In terms of organizational history, this period of forty-two months roughly parallels the time from November 1914 to May 1918, and includes the period of incarceration of the president, secretary-treasurer, publishers, and writers of the Watch Tower Bible and Tract Society. During their imprisonment, the preaching came to a near standstill – a situation they came to associate with mourning and sack cloth (see table 5; cf *WT* 1 January 1984, 8–9).

Another major prophetic period used to legitimize the organization's authority covers the time from the end of January 1919 to the first half of September 1922, at the Cedar Point, Ohio, convention. The scriptural reference for this period is Daniel 12:11: 'And from the time that the constant [feature] has been removed and there has been a placing of the disgusting thing that is causing desolation, there will be one thousand three hundred and thirty-five days' (*NWT*). As indicated in table 5, the convention at Cedar Point, which began on 8 September 1922, was to become a major landmark in the organization's history. During this gathering it was announced that the organization was once more prepared to function at capacity after the war years. The resumption of the preaching work was spurred on by Rutherford in his

TABLE 5

Prophecy and Organizational History

Prophecy	Time period	Interpretation
'SEVEN TIMES' or the appointed times of the nations (Dan. 4:16, 23, 25 and Luke 21:24).	Began in 7th lunar month (Ethanim – September to October) 607 BCE. Ended 7th lunar month, AD 1914.	End of the anointed times of the nations marks beginning of Christ's Second Coming.
'TIMES, TWO TIMES, AND HALF A TIME' (Dan. 7:25; 12:7; also compare 42 months of Rev. 11:2).	Began in first half of November 1914. Ended 7 May 1918, with arrest of Watch Tower society's officers and companions.	Satan the Devil ousted from heaven and with the nations of the earth whose time has ended strikes out at Jehovah's People.'
'THOUSAND TWO HUN-DRED AND NINETY DAYS' (Dan. 12:11).	Began the end of January 1919. Ended the first half of September 1922, at the Cedar Point, Ohio, assembly.	Period of reorganization, ends with announcement concerning the 'Other Sheep,' a new stage in preaching activity.
'THE THOUSAND THREE HUNDRED AND THIRTY-FIVE DAYS' (Dan. 12:12).	Began first half of September 1922, at Cedar Point assembly. Ended May 1926, at London International assembly.	Period of great 'happiness' as prophesied by Daniel. A period of unprecedented growth.
'TWO THOUSAND AND THREE HUNDRED EVEN-INGS AND MORNINGS' (Dan. 8:14).	Began in May 1926, at London International assembly. Ended 15 October 1932, with the official publication of notice in *The Watch Tower* that Jehovah's sanctuary had been 'cleansed.'	Period of decrease as some of membership gave up 'waiting.' Seen as a necessary 'in-house' cleaning before enacting written resolution's promise to world rulers that Jehovah would crush them.

best-remembered statement: 'The kingdom of heaven is at hand! ... You are his publicity agents. Therefore advertise, advertise, advertise, the King and his Kingdom!' (*JWDP*, 102).

The scriptural quotation which supported the next prophetic element is Daniel 12:12: 'Happy is the one who is keeping in expectation and who arrives at the one thousand three hundred and thirty-five days!' (*NWT*). 'One thousand, three hundred and thirty-five days' takes one from September 1922 to May 1926. These intervening years saw an annual increase in membership as follows: 1922 – 32,661; 1923 – 42,000; 1924 – 62,696; and 1925 – 90,434.* The significance of membership numbers as an indicator of Jehovah's blessings was taking root, but 1926, the end of the time for waiting, saw a temporary *decrease* in membership to 89,278. Disappointment over learning that only 144,000 individuals could qualify for heaven was augmented by the failure of a Rutherford prophecy of 25 September 1920 that the saints and prophets from the Old Testament would be resurrected in 1925. Rutherford went so far as to arrange housing for them in a huge mansion in San Diego called 'Beth Sarim.' The 'Ancients' failed to materialize, however, and Rutherford lived alone in the mansion until his death in 1942 (Stroup 1945, 42; Rogerson 1969, 48; Hewitt 1970, 90). The Witnesses' own official history ignores Beth Sarim entirely, offering another reason for discontent: 'The view had been somewhat general among the anointed that the remaining members of the body of Christ would be changed to heavenly glory that year' (*JWDP*, 107).

The combination of Rutherford's monetary extravagance in setting up Beth Sarim, his failure to predict accurately the comings and goings of Saints and Anointed Ones, and the failure of Armageddon to materialize as predicted in *The Finished Mystery* undoubtedly undermined morale and took its toll in terms of declining membership. This temporary threat to the organization's legitimacy as official spokesman for Jehovah was, however, dealt with to the satisfaction of the majority of the members by the organization's insistence that they had all passed through a 'test.' As the official history explained, 'A flood of new spiritual truths came to Jehovah's people, truths that further tested the devotion of those in line for the Kingdom' (*JWDP*, 107). Being tested implied that there was an external tester, and an appropriate scapegoat was sought. A drop in following coincident with the purported end of the waiting period indicated to the Witnesses that they had just come through a 'time of

---

* Note that 1925, like 1975, is the 48th year of a Jubilee cycle, that is, it is to be followed by two years of 'fallow.' The Witnesses have never capitalized on this coincidence, even though the surge in membership – the 'harvest' – would appear to corroborate Bible prophecy from their standpoint. The notion that Armageddon would come in 1925 was first introduced in 1917 in *The Finished Mystery*. The dynamics of the increase during the seventies were almost identical to those of the increase during the early twenties.

testing' and that some of their fellows had not measured up; but at a major assembly held in London, England, from 25 May to 31 May 1926, a formal resolution was drawn up which pointedly attacked world political leaders. In a show of strength designed to impress the membership with the power of Jehovah's organization they gave world leaders 'warning' that they had but '2,300 pathetic days to mark off when Jehovah's sanctuary should be restored to its rightful state' (*YWBDE*, 338 and *JWDP*, 102–4). This final period of 2,300 days was taken from Daniel's prophecy (8:14): 'Until two thousand three hundred evenings [and] mornings; and [the] holy place will certainly be brought into its right condition' (*NWT*). Anybody anticipating that the content of the original resolution was to bring woe to the world's religious and political leaders was to be disappointed. In actual practice, the end of 2,300 pathetic days was manipulated in a fashion inconsistent with the rest of the legitimization process and became an imperative for an in-house cleaning of the organization itself. This period ended on 15 October 1932, and in that month an announcement was made in *The Watchtower* concerning the discontinuation of the practice of 'electing' elders in a democratic process. They argued that a theocratic society had to be ruled from the top (God) down, not the other way around. From that time on the procedure for delegating responsibility was as follows: '"To the end that our service may be orderly, we will select certain ones of our company to perform specific service that may be necessary, including the following, to wit: A service director who shall be nominated by us and confirmed by the Society's executive or manager, and which service director shall be a member of the service committee of the company"' (*JWDP*, 127). This single move was declared to be the 'cleansing of the sanctuary' or the bringing of the 'holy place' into 'its right condition' in order for the preaching activity to develop. The target in the end had not been the religious leaders of the world but pockets of resistance and independence within the organization itself. In their own words, 'an unclean practice of the world' was eliminated with the end of the democratic process. Of all the prophetic analogies drawn, this final one stands as a clear example of the self-fulfilling type. Power had become absolutely centralized and the precedent set for any further 'cleansing of the sanctuary' which might be deemed necessary in the future.

Through these prophetic variations the organization was originally legitimized for the membership and its power established over their personal lives. Once the organization had been entrenched in this fashion it became, not only *one* mechanism for salvation, but the 'necessary agent' for all who wished

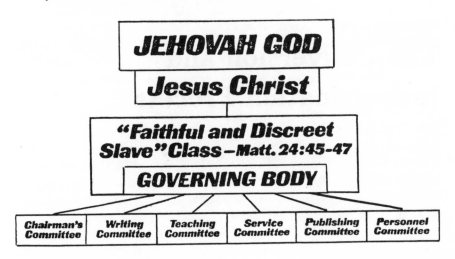

Figure 25 *WT* 1 January 1977, 16

to realize the vision of paradise. The *deus ex machina* of the Russell era had been transformed by Rutherford into the *machina ab deo* which persists to this day. The organization as it had existed under Russell had been a mouthpiece designed for the dissemination of novel, theologically revolutionary ideas through which people could assess their lives and strive for liberation from an oppressive larger society. Under Rutherford's leadership, the machinery for growth of the organization was expanded and rationalized, preaching and teaching techniques were standardized, and an efficient system for data collecting was established. Under Knorr, the machinery was refined and began to merge with the image of Jehovah himself until obedience to the organization had eclipsed in importance the individual's perception of and relationship with Jehovah. By 1977, when Frederick Franz officially took the president's chair, God had become imbedded in the corporate structure, as figure 25, published in a 1977 *Watchtower*, illustrates. Within this configuration, God is not *Logos* but merely a *logo*, an official seal of approval, the Governing Body's cosmic rubber stamp for use at its discretion in the quest for 'unity at all costs.' Like Big Brother, he is 'at the apex of the pyramid ... a focusing point for love, fear, and reverence' (*1984*: 209).

CHAPTER FOUR

The Conversion and Indoctrination Process

A Party member is expected to have no private emotions and no respites from enthusiasm. (*1984*: 212)

The non-ecstatic, non-carthartic quality of conversion as it applies to Jehovah's Witnesses has been dealt with previously by many scholars. One of the most succinct descriptions was offered by J.A. Beckford:

First and foremost we must report the virtual absence of anything which closely resembles the phenomenon of religious conversion as it is customarily understood. Jehovah's Witness converts certainly experience no sudden conviction that they have miraculously received God's grace nor that they have attained an immediate assurance of salvation. In fact, very few Witnesses can isolate a particular moment in time as a decisive turning point in their religious or spiritual development: Certainly none could remember having an overwhelming religious experience. (1975, 190)

For many, the conversion is a smooth transition from a state of doctrinal ignorance maintained through affiliation with another Christian group to one of relative enlightenment accompanied by a feeling of having come to a 'knowledge of "the Truth."' For some, this sense of enlightenment is heightened by an awareness that their own feelings concerning what is perceived to be wrong with other religions has been justified – that they themselves were right all along. And because the conversion is basically a cognitive one based on contrasts between light and darkness, error and truth, the rational approach of the society in presenting its perspective remains consonant with the nature of the conversion itself (Beckford 1975, 188 passim). As long as the convert relies upon the directions and instructions of the society, he is not likely to stray. Herein lies the crux of the conversion process within this group, as Beckford accurately concluded:

Only when converts willingly obey orders emanating from the Society's leaders, can one say that the conversion process has been successful. This frequently occurs long before individual converts have fully familiarized themselves with the movement's ideology and is, in this respect, a more important element of conversion than changes in religious ideas and feelings. Thus, in so far as there is a critical point in the conversion process, it centres around the acceptance or the rejection of the claims to authority made by the Society's officers at all levels of the hierarchy. (Beckford 1975, 192–3)

Two critical aspects of the Witnesses' proselytizing activities are designed to facilitate the conversion to the society: first, the formal study of Witness literature, and second, baptism by water immersion. The society states explicitly that all Bible studies should quickly show signs of 'real progress' to be deemed worthy of pursuit. The actual 'study' consists of question-and-answer coverage of one of the society's books. Eventually, the 'student' is introduced to the importance of prayer, of unity of action, of fellowship at the Kingdom Hall, and of preaching: 'As you study together week after week, keep in mind that for these persons to gain life they must eventually begin to bring forth fruit' (*OKPD*, 124; see also *YCLF* 200, 224).

Unless the potential converts are willing to give clear indication that they accept both the doctrines and the consequent responsibilities of attending meetings and going from door to door themselves, the study should be discontinued. Given that the Bible studies are held once a week for one hour at a time, the convert is often expected to make a choice based on approximately twenty-six hours of exposure to the doctrines in their simplest forms. However, it must be noted that in practice many Witnesses do continue non-productive studies for *years* in order to retain the 'good publisher' status which accompanies the regular recording of an ongoing Bible study.

The next stage of conversion is the process of baptism and the subsequent absorption of the convert into the social milieu of the organization. During this period the focus is gradually altered from studying the Bible directly to studying the society's own literature as an essential 'tool' to Bible understanding. Heavy emphasis is placed upon social imperatives in the Witness literature, a focus which helps bring the individual into a dependent relationship with the organization: 'If you have dedicated your life to the doing of Jehovah's will and are now contemplating baptism, you will be greatly aided by reading recent publications of the Watch Tower Society ...' (*OKPD*, 18). Of some eighty questions asked of the supplicant immediately prior to baptism, fifty are doctrinal and thirty are of social orientation (*OKPD*, 19–52; cf *OAOM*, 175–218). After this initial indoctrination, the baptized person is usually considered to be 'on his own' and is left to glean his information from the five weekly meetings. Although Bible studies may continue to be conducted with him, such studies are not counted in the society's statistics (*OKPD*, 127).

Once baptized, the individual is at the mercy of the organization, especially when it comes to discipline. A child who has been baptized at twelve can be disfellowshipped and ostracized, but 'non-baptized associates' of any age, although they may be 'named' by the congregation, cannot be formally expelled and, thus, are safe from the at times tyrannical application of justice manifested at the congregational level (see *OAOM*, 147–9).

Over the years, the Watch Tower Bible and Tract Society has published key primers of the basic Jehovah's Witness doctrines. The first of these books, published in 1946, was '*Let God Be True*' the first edition of which was printed in a run of a million copies. A second primer came out in 1958 and went through several editions totalling some ten million copies. *From Paradise Lost to Paradise Regained* in some ways resembled a Bible storybook, and it was used widely for Bible study with children; indeed, many Witness children learned to read for the first time using the book as a primer in a different sense. The simplistic language and repetition is hypnotic:

The simple language of this book is not because you are not a full-grown man or woman or do not have a mind old enough to understand hard things. But now you have something new to learn; you must find out about new people; you must learn new things that will be for your good, but different from anything you have heard or studied before. So you must get to know these things little by little. In that way you will understand these things from the very beginning and at last be able to understand the Bible itself when you read it ...

Besides using simple language this book has many pictures. There are so many good things to tell that there is not room enough in this book to write about them all. So we want these pictures to help in telling you some of these things ...

TABLE 6
Programme of Weekly Meetings

Public Talk
'These interesting Bible lectures are one of the best methods of helping those who are studying the Bible in their homes with Jehovah's witnesses to become acquainted with Jehovah's great purpose for mankind and to associate with God's organization regularly.'

The Watchtower Study
This is where 'spiritual truths are provided ... keeping one abreast with the application and fulfillment of Bible prophecy.' It is also where men, women and children learn their Christian roles.

The Kingdom Ministry School
The Theocratic Ministry School is 'designed for the purpose of teaching and equipping Jehovah's witnesses to preach the good news.' And 'unlike with most schools, there are no graduates, for the course is a lifelong one for young and old, male and female.'

The Service Meeting
'The service meeting ... give[s] Jehovah's witnesses practical instructions that will help them to become better qualified ministers and more efficient in carrying on their house to house ministry.' This is done through talks, demonstrations, question and answer parts, interviews and discussions between two or more persons.

The Book Study
Small groups meet, usually in private homes of members. 'The textbook is usually one of the latest Bible-study aids ... These studies make clear the light on Bible prophecies and the prophetic patterns needed to be understood at this time ...'

WT 15 January 1966, 45–6

At the bottom of each page there is a question or two. You can ask yourself these questions to find out whether you remember what you read on that page. In that way you can not only read this book but also make a study of it and teach others ...(7)

By far the most successful textbook published by the Watch Tower Bible and Tract Society was *The Truth That Leads to Eternal Life* (1968), which was designed to replace *'Let God Be True'* and covered the same ground: each of the twenty-two chapters covers a specific doctrinal issue. It remained the mainstay of home Bible study in the organization for fourteen years; the first edition had a run of 15,000,000 copies (unfortunately many of them were bound upside-down by mistake), and by 1982 the total number of copies printed had reached a staggering 115,000,000. Chapter 21 deals specifically with the leap every convert is sooner or later requested to make – dedication and baptism:

When love for God moves you so that you want to do his will, then it is proper that you go to him in prayer through Jesus Christ and express your desire to be one of his servants, walking in the footsteps of his Son. It is appropriate that you tell Jehovah that you want to belong to him and that you want to do his will both now and for all time to come. In this way you dedicate yourself to God. This is a personal, private matter. No one else can do it for you.

After you have made your dedication to Jehovah to do his will, he will expect you to keep it. It is no light matter ...

If you have made up your mind to serve Jehovah and want to be baptized, then make this known to the overseer of the congregation of Jehovah's witnesses with which you are associated. He will gladly assist you, without any charge for the baptism. (182–4)

Then the next step is broached: 'Of course, dedication and baptism are not the end of one's doing God's will. They are only the beginning ... A principal part of God's work for Jesus on this earth was to preach the kingdom of God ... It is God's will that this preaching work be done now ... Will you share in this work?'(184–5).

You Can Live Forever in Paradise on Earth (1982) covers much of the same material as *The Truth That Leads to Eternal Life* and *'Let God Be True'*, but presents it in a much more palatable form, including 150 colour illustrations and topical treatment of contemporary issues ranging from spiritism to marijuana. Many of the chapter headings are virtually identical to those of the earlier primers – a clear indication of how closely the society has adhered to the proven formula of its other best-sellers. Again the tone is seductive and the technique employed is the rhetorical question: 'Do you want to live forever on earth under God's government? Any person in his right mind would answer, Yes! Wonderful benefits will be enjoyed. But to receive them you cannot simply raise your hand and say: "I want to be a subject of God's government." More is needed'(127). What is needed is knowledge, righteous conduct, loyalty, and a willingness to 'tell others about it' (133), and the accompanying illustration shows a couple going from house to house, Witness style. In the chapter entitled 'Identifying the True Religion' two neighbours are shown chatting amiably over a fence. The caption reads: 'If you were to talk to someone about Jehovah and his kingdom, with what religion would people associate you?' (185).

The social imperative which demands active preaching as part of the responsibility of accepting membership in the group must be recognized as a critical factor in the conversion process itself. The Witnesses do not want among their membership persons who are not willing to carry out the social mandate of the group – to engage in proselytizing. As Beckford noted of those Witnesses who begin as avid evangelizers and cool off in their enthusiasm for the work: 'The dilemma is basically between tolerating partial defectors in the hope of eventually restoring them to full fellowship and running the risk of alienating practising Witnesses by appearing to condone rebellious or lax behaviour' (Beckford, 189). Backsliders create enough problems for the Witnesses without encouraging the involvement of people who from the outset clearly do not wish to spread the message of Jehovah's kingdom door to door. Active preaching is, in fact, one of the most effective boundary mechanisms the Witnesses have created (see figure 26).

To the Witnesses conversion provides important psychological rewards, as described by Alan Rogerson:

What sort of people choose to become Jehovah's Witnesses? One answer to this is that the chief field for converts appears to be amongst disillusioned church members – people with a 'religious' outlook searching for the answers to the questions: Why is there evil? Why are we here?, etc. The relatively sophisticated orthodox churches feel there is no definite answer to these queries, but the Witnesses provide an answer to all such questions – their remedy is no less than a universal panacea! Hoekema recalls the expression: 'the cults are the Unpaid Bills of the Church'; and it often seems as though the Witnesses have set out to accomplish what the established churches have failed to do. (1979, 175–6)

Within the symbolically constituted world of the Witnesses, the disinherited souls of other churches are provided with answers to all their questions as well as formulae for action in which they feel a sense of power in being able to function productively within their newfound community. Inevitably, they are led to dedication and baptism through water immersion – the contract that binds the individual with the organization and puts him formally on the 'road to life.'

Besides undergoing baptism and participating in the active distribution of Watch Tower literature, newly converted Jehovah's Witnesses are also expected to adopt a new personality: 'Because we are all sinners, changes in our attitude, our speech and our conduct are required in order for us to reflect the personality of our God. We need to put on the 'new personality' ... Counsel

Figure 26 *WT* 1 June 1978, cover

and discipline help us to identify areas where adjustments are needed and then to see how to make these' (*UWTG*, 130). Such adjustments in personality are monitored carefully by the congregation elders, for 'those who have spiritual qualifications bear responsibility to use the Scriptures to readjust others when they discern a need' (131). Jehovah's Witnesses must be seen to be 'gathered together in unity of thought and action regardless of their physical location on earth' (*OAOM*, 154); such international unity allows the organization to claim that it has already constructed a 'spiritual paradise': 'Building and maintaining the spiritual paradise also means "doing nothing out of contentiousness or out of egotism, but with lowliness of mind considering that the others are superior to you"' (157). Those who do not conform totally to Watch Tower doctrine 'could be exerting an unhealthy influence on others'; and so each must be 'marked' by the elders and treated 'as a "marked" individual': 'Occasionally, in the congregation today, there may be those who, although not known to be guilty of practicing a grave sin for which they could be expelled, nevertheless continue to display flagrant disregard for theocratic order' (152–3). Such a 'marked' person would be watched carefully for signs of wrongdoing, and would be avoided socially: 'Theocratic subjection affects all aspects of our life' (16).

Despite ongoing pressure to conform socially and to adopt a 'new personality,' a long time must be spent by new converts in learning the theocratic language of the Witnesses through which their vision is transmitted and which distinguishes them as a unique community. As Rogerson noted, 'a new convert's conversation conspicuously lacks the "stock phrases" used and sanctioned by the Society ... The Witnesses themselves approve of such a special vocabulary which they feel helps to ensure their loyalty to the Society – a situation similar to that in George Orwell's novel *1984* where the creation of *Newspeak* eliminated the possibility of thoughtcrime!' (Rogerson 1969, 178). The Witnesses refer to each other as 'brother' and 'sister' and collectively as 'the Friends,' who are all 'in the Truth.' 'Brother' and 'Sister' are also used as titles of address up and down the ladder of command, from the mere child to the president of the organization; 'Mr' or 'Mrs' are titles reserved for 'worldly' people. Hence, the president is referred to as 'Brother Franz' and his wife as 'Sister Franz.' To call him 'Mr Franz' would be an insult. If a newly interested person comes to the Kingdom Hall, he is introduced either by his first name or as 'Mr.' Immediately the Witnesses know his status, and treat him deferentially as a newcomer. The incumbent must earn his status as 'brother' (as 'one of the Friends') by becoming active in the ministry.

The adoption of different language patterns by Witnesses is automatic and largely unconscious even though they readily accept the existence of 'theocratic language.' Just as Newspeak reflects Party status in Oceania, theocratic language in many ways helps define Jehovah's Witnesses as a cultural group; it is often possible to detect a Witness just by listening to his or her social conversation. The 'theocratic language' includes the redefinition of standard English words, the emotional charging of words, the peculiar use of metaphor in argument, and the adoption of particular mannerisms of speech. While the Witnesses have not actually coined any new words, they do alter extant words. For example, they write of the many forms of 'happinesses' and talk of 'happifying' experiences. They also embellish many words with idiosyncratic connotations or ascribe peculiar meanings to them. Thus, 'theocratic' is not only used to describe the organizational structure of the Witnesses, which they firmly believe to be under the control and inspiration of God, but it is also used in adjectival or adverbial form to modify any 'godly' or 'faithful' or 'good' behaviour on the part of the Witnesses – behaviour that sets them apart *as* Witnesses. It is 'theocratic' to refuse a blood transfusion and 'untheocratic' to accept one.

Among those terms which have been redefined to accommodate the Witnesses' theocratic conceptions are 'Christendom' and 'Christian.' The former refers to all Catholic and Protestant religions *other than* Jehovah's Witnesses, and the latter refers to the Witnesses alone; they regard themselves as the only true 'Christians.' The notion that all religions of the world (collectively known as 'Babylon the Great') are outlets for doctrines of the Devil deceptively disguised was responsible for the long-lasting reluctance of Jehovah's Witnesses to be known as a 'religion' or 'church.' In the words of Rutherford: '"Religion" is doing anything contrary to the will of Almighty God' (*Yearbook* 1941, 14). However, these terms have finally gained a modicum of acceptance within the organization (*WT* 1 January 1982, 7).

An issue closely connected with the perception of 'religion' as a negative word is the traditional spelling of the name of the group with a lower-case 'w'. As Rogerson explained 'The Witnesses today insist on spelling their name with a small 'w' – *Jehovah's witnesses*. They believe they are not just a new cult or sect (Jehovah's Witnesses) but they are simply God's servants, God's present-day *witnesses* to His name and glory' (1969, 56). The Witnesses insisted upon the use of the lower-case 'w' until 1976. All literature published by them prior to 15 March 1976 followed this convention; then without one word of explanation, the 1 April 1976 *Watchtower* abandoned the practice, capitalizing 'Witnesses' throughout the text. Owing to a proofreading oversight, the inside front cover and masthead containing publishing details continued to use the lower-case 'w' until 1 August 1976. Several Witnesses were questioned about this change of policy and not even the elders seemed to have noticed – each expressed surprise when the change was pointed out. Now, years after the revision of what was originally perceived to be a major policy, no one seems to remember that there ever was an issue made of the capitalization of the name.

Once adopted, the name 'Jehovah's Witnesses' enabled the members (in their own minds) to have a feeling of intimacy with God: 'Our having an approved relationship with Jehovah, knowing him as a real Person, and making his name known to others will result in his holding us in mind for our lasting good' (*WT* 1 May 1978, 14). *The Watchtower* often refers to the Witnesses as 'Jehovah's name-people' or 'people for His name': 'That people for Jehovah's name would be his witnesses, gathered together in unity of thought and action' (*OAOM* 1983, 154).

The Witnesses recognize clearly that the extent of the idiosyncratic nature of their expressions goes beyond their adoption of a specific name for God. This was pointed out explicitly in the January 1965 *Kingdom Ministry*, a four-page news sheet designed to organize the weekly Service Meeting: 'It is also good to be careful in the terms we use. Words such as "Kingdom," "Armageddon," "remnant" and "great crowd" are everyday expressions to us, but they probably would not be correctly understood by most people we meet in the house-to-house work; so it is wise to add something that will make clear just what they mean' (3). On the other hand, some words that are everyday expressions to most of the world, such as 'good luck,' are frowned on by the Witnesses. The acceptability of a particular phrase or word may change from time to time, and good Witnesses stay on their toes. In fact, catching a fellow Witness using a *verboten* expression is a popular game – a form of social one-upmanship – not unlike the one that O'Brien plays with Winston Smith: '"I noticed you had used two words which have become obsolete. But they have only become so very recently"' (*1984*, 159).

Not only the spoken or written word comes under scrutiny. Much attention is placed in the Ministry School on gesture and facial expression, and in the *Theocratic Ministry School Guidebook* (1971) the Witnesses were reminded, 'Our manner of speaking is important. This includes even our facial expressions and tone of voice' (54). This position was reinforced in circuit assemblies in 1982: 'Sisters should not express disagreement with judicial decisions of the elders EVEN BY THEIR FACIAL EXPRESSIONS' (*Comments from the Friends* March 1982, 2). In Orwell's Oceania, 'To wear an improper expression on your face (to look incredulous when a victory was announced, for example) was itself a punishable offence. There was even a word for it in Newspeak: *facecrime*, it was called' (*1984*, 62).

So concerned is the society to avoid the accusation of being lewd that its publications overuse euphemisms, with a strange lexiphanic effect, as in this description of the sex act in *Your Youth: Getting the Best Out of It* (1976): 'The husband lies close to his wife so that his male organ fits naturally into her birth canal' (22). We have yet to see the words 'penis' and 'vagina' in any of the Witnesses' literature. In fact, a recent review of the movie *E. T. – The Extra-Terrestrial* in *Awake!* (8 July 1983) castigated the film partly because 'some of the language used by these children is gross profanity' – an allusion to Elliott's calling his older brother 'Penis-Breath' (27).

Sometimes, a similar effect is achieved in Witness literature by unwitting *non sequitur*, as in the booklet *Unseen Spirits: Do They Help Us? Or Do They Harm Us?* (1978). After denouncing certain *funeral* rites as 'pagan' the booklet states, 'Yes, deaths, funerals, marriages, pregnancies, births, circumcisions are all occasions to be alert. God's Word warns: "Awake! be on the alert! Your enemy the devil, like a roaring lion, prowls round looking for someone to devour"' (53).

The Witnesses cultivate their language carefully, specifically in the weekly Ministry School Meeting during which five or so members (chosen on a rotating basis) each present a short talk. Male speakers stand before the podium and address the audience directly, but the women present skits, talking to each other on the platform, as they are not allowed to take part in the direct instruction of fellow Witnesses. (If a woman ever feels moved to correct a man on some detail of doctrine, or if she prays or says grace aloud in the presence of other baptized Witnesses – male or female – she must first cover her head, be it with a hat or a Kleenex, to indicate that she understands her place within the divine scheme of things.) At the end of each five- to seven-minute presentation, the Ministry School Servant (an elder appointed to the task) counsels the speakers on three specific points contained on the 'Speech Counsel Form' (see figure 27). Not until a speaker has received a 'Good' on a given point is he or she allowed to proceed to the next focus of emphasis during the subsequent scheduled presentation.

The Theocratic Ministry School Guidebook (1971) is a 192-page reference manual for improving one's teaching skills. It is designed to help the member achieve the desired patterns capsulized in the Speech Counsel Form.

SPEECH COUNSEL

Speaker _____
(Full Name)

Marks: W - Work on this
I - Improved
G - Good

Date

Talk No.

Informative material (21)*
Clear, understandable (21)
Introduction roused interest (22)
Introduction appropriate to theme (22)
Introduction of proper length (22)
Volume (23)
Pausing (23)
Audience encouraged to use Bible (24)
Scriptures properly introduced (24)
Scriptures read with emphasis (25)
Scripture application made clear (25)
Repetition for emphasis (26)
Gestures (26)
Subject theme emphasized (27)
Main points made to stand out (27)
Audience contact, use of notes (28)
Use of outline (28)

Remarks: _____
_____
_____

* Each number in parentheses refers to the Study in Theocratic Ministry School Guidebook that discusses the designated speech quality.

S-48   6/71   Printed in U.S.A.

Date

Talk No.

Fluency (29)
Conversational quality (29)
Pronunciation (29)
Coherence through connectives (30)
Logical, coherent development (30)
Convincing argument (31)
Audience helped to reason (31)
Sense stress (32)
Modulation (32)
Enthusiasm (33)
Warmth, feeling (33)
Illustrations fit material (34)
Illustrations fit audience (34)
Material adapted for field ministry (35)
Conclusion appropriate, effective (36)
Conclusion of proper length (36)
Timing (36)
Confidence and poise (37)
Personal appearance (37)

NOTE: For each talk the counselor will check the student on the next points in order on the Speech Counsel form, covering whatever is grouped together in a single Study in Theocratic Ministry School Guidebook. Whenever there are adjustments made in that procedure the counselor will note that in advance under "Remarks." The blank spaces on the form may be used for counseling students on points not listed, such as accuracy of statement, articulation, bearing, choice of words, grammar, mannerisms, relevancy, teaching techniques and voice quality when the need arises.

Figure 27

Given the intensive indoctrination in language itself, it is not surprising that the classic 'Good morning! It's a lovely day today, isn't it?' one uses in greeting a householder could be replaced with a string of nonsense syllables and still the inflection, tone, and facial gestures would indicate clearly that the speaker was a Witness. This adoption of specific physical attitudes and gestures, analogous to the *mudras* of the Yoga tradition, adds 'meaning to your speech' and 'should become a matter of course' (*TMSG*, 133); or, in Orwellian terms, 'Zeal was not enough. Orthodoxy was unconsciousness' (*1984*, 56).

The rhetorical question is a major linguistic tool used by the Witnesses. So ingrained is its use that even casual conversation around the dinner table is permeated with self-answered questions. Orwell described this type of language ('a trick of asking questions and then promptly answering them') as being typical of Big Brother (*1984*, 47). Conversations among Witnesses, or talks formally delivered – indeed, much of the literature – are spattered with such statements as 'We *are* privileged to be among Jehovah's chosen people, *aren't* we?' and 'We can't be too careful of bad worldly associations, *can* we?' If the person being referred to is lax in some way the questions can become pointedly mordacious. 'She *does* look dreadful in those clothes, *doesn't* she?' or 'You *won't* get through Armageddon acting that way, *will* you?' Even brief encounters with this form of conversation are extremely irritating to anyone not considered to be a part of the elite 'we,' yet among the Witnesses the stock answers to the stock questions provide a verbal feedback system for consolidating social integration within the faith. It also obviates the necessity of thinking when presented with a question. When lured off the course of their carefully prepared house-to-house rhetorical interrogation presentations, many Witnesses become flustered and are unable to continue.

The use of specialized language and the rhetorical question is often complicated by the use of analogy. One example of this combination is to be found in the Witnesses' attack on the theory of evolution. This often-treated subject was dealt with 'in depth' in a 1967 publication entitled *Did Man Get Here by Evolution or by Creation?* In presenting the subject matter to a membership already acculturated to the tongue-in-cheek pronunciation of the word as 'evil-you-shun,' the society asks: 'Do you believe that these creatures achieved this ability by *blind* evolutionary *chance*? Is it not obvious that an intelligent Creator with a perfect understanding of physical laws designed their bodies? And since man learns from this, does not that show there had to be a teacher?' (*DMGHE*, 122; italics added). The whole tone of the book is established in the first sentence of the text: 'Are you a descendant of an apelike beast that lived millions of years ago?' (*DMGHE*, 5). One is aware from the first that the Witnesses consider evolution to be so ridiculous as to hardly warrant refutation. The Witnesses, however, do not notice the inappropriateness of the analogies often used in the process of debating the issues. For example: 'Mutations are compared with accidents in the genetic machinery of living things. They are more like the wrecking of an automobile, not the building of one. An accident is not associated with improvement, but with disaster. Dropping a delicate watch or throwing a wrench into a computer's mechanism is not calculated to improve performance' (*DMGHE*, 64). Not even the obvious problem of comparing inanimate objects with living organisms poses a problem for the Witnesses who read and study this book. Surprisingly, even Rogerson liked the book: 'The tone is reasonable and there are few errors of logic and reasoning ...' (1969, 117).

So compartmentalized is the thinking of the Witnesses that their own theory of speciation poses no problem for them in spite of their adamant rejection of evolution. They firmly believe that the flood destroyed all non-aquatic animal life approximately 4,000 years ago. Therefore, all extant forms of animal life are directly descended from archetypal 'types' or 'kinds' that survived the global flood in Noah's ark. All members of the *Felis* genus, for example, including the mountain lion and the housecat, 'sprang' (but did *not* 'evolve') from the two archetypal cats on the ark which contained all the genetic variables that have come to be expressed in the last 4,000 years (see *IBRWG*, 43). As Rogerson noted:

A long acquaintance with the literature of the Witnesses leads one to the conclusion that they live in the intellectual 'twilight zone'. That is, most of their members, even their leaders, are not well educated and not very intelligent. Whenever their literature strays onto the fields of philosophy, academic theology, science or any severe mental discipline their ideas at best mirror popular misconceptions, at worst they are completely nonsensical. (Rogerson 1969, 116)

The linguistic peculiarities of the Witnesses serves to define and support their world view – their apprehended reality. When threatened by dissonant messages from the broader culture, they may retreat into their own intellectual world where standard definitions and the rules of formal logic have no power. As in *Nineteen Eighty-Four*, 'The empirical method of thought, on which all the scientific achievements of the past were founded, is opposed to the most fundamental principles of Ingsoc' (194).

One final point must be made concerning those who become members through conversion. Much of the extant literature on the Witnesses suggests that they become involved in the movement as a result of low intelligence. This attitude belies the power of the processes operative within the group and serves only to mask certain basic issues. That the organization does have an 'anti-intellectual' bent is demonstrated, not only in the literature (see *WT* 15 July 1982, 12–5), but also by the fact that even those who have served the society well as lawyers and apologists – such as H.G. Covington or Dr James Penton – often find themselves in disfavour during a period of internal conflict. These people often have extensive knowledge of the internal workings of the organization and, like Syme in *Nineteen Eighty-Four*, may find themselves removed to prevent them from disseminating damaging knowledge or information about the society from the 'inside.' Most Witnesses, although *capable* of intelligent, reasonable thought, have as part of the payment for paradise delegated authority to the organization for directing their lives in accordance with their desires for realizing the ultimate goal, and finally abrogate *all* responsibility and rights over their personal lives – in effect, allowing the society to do their thinking for them.

The punishment most commonly meted out to Jehovah's Witnesses who reject or challenge the fundamental doctrines of the Watch Tower Society – or who ignore Watch Tower taboos such as those against smoking or oral sex – is 'disfellowshipping,' a form of social and spiritual ostracism the effects of which are legendary. Jehovah's Witnesses have a closed society in that they try to ensure that the majority of their friends and acquaintances are from within the congregation. Since the Witnesses discourage the pursuit of post-secondary education ('Many parents feel that the potential benefits of a university education are not worth the possible horrendous costs, especially where the children would have to go unsupervised to another city or country' [*WT* 15 July 1982, 14]), if a Witness should become disfellowshipped, he not only loses most of his friends but finds himself out in the world with limited employment opportunities. The very focus of his 'spiritual education' that makes him successful as a Witness leads to difficulties in coping with the larger world.

But the social and economic implications of disfellowshipping are comparatively minor in the mind of the committed Witness when assessed against the implications of the threat of eternal condemnation by God – oblivion. Even more serious are the implications of disfellowshipping a member of the anointed Remnant. As one of the 144,000 anticipating kingship in heaven with Christ, the stakes are much higher than for a member of the Great

Crowd. Furthermore, once a member of the 'Faithful and Discreet Slave' Class becomes disfellowshipped, he is automatically branded as a member of the 'Evil Slave' Class – tantamount to being branded a demon – and the chances of reinstatement are very slim indeed.

In recent years, the Watch Tower Bible and Tract Society has clamped down on disaffection by insisting that inactive Witnesses either become active or declare themselves 'disassociated.' Usually people in this category are asked to declare that they no longer believe key Watch Tower doctrines. Since 1980, any written indication of a willingness to disassociate oneself has been taken as tantamount to apostasy, no matter what the reason (*WT* 15 September 1981, 29). Other Witnesses are not allowed to socialize with those who have been disfellowshipped or who have disassociated themselves. If they do so, they may themselves be punished by disfellowshipping. In *Nineteen Eighty-Four*, the rebellious Jones, Aaronson, and Rutherford are treated in a similar manner: 'It was not wise even to be seen in the neighbourhood of such people' (*1984*, 75–6). The Witnesses' latest handbook, *Organized to Accomplish Our Ministry* (1983), gives a broader definition of disassociation: 'a person might renounce his place in the Christian congregation by his actions, such as by becoming part of a secular organization the objective of which is contrary to the Bible ... If a person who is a Christian chooses to join those who are disapproved by God, it would be fitting for the congregation to acknowledge by a brief announcement that he has *disassociated himself* and is no longer one of Jehovah's Witnesses. Such a person would be viewed in the same way as a disfellowshipped person' (151; italics in original).

Witnesses who are charged with a disfellowshippable offence, or who are deemed to have disassociated themselves by their actions rather than by a formal letter, are presumed to be guilty until found innocent. The onus is on the accused to prove his innocence, and if he makes no effort to do so – if, for example, he does not show up for a unilaterally and often arbitrarily scheduled judicial committee hearing – then he is assumed to be unrepentant and 'guilty' and may be disfellowshipped, despite the fact that guilt has not been established; the rule of *habeas corpus* is not recognized. 'The wrongdoer may have become hardened in his course of wrong conduct and fail to respond to the efforts of his brothers to help him. Fruits, or works, befitting repentence may not be in evidence, nor may genuine repentence be apparent at the time of the hearing. What then? In such cases it would be necessary for the responsible overseers to expel the unrepentant wrongdoer from the congregation' (*OAOM*, 146).

After any disfellowshipping, the individual has one week to appeal, and the appeal hearing is held within a week of the committee's receiving 'a letter clearly stating his reasons for the appeal' (147). A disfellowshipped person can be reinstated only by the congregation that initially disfellowshipped him and preferably by the same committee. If the person has moved to another congregation in the meantime, reinstatement hearings must involve both congregations, but the disfellowshipping congregation makes the final decision on his status (147–50).

One of the key factors in maintaining the adherence of converts to the sect is the degree to which they focus on the collective vision of symbol and imperative that the Watch Tower Bible and Tract Society presents to them. To ensure absolute obedience, Watch Tower literature increasingly emphasizes the importance of avoiding or fighting against 'independent thinking,' by which the society means 'thinking that we know better than the organization' (*WT* 15 January 1983, 27):

From the very outset of his rebellion Satan called into question God's way of doing things. He promoted independent thinking. 'You can decide for yourself what is good and bad,' Satan told Eve. 'You don't have to listen to God. He is not really telling you the truth.' (Genesis 3:1–5) To this day, it has been Satan's subtle design to infect God's people with this type of thinking. – 2 Timothy 3:1,13.

How is such independent thinking manifested? A common way is by questioning the counsel that is provided by God's visible organization. (22)

The society argues that Jehovah's Witnesses are God's organization, for 'Jehovah has always guided his servants in an organized way. And just as in the first century there was only one true Christian organization, so today Jehovah is using only one organization':

Yet there are some who point out that the organization has had to make adjustments before, and so they argue: 'This shows that we have to make up our own mind on what to believe.' This is independent thinking. Why is it so dangerous? ... If we get to thinking that we know better than the organization, we should ask ourselves: 'Where did we learn Bible truth in the first place? Would we know the way of the truth if it had not been for guidance from the organization? Really, can we get along without the direction of God's organization?' No, we cannot! (27)

A similar attitude was described by George Orwell in *Nineteen Eighty-Four*, in which O'Brien insists that 'whatever the Party holds to be truth, *is* truth. It is impossible to see reality except by looking through the eyes of the Party' (252); Winston is required to 'make complete, utter submission' and 'escape from his identity' to allow him to 'merge himself in the Party'; this is Winston's only chance to become 'immortal' (267). Furthermore, 'The two aims of the Party are to conquer the whole surface of the earth and extinguish once and for all the possibility of independent thought' (194). The power of the Party over its members is the assumption and belief that 'the Party is always right' (156; see also 133, 137, 211–14), but the 'more the Party is powerful, the less it will be tolerant' (271). All of these precepts of Orwellian theocracy apply to Witness theocracy as well: proscriptions such as those against 'independent thinking' lead the new convert to place all his trust and focus all his faculties on the *collective* rather than individual vision – as must the Party members of Oceania.

CHAPTER FIVE

Watch Tower Literature

Books, also, were ... rewritten again and again, and were invariably reissued without any admission that any alteration had been made. (*1984*, 41)

The power that the Watch Tower Bible and Tract Society has subsumed for itself over the past century presupposes a sophisticated system for maintaining and sustaining the symbolic vision for the membership and interpreting it in meaningful ways. The onus has thus devolved upon the society itself to keep the symbolic corpus alive within the minds of its members. Since the early 1940s, the symbolic superstructure of the sect has remained essentially stable, new revelations building upon, or only marginally modifying, the mythic fabric already in place. A primary function of the organization has thus become symbol management, or more specifically symbol manipulation, which includes reiterating and reaffirming for the community the continued veracity of specific symbols, and the quiet shelving of others considered to be outdated. Some 'truths' are maintained; others are allowed to die (*WT* 1 December 1981, 26–31).

The vast quantity of literature produced by the society in order to keep the current body of symbols alive for the membership consists necessarily of a constant repetition of the basic viable symbolic themes. This repetition becomes mantric in quality, and the society's constant rephrasing and re-presentation of the basic corpus of recognized belief becomes for the membership the rhythmic life-breath of *the* symbol, *the* truth, *the* ultimate security. Mesmerized by the repetitious drumbeat of familiar doctrine, the membership soon forgets that part of the symbol that has been sloughed off without comment or apology. Anything that is not constantly repeated is forgotten in time; doctrinal memory is definitely not one of the long suits of the membership. The literature is used both for the transmission of the symbolic vision to potential converts and for the ongoing indoctrination of the membership. The importance of social control is recognized explicitly by the organization, and the literature gives constant voice to the need for absolute conformity and obedience to its dictates if the ultimate symbolic vision – the New World promised by God – is to be achieved.

The official mouthpiece of the society is *The Watchtower*. With a circulation of 10,200,000 copies per issue, it is considered to be God's channel of communication with mankind, produced through the graces of the 'Faithful and Discreet Slave' or 'Little Flock' Class represented by the Governing Body. A semi-monthly periodical, *The Watchtower* is constantly before the Witnesses and contains the question-and-answer material for the 'principal meeting of Jehovah's Witnesses,' the Sunday *Watchtower* study which, with the exception of specifically public meetings, attracts larger numbers of the membership and interested individuals than any other meeting. In the Witnesses' own words: 'It is at the *Watchtower* study where doctrinal points are established and timely new spiritual truths are provided – keeping one abreast with the application and fulfilment of Bible prophecy' (*WT* 15 January 1966, 44). With specific reference to the social value of the *Watchtower* study, they add:

A man can learn how to care for his responsibilities within the family circle. He can receive information on how to be a good and wise father, how to keep unity and peace among the members of his family and how to exercise his headship properly. A woman can learn her Christian place, not only in the home, but also in the theocratic organization, and how she can serve God and her family in a pleasing manner. Children are taught proper respect for God and parents as well as receive instruction and discipline, which will contribute to their physical and spiritual growth. (44–5)

In order to demonstrate the relative importance of theological doctrine with social imperative within the organization, we analysed 144 consecutive issues of *The Watchtower*, from 1 January 1975 to 15 December 1980. As the magical moment envisioned for 'no later than October, 1975' approached, blatantly social articles dominated the pages of *The Watchtower*; 69 per cent of the articles were dedicated to various social imperatives and only 31 per cent of the articles were concerned with doctrine. This emphasis was even more pointed in the central articles used for study, of which 89 per cent were predominantly social in content.* Two possible explanations could be advanced for this conspicuous emphasis: first, that the Witnesses wished to focus community attention on the necessity that their organization be in a 'clean state' for the final glorious moment; second, that the period under consideration was concurrent with the traumatic decline in health of the president, Nathan H. Knorr. Since F.W. Franz had long been in control of official doctrine, the second explanation is not likely; besides, when Armageddon failed to arrive by the end of 1975, the articles abruptly reverted to a balanced configuration of emphasis.

As the membership became aware of the ramifications of alleged 'failed prophecy,' the Brooklyn headquarters was deluged with letters of complaint and demands that the society frankly admit that it had made a serious mistake in its suggestions. But pressure from the grass roots did nothing to move Brooklyn to an admission of oracular error. Rather, over the following years, the articles of the official mouthpiece became increasingly doctrinal in content. It was becoming imperative to maintain the focus of the attention of the membership on the collective vision of Armageddon, which, if delayed, none the less remained a major concern of every believer. The trend towards heavier emphasis on doctrine finally peaked in 1979, although no direct apology for the prophetic failure of 1975 came through the pages of *The Watchtower* until March 1980.

The doctrinal content of *The Watchtower* between 1977 and 1979 cast yet another light on the need for the internal reaffirmation of ultimate goals and the struggle to attain them. Concern began to focus more and more heavily upon theological interpretations of 'good behaviour' – of what was demanded by God if Jehovah's Witnesses were to retain or regain Jehovah's approval. The Governing Body blamed the presumptuousness of the masses for the delay of Armageddon. Through what appeared to be an obsession with eroto-pathological behaviour in the finest detail – including the sexual indulgences of married couples – the Governing Body deflected attention away from more fundamental theological and doctrinal problems. As early as 1974, the organization had redesignated what had been mere 'undesirable practices' such as

---

* For a detailed analysis, issue by issue, see Heather Botting, 'The Power and the Glory: The Symbolic Vision and Social Dynamic of Jehovah's Witnesses' (Doctoral dissertation, University of Alberta, 1982: 514–68).

smoking and oral sex as disfellowshippable offences. Not only were the Witnesses intent on being found in a clean state by Jehovah at the penultimate judgement, but the leaders in particular were concerned that any sources of dissension be cleared before the reverberations of any possible failure could shake the community.

Similar processes of deflection of attention of the membership away from crises are used in *Nineteen Eighty-Four*. Interestingly, Winston Smith works in the Records Department of the Ministry of Truth, where books and periodicals are rewritten and reissued again and again: 'Even the written instructions which Winston received, and which he invariably got rid of as soon as he had dealt with them, never stated or implied that an act of forgery was to be committed: always the reference was to slips, errors, misprints, or misquotations which it was necessary to put right in the interests of accuracy' (41). In this manner, mistaken prophecies uttered by Big Brother are eradicated from human memory and the *illusion* of infallibility is maintained (213–16).

The notion of books being rewritten and reissued – and even recalled – is not new to Jehovah's Witnesses. There have, of course, been several editions of some books, each of which contain insignificant changes; but the 1981 edition of the *New World Translation of the Holy Scriptures* included some fairly major modifications in translation without much fanfare. Certain motifs and drawings are repeated again and again in the literature – especially in *The Watchtower* and *Awake!* magazines – sometimes with tiny alterations reflecting shifts in doctrine. A beardless Christ or Adam depicted in a drawing in the literature of the sixties may well appear in the literature of the seventies complete with beard but without specific reference to the tacit shift in official stance. An illustration of a Witness family in which one boy had longish hair, first printed in *The Watchtower* of 1 March 1981, was reprinted in the *Awake!* of 8 March 1982 – minus the hair: in the interim, the society had changed its stance on looking different from the world. As we have seen, certain doctrinal primers are repetitions of each other, but often almost identical books – some of them fairly long – are released by the society under different titles, without mention that the books are virtually identical (compare, for example, *Your Word Is a Lamp to My Foot* [1967] and *Organization for Kingdom-Preaching and Disciple-Making* [1972]). As Orwell wrote of Oceania, 'every book has been rewritten, every picture has been repainted' (*1984*, 156).

There are several reasons for this reprinting and reissuing of the same material under different covers. One obvious reason is that each new book released has an automatic readership of two million; but this suggests a mercenary motive that does not do justice to the society. A second reason has to do with familiarity of material: the wording of given articles in the magazines may *seem* familiar to Witnesses of long standing, partly because the same writer may well be presenting the same ideas in a slightly different way, or because a novice writer (the Writing Department has a regular turnover of staff) is trying to imitate the style of a predecessor. Again, the writers rely heavily for their research on extant materials in their library and, as a result, use some ideas many times over. After all, if some aspect of doctrine has not changed, why not use it over again *verbatim*? The interesting thing is that the Witnesses usually accept the repetition and, in fact, rarely notice it.

While *The Watchtower* is the official organ of Jehovah's Witnesses, the Holy Bible remains the fundamental touchstone for doctrinal deliberations. In fact, Jehovah's Witnesses have their own version of the Bible, *The New World Translation of the Holy Scriptures*, prepared and published by the Watch Tower Bible and Tract Society under the guidance of F.W. Franz. Produced over several years by a process of translation-by-committee and with reference to numerous polyglot versions and dictionaries, *The New World Translation*, which is the version most often used by the Witnesses both in their publications and in their preaching, has a decided bias in favour of the Witnesses' concept of natural order. In particular, the name 'Jehovah' has been inserted in the place of 'God' or 'Lord' throughout, the translators insisting that the name has been simply reinstated in places where superstitious scribes had arbitrarily removed it in ages past. The name has also been restored to the Hebrew Scriptures, in the preface to which the Witnesses declare, 'The tetragrammaton [YHWH] occurs, 6,161 times in the original-language text ...' (see *ABU*, 885, 888), and to the Christian Greek Scriptures (the current edition uses the name 'Jehovah' 237 times). Interestingly, when confronted with an elementary passage of Hebrew from Genesis, F.W. Franz, the chief translator, could not make any sense of it, although he claimed he could read Hebrew (see Transcript of the Walsh case, 92). The other committee members, N.H. Knorr, A.D. Schroeder, G.D. Gangas, and M. Henschel, had even less linguistic background (Gruss 1979, 74).

In assessing the net result of *The New World Translation*, Alan Rogerson noted, 'It reads like a legal document; in striving to be exact the translators have made the text sound clumsy and sometimes ludicrous' (1969, 166). For example, note the variation in the translation of Ephesians 6:4 as set out in table 7 (all three renditions were taken from versions of the Bible printed by the Watch Tower Bible and Tract Society).

TABLE 7
Comparative Translations of EPHESIANS 6:4

Version	Text
King James (1942)	And, ye fathers, provoke not your children to wrath: but bring them up in the nurture and admonition of the Lord.
New World (1950 and 1961)	And you fathers, do not be irritating your children, but go on bringing them up in the discipline and authoritative advice of Jehovah
New World (1981)	And you, fathers, do not be irritating your children, but go on bringing them up in the discipline and mental-regulating of Jehovah.

The King James Bible was used by the Witnesses prior to the release of their own version, which began with the Greek Scriptures, in 1950. The progression from 'nurture and admonition' through 'discipline and authoritative advice' to 'discipline and mental-regulating' of Ephesians 6:4 reflects the increasingly tight regulation of the membership over the years; as Orwell wrote, 'The more the Party is powerful, the less it will be tolerant' (*1984*, 215).

The specifically *doctrinal* shifts of Jehovah's Witnesses away from more traditional forms of Protestant theology can, perhaps, best be described metaphorically in terms of 'for want of a nail ...' Much of Witness doctrine hangs precisely on the placing of a comma, the insertion of parentheses, and the addition of an indefinite article. Examples of three crucial alterations to the traditional text are to be found at Luke 23:43, John 1:1, and Revelation 20:5 (see table 8).

The change at Luke 23:43 is significant in terms of the Witnesses' view of the earthly resurrection as a *future* event – the resurrection to heaven did not commence until this century. Therefore, the Witnesses argue, the thief hanging on the torture stake beside Jesus could not have been promised that he would be with Christ in paradise on 14 Nisan AD 33. By placing the comma after 'today' instead of before it, the implication becomes that Jesus was merely telling the thief that *some day* they would be together in paradise, not

TABLE 8

Comparative Translations of Three Key Scriptures

King James Version 1942	New World Translation 1961
Luke 23:43	
And Jesus said unto him,	And he said to him:
Verily I say unto thee, Today	'Truly I tell you today,
shalt thou be with me in paradise.	You will be with me in Paradise.'
John 1:1	
In the beginning was the Word,	In [the] beginning the Word was,
and the Word was with God,	and the Word was with God,
and the Word was God.	and the Word was a god.
Revelation 20:5	
But the rest of the dead lived not again	(The rest of the dead did not come to life
until the thousand years were finished.	until the thousand years were ended.)
This *is* the first resurrection.	This is the first resurrection.

that particular day. The Witnesses' substitution of 'a god' at the end of John 1:1 refutes the conventional trinitarian doctrine which holds that God and Christ are one. The Witnesses insert the indefinite article and remove the capital 'G,' thus allowing them to claim that, although the Word (i.e., Christ) was regarded as 'godlike,' he was not actually God himself.

The insertion of parentheses around a portion of Revelation 20:5 is another example of arbitrary determinism: there is nothing in the Greek manuscripts to indicate the need to introduce parentheses, but if that portion of the text is not considered to be parenthetical, the text does not fit in comfortably with the Witnesses' vision of the unfolding of events. They believe that the events concerning the resurrection described in the verses immediately following Revelation 20:5 will occur during the millennium, not *after* it as is clearly implied in a straightforward reading of the text. Enclosing the maverick scripture in parentheses allows the Witnesses to discount it, as their literature invariably does. Whereas most of Revelation 20 is interpreted literally, the Witnesses believe that verse 5 refers to a *figurative* resurrection of those who have already been resurrected once, and of those who survived Armageddon: 'As long as persons in both categories are not free of inherited sin, they will in a sense be "dead" in God's sight ... Hence, by the end of the Millennium persons serving God on earth, "the rest of the dead," will "have come to perfect human life." Jesus successfully will be able to turn over to his Father a race of perfect humans ... Satan will then be let loose for a decisive test of mankind. Those proving loyal to Jehovah under that test will qualify for everlasting human life in Paradise' (*WT* 1 December 1982, 31; see also *GKTY*: 36).

Two anomalies spring from this interpretation of the Scripture if it is viewed from the perspective of the average Jehovah's Witness. First, the average Witness believes – has been told many times – that he will survive Armageddon into God's New World. For him, the attainment of paradise is a simple matter of hanging on to the faith until he gets through Armageddon. He lives in expectation of 'the Millennial Hope.' Clearly, this is a naive hope if Armageddon survivors are still to be considered 'dead in God's sight' and must wait another thousand years of 'Judgement Day' before qualifying for 'everlasting human life in Paradise.' Most Witnesses do not understand the implications of this long wait even though Witness literature is quite explicit about it; the 'New World' is synonymous in their minds with 'the Kingdom.'

Second, the Witnesses hold that reading the Scriptures 'in context' is an important way to assess the accuracy of a biblical understanding:

When a question is raised as to the meaning of texts that appear to conflict, it is always wise to examine the context or surrounding material. Perhaps you yourself have had the experience of being misrepresented because something you said was taken out of context. You can appreciate, then, that any use of a scripture in a way that is not in harmony with its context would misrepresent it ...

Reading the context then, helps to clear up seeming contradictions, and helps one to get a proper view of the Bible. (*IBRWG*, 86, 88)

Yet it remains that if this crucial chapter of the Bible is read in its entirety and in context the earthly resurrection would logically come *not* after Armageddon but after the *end* of the thousand-year reign of Christ.

Within the medium of their literature, Jehovah's Witnesses receive an important portion of the message through visual images. As Roberto Assagioli has pointed out: 'Images constitute another means through which affirmations can be focused; their dynamic potency is well known. One can use the image, or vision, of what is wanted *as if it were already accomplished*' (1973, 173; italics in original). The overriding image in Witness literature is that of community – the *ideal* community of the present and of the future. Images

Figure 28 *WT* 15 November 1975, 685

Figure 29 *PLPR*, 241

are also used to depict the process of attaining the ideal future, and those images are frequently juxtaposed with images of the evil one must avoid if one's quest is to be successful. One of the most frequent images in Witness literature is that of the group of believers – the Great Crowd – invariably portrayed as racially varied and integrated (see figure 28). These multiracial representations are an important example of visual manipulation of the symbols by a multinational corporation in the business of presenting Jehovah to the nations of the world. Figure 28 captures the compact quality of the social unit and typifies the conscious self-image of the Witnesses as they see themselves within the congregation in particular and the organization in general. There is literally no room in the consciousness of the Christian looking forward to salvation for anyone or anything but the other members of Jehovah's organization, and within this close group, they are united specifically in the sense of looking forward to a common goal.

The image of the Great Crowd is not limited to the context of the present world. Rather it is projected forward into the vision of the New World which the Witnesses believe awaits the faithful after Armageddon (see figure 29). Paradise too is to be teeming with the Great Crowd of Jehovah's people and represents a future for which they yearn as a reward for faithful service now.

It should not be assumed that these images of paradise are not carefully conceived. In *Aid to Bible Understanding* (1971), calculations concerning the nature of life in the New World were carefully set out:

A very liberal estimate of the number of persons that have lived on earth is twenty billion ... Not all of these ... will receive a resurrection, but even assuming that they did, there would be no problem as to living space and food for them. The land surface of the earth at present is about 57,000,000 square miles ... or more than 36,000,000,000 acres ... Even allowing half of that to be set aside for other uses, there would be more than half an acre for each person ... One-half acre ... will actually provide much more than enough food for one person ...

Let us assume that those who compose the 'great crowd' of righteous persons who 'come out of the great tribulation' on this system of things alive ... number one million (about ... 1/3500 [one thirty-five hundredth] of earth's present population). Then if, after allowing, say, one hundred years spent in their training and 'subduing' a portion of the earth ... God purposes to bring back three percent of this number, this would mean that each newly arrived person would be looked after by thirty-three trained ones. Since a yearly increase of three percent, compounded, doubles the number about every twenty-four years, the entire twenty

What Is This Thing Called
DEATH?

How grand it will be when one's own family members
return from the dead!

Figure 30 *Awake!* 22 October 1976, 9

billion could be resurrected before five hundred years of Christ's thousand-year
reign had elapsed. (1400)

For most Witnesses this vision of a populated paradise is reassuring and
anticipated with joy and confidence, not as a hypothetical proposition but as

an apodictic certainty. The focus of the vision of the Great Crowd in paradise is not simply a matter of security but also includes the collective hope of life in the New World without pain and death. The promise held out to those who survive Armageddon is explicitly that of eternal life. Many Witnesses are so totally involved with this imagery that they thoroughly purge the idea of personal death from their minds, and then, when finally faced with death, are totally unprepared for life's most traumatic rite of passage. Still, when death does threaten there is comfort in the promise of the resurrection, and again visual imagery captures the goal towards which the collective will is directed (see figure 30). The 'reality' of this goal is underscored by the judicious mixing of numerous articles discussing the basic theology of the resurrection with occasional emotional articles of a personal nature. The fact that the boy who is mourning his father in figure 30 has not aged appreciably at the time of the resurrection is anomalous with Watch Tower belief.

Yearnings for paradise must, however, be tempered by the exigencies of the contemporary world within which the Witnesses live. The very fact that their vision demands the destruction of this world makes it necessary for them to define what is wrong with a world in such imminent danger. Thus the goodness of the New World must be juxtaposed with the evil of the existing one. Ugliness and entrapment are constant themes applied to the images of the existing world (see figures 31 and 32). To be caught in the web of 'this world' is to partake of a bleak future in which only disease, war, crime, and death persist as forms of oppression. Care is taken to impress the hopelessness of 'this world' upon the reader with illustrations of starving children, violent crime, and victims of earthquakes and wars.

The cause of global misery, the Witnesses believe, is Satan the Devil, most frequently represented as the dragon, the arch-enemy of God who attacks with particular ferocity the Bride of Christ or the 144,000 chosen anointed ones of Jehovah. The human agents of the Devil are believed to be the leaders of all other world religions; they are slated for destruction, along with their followers, by the 'wild beast' of world government upon which 'false religion' rides. The projected fate of Christendom is portrayed in figure 33 proleptically 'as if it were already accomplished.'

To the outside observer, such images of rampant destruction expected to occur at Armageddon may appear so distasteful as to suggest that the Witnesses themselves must surely fear this impending holocaust. In fact they pray for it fervently and look forward to it with joy (see figure 34). Similarly, in *Nineteen Eighty-Four*, 'no Inner Party member wavers for an instant in his mystical belief that the war *is* real, and that it is bound to end victoriously' (193–4).

Figure 31 *WT* 1 June 1979, cover

Wrong beliefs hold many people in a "web" of fear

Figure 32 *USHH*, 37

The most critical social imperative for the Witnesses is to become and remain regular publishers engaging actively in the distribution of Watch Tower literature – an activity which accounts for about 90 per cent of the total preaching time recorded. In considering action necessary for the achievement of their goals, the Witnesses apply literally the words of James 2:26: 'Indeed, as the body without spirit is dead, so also faith without works is dead' (*NWT*). Consequently, no matter how long a Witness remains an active distributer of literature, the moment he ceases to be active he is regarded by his peers as as good as dead in terms of achieving the ultimate goal of life everlasting in an earthly paradise. This emphasis on the individual's personal track record results in a situation in which salvation must be bought. But few realize upon entering the movement that the purchase price is open-ended and that the bill can never be paid in full until death or the advent of Armageddon.

The implications of the Witnesses' emphasis on never-ending distribution work becomes apparent to the member only as the years pass without respite from active service and Armageddon gets no closer than 'just around the corner.' Many faithful Witnesses, after thirty, forty, or fifty years of active service, do stop publishing. These individuals create a great deal of concern

Figure 33 *WT* 1 November 1979, 23

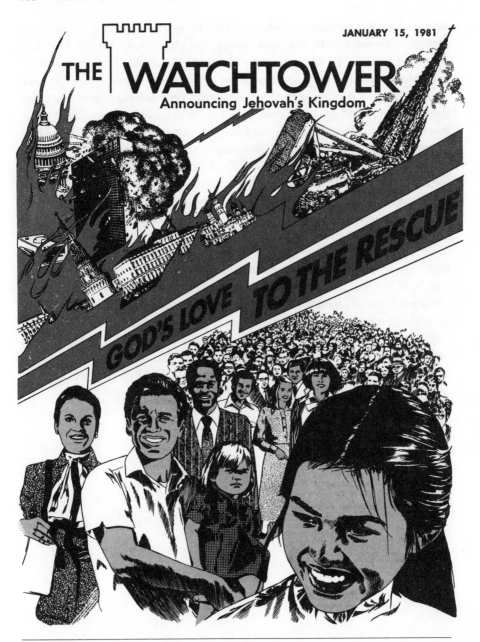

Figure 34 *WT* 15 January 1981, cover

among their fellow believers, who fear that by relaxing in zeal, despite their long-term investment in time and energy, the older Witnesses will lose their chance at paradise by not remaining faithful to the demand for service to the end. Many of these older members, however, seem to come to a personal arrangement (as it were) with God concerning their salvation, and as a result the tension created by their slacking off is perpetuated and exacerbated as more and more members slide into this velleitic group (*YWLF*, 209). These members never clarify their beliefs concerning their personal trust in Jehovah's discretion because such beliefs fly directly in the face of the society's social imperatives: they convince themselves that their long years of service – their thousands of placements of literature – must count for *something*, and that beyond a point no reasonable God could deny them paradise. It is for them not a question of the principle of whether they *want* paradise so much as it is a question of the total price or cost of their investment over the long run. In addition, there are some members who reject the vision or lose faith in it; but, out of fear of losing their families and of the humiliation of total ostracism, they too, having ceased their active distribution work or publishing, become meeting attenders only. Because people in neither group dare voice their positions, it is difficult to distinguish between those who have given up on the hope of paradise and those who assume that, despite organizational warnings to the contrary, they have earned a place in the New World already.

CHAPTER SIX

Discipline and Mental-Regulating of Youth

Thoughtcrime does not entail death: thoughtcrime IS *death.* (*1984*, 29)

Within the rigorously controlled social world of the Witnesses, parents are held personally responsible for bringing their children up in the 'discipline and mental-regulating of Jehovah.' The purpose of the regulation of the child is to encourage him to accept the vision of the organization as a whole, and the status the parents will continue to enjoy within that world depends largely upon their success as parents. As the 1 August 1975 *Watchtower* indicated: 'An elder must be a man presiding over his own household in a fine manner, having children in subjection, namely, "If indeed any man does not know how to preside over his own household, how will he care for God's congregation?" (1 Tim. 3:5)' (469). Accordingly, children are taken to the weekly round of meetings from the time of birth and begin to accompany parents in their door-to-door visits as soon as they may be trusted to behave, often as early as five or six years of age.

From the time a child becomes aware of the proceedings around him, he is fed on the imagery of destruction and paradise which looms ahead, which is always 'just around the corner,' and in order to avoid the former and attain the latter, children are admonished to obey their parents and the society: 'Children, be obedient to your parents in union with [the] Lord, for this is righteous: "Honor your father and [your] mother"; which is the first command with a promise: "That it may go well with you and you may endure a long time on the earth"' (Ephesians 6:1–3, *NWT*). Throughout the pages of the

Witnesses' literature, parents are reminded of the proverb which advises: 'Train up a boy according to the way for him; even when he grows old he will not turn aside from it' (Prov. 22:6). Children in turn are urged to obey their parents in all things. With reference to the book of Proverbs, the 8 April 1981 *Watchtower* noted its value as a training manual for the young: 'If they are to turn out well, they are urged to "listen to," "measure up," "not forget," "pay attention [to]," "observe" and not "forsake" the commandments and discipline of parents. Over *four times as much* counsel is given to children as is given to parents in just this one book of the Bible!' (12). To ensure that their children benefit from biblical ordinances, parents are directed to study the Bible (more specifically and accurately, the society's literature) with their children; within that literature, safety is attainable only in the practice of Bible study (see figure 35).

Parental vigilance is measured in terms of the conviction and energy demonstrated by their children, as shown by their record in the ministry; spiritual strength is assessed according to the number of hours spent in proselytizing work and the number of magazines or books placed from week to week. To lose a son or daughter to 'the world' is to taint one's personal record; indeed, parents often cover the weaknesses of their children to avoid being shamed themselves, working all the more earnestly in the ministry to offset any perceived slackness among their children. Men and boys are constantly thrust into the forefront of activity in the essentially patriarchal society, despite the fact that they are outnumbered by women members.

The type of pressure on young people is easily demonstrated by reference to the types of questions – real and rhetorical – that were asked of youth in a recent *Watchtower* article, 'Happy Youth in a Corrupt World':

Do you pursue privileges of Christian service? Do you have a personal goal of putting a certain amount of time in the house-to-house teaching work each week or month? Do you encourage other young people to come with you? Do you have a goal of becoming more capable of teaching during return visits and home Bible studies? Some young people have a yearly goal of being a pioneer (full-time volunteer preacher) during school vacation. (15 January 1982, 21)

As the Witnesses' best-selling book, *You Can Live Forever in Paradise on Earth* (1982), puts it, 'the Bible compares the position of a child to that of a slave' (242).

Even in the eyes of parents, the level of faith and commitment in their children is measured in terms of the record card – hours put in, magazines

Bible study will help you to "take up the large shield of faith, with which you will be able to quench all the wicked one's burning missiles."—Eph. 6:16.

Figure 35 *WT* 1 August 1976, 467

placed, and so on. To come out on top in magazine placements on a given Saturday morning has long been considered something of a *coup*, and frequent success in this area, a definite plus to the entire family's status and security despite the society's discouragement of blatant competitiveness: 'There is no reason for us to become competitive in making our reports, comparing our service with that of another individual. Individual circumstances vary greatly, making it unwise for us to make such comparisons' (*OAOM*, 108).

The society views the children of its members as a ready source of growth and warns parents pointedly to guard this important resource.

Yes children require time, attention and money. It has been estimated that it takes thousands of dollars to raise a child to adulthood. A sure way to lose that investment of money, as well as of time, is to fail in giving proper spiritual oversight to those we bring into the world.

... That is the parent's Christian responsibility. Ministers of God will not forget this obligation they have resting on their shoulders. (*WT* 1 January 1982, 19–20)

Any child who turns his back on 'the Truth' by rejecting the teachings of the Watch Tower Bible and Tract Society is regarded as a dead loss, irredeemably damned to total obliteration – unless, of course, he should embrace the faith again and become an active distributer of Watch Tower literature.

Much of the rationale for such intensive involvement within the context of the organization lies in the Witnesses' preoccupation with 'worldly' contamination; as the often-quoted scripture warns: 'Bad associations spoil useful habits' (1 Cor. 15:33). Great care is taken to isolate the child as much as possible from 'the world,' and where such isolation is impossible, as in the compulsory education system of most countries, the value of the academic components of education is denigrated. This is especially the case where science is involved; the Witnesses, in step with the temper of the late nineteenth century, interpret science to be the natural enemy of religion. For example, in the 8 December 1976 issue of *Awake!*, in an article entitled 'How Much Confidence Should You Have in Science?,' the writers blame science for everything from the Second World War to thalidomide babies (4–6). They then embark on an attack of evolution, using the case of the Piltdown man to tar with the brush of 'fraud' everything from Neanderthal finds to cave art (7–9). One may recall that in *Nineteen Eighty-Four*, 'The Party told you to reject the evidence of your eyes and ears. It was their final, most essential command' (81).

Like the Oceanian child, each Jehovah's Witness child undergoes an elaborate mental training or 'mental-regulating' along the lines described in *Nineteen Eighty-Four*:

If he is a person naturally orthodox (in Newspeak a *goodthinker*), he will in all circumstances know, without taking thought, what is the true belief or the desirable emotion. But in any case an elaborate mental training, undergone in childhood and grouping itself round the Newspeak words *crimestop*, *blackwhite*, and *doublethink*, makes him unwilling and unable to think too deeply on any subject whatever.

... The first and simplest stage in the discipline, which can be taught even to young children, is called, in Newspeak, *crimestop*. *Crimestop* means the faculty of stopping short, as though by instinct, at the threshold of any dangerous thought. It includes the power of not grasping analogies, of failing to perceive logical errors, of misunderstanding the simplest arguments if they are inimical to Ingsoc, and of being bored or repelled by any train of thought which is capable of leading in a heretical direction. (212–13)

Some Witness children grasp hold of Witness orthodoxy with fanatic zeal, to the point of feeling less loyalty to their parents than they do to the society. Sometimes, like Parsons' daughter, they may inform on their parents, an act which may eventually lead to their parents' being disfellowshipped and which causes unexpected reverberations and recriminations throughout the family for a long time to come. As one Melbourne member was quoted as saying: '"No one escapes being watched. If a member is suspicious that a fellow member is breaking a law he is obliged to report it to the church committee. Even if that person is your mother or your husband or wife."'

Winston regards his neighbour's kids with detached cynicism:

With those children, he thought, that wretched woman must lead a life of terror. Another year, two years, and they would be watching her night and day for symptoms of unorthodoxy. Nearly all children nowadays were horrible. What was worst of all was that by means of such organizations as the Spies they were systematically turned into ungovernable little savages, and yet this produced in them no tendency whatever to rebel against the discipline of the Party. On the contrary, they adored the Party and everything connected with it. The songs, the processions, the banners ... the worship of Big Brother – it was all a sort of glorious game to them. (*1984*, 25)

Although this may seem to apply more to the Chinese Red Guard than to the children of Jehovah's Witnesses, the degree of fanaticism adopted by many Witness children, especially in their teens, can be misdirected out of a sense of righteousness and duty. This is especially true of those young Witnesses who are taught by authoritarian parents that the Watch Tower Society teaches the truth, and that 'worldly knowledge' is, therefore, all a lie. Dependent upon Watch Tower teachings as the sole source of intellectual stability, such children either demonstrate fanatic zeal, or become totally rebellious. And sometimes their zeal *becomes* rebellion, so that a type of dual personality develops: a child may well preach on weekends and run with the gang during the week. Encouraged to believe that secular authorities such as teachers are 'of the world', or more specifically 'of the devil,' he may develop a definite discipline problem, even resorting to vandalism and other crimes.

The threat of Armageddon just around the corner is one factor that serves to keep the child from taking 'worldly education' too seriously. Parents make a point of stating often that 'Susy won't make it into primary school before Armageddon comes,' 'Susy won't make it into junior high before Armageddon comes,' 'Susy won't make it into high school before Armageddon comes,' 'Susy won't graduate before Armageddon comes,' 'Susy won't get married before Armageddon comes,' 'Susy won't have children before Armageddon comes,' 'Susy's little Jim won't make it into primary school ...' On and on it goes. At least four generations of Witnesses who were themselves never going to make it into primary school have married off their children before the advent of Armageddon. Anyone who does aspire to post-secondary training in spite of Armageddon's imminence is subjected to accusations of self-aggrandisement, pride, and 'thinking he's *too good for us.*'

When Witness children do enter the school system, care is taken to direct them away from academic interests, especially science. Only practical training is valued – and then only because such training can lead to a job with which the individual can support himself in his volunteer ministry (*WT* 1 January 1984, 19). Students endowed with above-average intelligence may be frustrated by this type of education (see *WT* 1 April 1979, 10–11 and *School and Jehovah's Witnesses* 1983, 5).

The Watch Tower Bible and Tract Society tends to see university education as a threat to faith, and periodically cites examples of students who 'stopped associating with fellow Christians and ceased to serve Jehovah':

A young man enrolled in a university in his own country, but far from home ... All the things he had learned 'from infancy' left him, and now he even questions the teachings of the Bible.

Unfortunately, this young man is not alone. There are others who were brought up to serve God who are now evolutionists, atheists and critics of Biblical truth. Is this because the Bible is wrong and modern philosophy is right? Not at all. It is because they were subjected to a constant onslaught of ungodly ideas at college while separated from other Christians. As a result their faith weakened and finally died ...

... Some of the worst associations possible for a Christian – spiritually and morally speaking – have been found on university campuses. (WT 15 July 1982, 14)

Attending university is not a decision to be made by the individual young adult; rather 'this is something each parent should decide for his own child' (15).

Undoubtedly, university education is a challenge to faith and a particular threat to the doctrines of the Witnesses is the theory of evolution that is taught as a central assumption in many courses in high schools and colleges. From time to time, the Witnesses release treatises refuting evolution, including the mainstay of Witness creationist belief, *Did Man Get Here by Evolution or by Creation?* (1967). This text, and a similar one, *Is the Bible Really the Word of God?* (1969), use a pseudoacademic approach, footnoting secular sources as diverse as *The Fresno Bee* and *Reader's Digest*. Fully half of the 248 footnote references in 'The *Evolution* Book,' as the 1967 title is affectionately known, are to popular magazines, newspapers, and encyclopedias; other references (*Biology for You* and *Review Text in Biology*) are to school texts. The premises put forward for refuting evolution are at odds with what most children are taught in school, and Watch Tower observations about analogous but fundamentally dissimilar situations confuse the child. For example, evolutionists theorize that the atmosphere of the earth was radically different during its formation than it is now: it was a seething vat of methane, ammonia, water, and other chemicals combining and recombining in accordance with chemical laws over millions of years as temperatures fluctuated and electrical storms slashed the firmament. The Witnesses clearly misrepresent the stance of the evolutionist when they show a man sitting in a furnished living room and ask, 'Did these things evolve or were they made?' (*YCLF*, 70), or state, 'Machine left to itself decays, as inanimate matter tends downward, not upward' (see figure 36).

The Witnesses thus use a form of analogical conceit; few have any idea of current definitions of evolution other than those proferred by the society, and the society tends to view the process piecemeal: 'If the mammary glands in females came about by slow evolution, how did these females feed their offspring in the meantime? If they already had another way to feed them, then why develop breasts? And if breasts were developed because they were a superior way of feeding, then why do we still have animals that feed otherwise and survive just as well?' (*DMGHE*, 36). For the average child, these are ponderous questions. The key word in this passage – and one which the Witnesses and evolutionists would define radically differently – is 'slow.' The Witnesses believe that the world was created in seven creative periods of 7,000 years each. Although the planet may be much older, life did not appear, the Witnesses believe, until about 34,000 years ago (see *Is the Bible Really the Word of God?* 19–27). They cannot conceive of life existing on this planet millions of years ago; nor can they concede that genetic changes are controlled by subtle shifts in the chemistry of organisms: mutations must necessarily be destructive, like a car wreck. And yet their own assumptions about speciation and adaptation seem to be totally implausible to the student of biology, because they *assume* genetic instability.

In addition to pejorative attitudes towards school expressed in the home, other situations are created to ensure that the children will remain misfits in relation to the larger cultural world. Being isolated from their 'worldly' peers by organizational prohibitions against the singing of anthems, saluting of flags, participation in 'pagan' Christmas, Hallowe'en and Valentine's Day parties, running for office, and other activities, generally make 'loners' of the Witness children. 'The World' becomes a most unpleasant and alien place. As a misfit in the broader society, the child *must* seek companionship within his family and religious community. Children are told why they may not participate in such 'worldly' activities, and may ask for clarification of such explanations; however, there is no room for debate. If the child indicates a desire to argue he is cut short with a stern, 'Don't you ever question Jehovah's will if you want to live in the new world!'

Wagon will not move by itself unless acted upon by outside force

Machine left to itself decays, as inanimate matter tends downward, not upward

Time produces disintegration, eroding cliffs. It is destructive, not constructive

Ball will not pick itself up off the ground

Figure 36 *DMGHE*, 25

One fundamental problem in rearing children within the anomalous belief and social system of Jehovah's Witnesses is that a culture gap often exists between the children and the parent in terms of perspective, especially if the adult came to the group as an adult and hence has no childhood memories of his own to help him understand the child's feelings of disjointedness occasioned by the peculiar beliefs and customs. The classic example of such a gap appears time and time again in the writings of people who were raised as

Figure 37 *WT* 15 December 1975, 739

Witnesses: Christmas. To the Witnesses, Christmas is a blasphemous perversion of a pagan rite: 'It was the absorbing of a pagan ritual into a celebration in pretended honor of God and Christ' (*WT* 15 December 1977, 740). Most Witness parents assume that the presents are all that figure in the minds of children anyway and their yearning after Christmas is nothing more than an expression of greed (note figures 37 and 38).

Still, most Witness children do survive the absence of Christmas festivities and scores of other similar crises, and grow up, eventually finding themselves dedicating their lives to Jehovah and his organization through the act of baptism. However, it is also among those born into the sect or brought into the organization through parental conversion that much of the defection occurs. The adult convert has made his choice against a backdrop of dissatisfaction with the world, and yearns within his own imagination for paradise only. The imagination of the child who has never experienced 'this world' is, however, not so easily bridled or contained.

As Barbara Harrison has remarked: 'The imagination of very young Witnesses is fueled and fired by the rich imagery of destruction and creation with which they live' (1978, 97). Much of the imagery to which Harrison alludes is

Figure 38 *WT* 15 December 1977, 741

contained within the vision of the destruction of the old world and the reconstruction of the new, a vision augmented at every turn by images of the innate
evil of the existing world. The child is expected to relish the apocalyptic
advent of Armageddon while fearing the day-to-day world in which he
lives – a world inhabited by the Devil as agent of false religion, science, politics, and death. Many of these children do grow up in anticipation of God's

great war as they struggle to avoid the vicissitudes of the Devil transmogrified into the personage of the 'soul-catcher' or 'grim reaper.'

In *Nineteen Eighty-Four*, Winston Smith's first overt act of rebellion is to start keeping a diary to record the 'interminable restless monologue' that runs inside his head. The first thing he describes in his diary is an incident that occurred the day before – on 3 April 1984 – when he went to the theatre to see a war film. It was a mixed audience, apparently, containing Party members and proles, adults and children, men and women. The incident that he describes had bothered Winston profoundly, and he records it 'in sheer panic, only imperfectly aware of what he was setting down.' The incident was a catalyst for Winston's revolt against the Party and his expression of contempt for Big Brother and the Thought Police and everything they stand for. One of the films was:

[a] *very good one of a ship full of refugees being bombed somewhere in the Mediterranean ... there was a middle-aged woman might have been a jewess sitting up in the bow with a little boy about three years old in her arms. little boy screaming with fright and hiding his head between her breasts as if he was trying to burrow right into her and the woman putting her arms round him and comforting him although she was blue with fright herself, all the time covering him up as much as possible as if she thought her arms could keep the bullets off him. then the helicopter planted a 20 kilo bomb in among them terrific flash and the boat went all to matchwood. then there was a wonderful shot of a child's arm going up up up right up into the air a helicopter with a camera in its nose must have followed it up and there was a lot of applause from the party seats but a woman down in the prole part of the house suddenly started kicking up a fuss and shouting they didnt oughter of showed it not in front of kids they didnt it aint right not in front of kids it aint until the police turned her turned her out i dont suppose anything happened to her nobody cares what the proles say typical prole reaction they never –* . (10)

From the Party perspective, Armageddon is being enacted before their eyes: theocracy is conquering the infidel; Big Brother will be victorious and His Party and Oceania will become 'the undisputed master of the entire world' (194). So '*there was a lot of applause from the party seats*' but there was a protest from the proles. The nature of the woman's protest is simply that such violence should not have been shown '*in front of kids.*' Obviously, the Party regards the film to have some educational value, either as a deterrent from rebellion or as a catalyst to rally to the cause of Big Brother; but for whatever the reason of its acceptance by the Party, Winston cannot hide his disgust at the way the woman was treated and his concern for her welfare. This constitutes 'thoughtcrime,' of course, because he should not be concerned about people in the prole world, let alone the aliens in the boat. Winston, therefore, has been moved to vent his wrath on Big Brother by writing his thoughts in the diary – beginning with this 'outrage.'

The description of the war film is not unlike those given of Armageddon in Watch Tower literature on a regular basis. The full impact of the imagery of the symbols fed into the growing consciousness of the child, year after year, can perhaps best be appreciated by examining actual pages of the society's publications. *From Paradise Lost to Paradise Regained* was released in 1958, mainly for the purpose of home Bible study with children. The book shows buildings toppling on little children (see figure 39) and provides this text:

Soul-chilling terror will spread through the masses of people so that they will lose control of themselves; they will begin killing one another ... But their selfish fight to live will be all in vain. Those who escape being killed by their neighbours will be destroyed by God's heavenly armies.

Christ's angels will smite all the opposers of God's kingdom and his kingdom witnesses with a terrible destruction. A flesh-eating plague will destroy many. Says Jehovah: 'Their flesh shall rot while they are still on their feet, their eyes shall rot in their sockets, and their tongues shall rot in their mouths.' ... Eaten up will be the tongues of those who scoffed and laughed at the warning of Armageddon! Eaten up will be the eyes of those who refused to see the sign of the 'time of the end'! Eaten up will be the flesh of those who would not learn that the living and true God is named Jehovah! Eaten up while they stand on their feet!

... Closed will be all avenues of escape! Wherever they flee God will find them and destroy them ...

Dead bodies will be everywhere – from end to end of the earth ... Ungathered, unwept for, the bodies will be like so much fertilizer ...

... To all surviving flesh the dead bodies will be disgusting, hateful things. Worms will not stop swarming over the millions of bodies until the last body is eaten up. (208–11)

These and similar passages were required reading for a whole generation of juvenile Jehovah's Witnesses, who were instructed to pray for these events to occur. Obviously these teachings led to a feeling of alienation from 'worldly' friends and classmates whose destiny was so graphically delineated; more

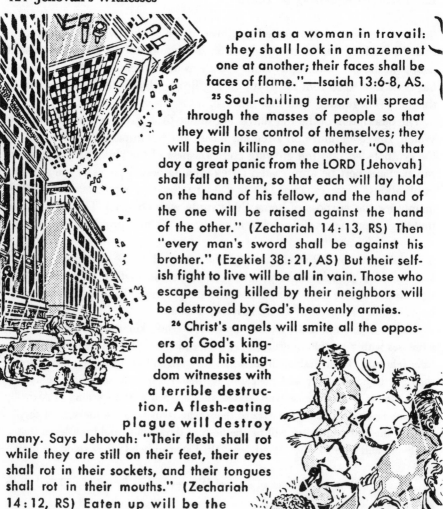

pain as a woman in travail: they shall look in amazement one at another; their faces shall be faces of flame."—Isaiah 13:6-8, AS.

25 Soul-chilling terror will spread through the masses of people so that they will lose control of themselves; they will begin killing one another. "On that day a great panic from the LORD [Jehovah] shall fall on them, so that each will lay hold on the hand of his fellow, and the hand of the one will be raised against the hand of the other." (Zechariah 14:13, RS) Then "every man's sword shall be against his brother." (Ezekiel 38:21, AS) But their selfish fight to live will be all in vain. Those who escape being killed by their neighbors will be destroyed by God's heavenly armies.

26 Christ's angels will smite all the opposers of God's kingdom and his kingdom witnesses with a terrible destruction. A flesh-eating plague will destroy many. Says Jehovah: "Their flesh shall rot while they are still on their feet, their eyes shall rot in their sockets, and their tongues shall rot in their mouths." (Zechariah 14:12, RS) Eaten up will be the tongues of those who scoffed and laughed at the warning of Armageddon! Eaten up

25. In their fear, what will people do to one another? 26. What kind of plague will Jehovah bring upon those who fight against his people?

Figure 39 *PLPR*, 208–9

will be the eyes of those who refused to see the sign of the "time of the end"! Eaten up will be the flesh of those who would not learn that the living and true God is named Jehovah! Eaten up while they stand on their feet!

²⁷ Where can people hide from this destruction coming from God? Nowhere! Jehovah says: "Not one of them shall escape. Though they dig into Sheol, from there shall my hand take them; though they climb up to heaven, from there I will bring them down. Though they hide themselves on the top of [Mount] Carmel, from there I will search out and take them; and though they hide from my sight at the bottom of the sea, there I will command the

27. When Armageddon begins, will there be any way for people to escape destruction?

importantly, for some they led to a sense of nightmarish confusion. Where, in all this, was 'Gentle Jesus, meek and mild'?

Your Youth: Getting the Best out of It was prepared for an older group, those entering puberty to those in their early twenties who were contemplating marriage. This work, released in 1976, was a guide for the youth of the movement to the highly restrictive moral code dictated for them. All forms of socialization with 'the world' were roundly condemned and emphasis was placed upon sex as an activity for married couples only. The book is rich in its own form of imagery:

Because [God's law] is so clear and forceful it helps us to keep our senses, bolsters our moral courage and, most important, it helps us to learn to hate the wrong course. Do you actually hate the course of sexual immorality? ... If not, then isn't that course worth hating? Surely you would not want to make yourself like a public towel on which any man or woman can wipe his or her hands by means of immorality. (138)

It is within this context of explosive and graphic imagery of wholesale destruction and vile contamination (see figure 40) that every individual must assess his own role and worth within the organization. This is especially crucial for those who grow from childhood within this symbolic system. Although most Witness children do not become baptized until they are at least sixteen, some are expected by overeager parents to declare their dedication to Jehovah's Will by water immersion at the age of twelve or thirteen. The contract is as binding on them as on those who enter as adults and take the vow, as it were, in middle age. That Jesus was thirty before committing himself in the form of baptism does not seem to bother the Witnesses. Nor does the fact that the Witnesses claim that emotional maturity (for purposes of making decisions regarding marriage, at least) comes comparatively later than the optimum baptism age:

Right now you are in a transition time, a period of change. Your body for example, is moving toward physical maturity. But it doesn't reach that stage until sometime between the ages of twenty and twenty-three. It can take still longer for you to reach emotional maturity. Some of the changes taking place in you could make you feel confused and unsure of yourself. (*YYGB*, 6)

On the one hand the society encourages Witness children to postpone marital commitment until they are more mature but on the other there is definite

Figure 40 *YYGB*, 138

pressure to co-opt young people into baptism before they reach the age of majority and leave home. Hence, young people come out from under the wing of parental control only after commitment to societal control: punishment, such as probation and disfellowshipping, is applicable only after the individual has been publicly baptized. Baptism is parallel to induction into the Party; to be in an unbaptized state is to be a prole:

There was a vast amount of criminality in London, ... but since it all happened among the proles themselves, it was of no importance. In all questions of morals they were allowed to follow their ancestral code. The sexual puritanism of the Party was not imposed upon them ... For that matter, even religious worship would have been permitted if the proles had shown any sign of needing or wanting it. They were beneath suspicion. (*1984*, 72)

Although a congregation may publicly 'name' an unbaptized person as being unfit company for baptized Witnesses – especially Witness children – it would not encourage such a person to become a 'Party member,' so to speak, until he had adjusted his life to conform to the puritan standards of Jehovah's Witnesses. Thereupon, of course, he would have ceased to be a problem and would be welcomed into the fold upon his baptism just like anybody else. But if he should backslide and begin to adopt prolish habits – the habits of 'the world' – he would find himself subject to much harsher treatment than that he received as an unbaptized associate. Increasingly, Witness children are under great pressure to get baptized, pressure originating from parents and elders in the congregation and from peers in the same age group.

Fornication is one of the most common expressions of rebellion to be found among young Witnesses; indeed, this explains why the society prints many articles on sexual immorality, adopting a no-nonsense stance even for such habits as masturbation. Young Witnesses are discouraged from kissing before marriage, although few take such censure seriously. Those who do commit fornication are often already on the way out, spiritually or socially speaking, and find illicit sex to be a pleasurable expression of their discontent. Such ones are usually discovered and punished, or disassociate themselves from the congregation before they can be formally disfellowshipped. In many cases, however, young people are led to 'drift into sin' by the onset of physical attraction and desire, and ultimately commit acts that, outside marriage, are considered to be 'unnatural.' Many young people develop sin complexes after finding themselves in an uncompromising sexual predicament; indeed, many develop such complexes without ever having experienced sex.

Once young Witnesses start dating, they may find themselves in a situation similar to that experienced by Winston and Julia in Oceania, where:

The unforgivable crime was promiscuity between Party members ... Not love so much as eroticism was the enemy, inside marriage as well as outside it ... The only recognized purpose of marriage was to beget children for the service of the Party ... This again was never put into plain words, but in an indirect way it was rubbed into every Party member from childhood onwards ... The Party was trying to kill the sex instinct, or, if it could not be killed, then to distort it and dirty it. He did not know why this was so, but it seemed natural that it should be so. And as far as the women were concerned, the Party's efforts were largely successful. (*1984*, 65–6)

Dr James Penton, a religious historian, has written that 'for years the Watch Tower Society discouraged marriage as something which should not be countenanced until after the start of the millennium. Normal family obligations were openly discouraged also if they failed to serve the primary aim of the Watch Tower Society – its "preaching work." Hence, many Jehovah's Witnesses long delayed or put off marriage entirely while couples frequently refrained from having children' (*TBE* 3: 2, 5). A current suit against the Watch

Tower Society in Calgary, Alberta, alleges just that. Michael and Helen Zebroski, who pioneered in Alberta for many years before being disfellowshipped for allegedly 'being uncooperative,' claimed that they had been instructed by the Watch Tower Society not to have children. Initially, their case was rejected by the Canadian courts, but their appeal to the Court of Queen's Bench on 9 December 1983 was upheld in the Zebroski's favour; the court rejected the arguments of Glen How that a statute of limitations applied to their case and that the Governing Body was immune from court proceedings in Canada and allowed the Zebroskis to reopen their suit on the grounds that they had not been given a hearing or clear reason for their ejection from the sect. The finding is likely to have widespread ramifications for disfellowshipped Jehovah's Witnesses in Canada who wish to appeal arbitrary excommunication.

When Winston and Julia finally make love, 'Their embrace had been a battle, the climax a victory. It was a blow struck against the Party. It was a political act' (*1984*, 104). These are similar to sentiments expressed by several of the couples interviewed, subsequent to their leaving the Witnesses after confessing to fornication. After alluding to the increase in apostasy within the sect, *The Watchtower* of 1 January 1984 added, 'However there is other uncleanness that today claims many times more victims than does apostasy – *moral uncleanness*. We need to be on guard against the world's pressures to indulge in immorality! ... There is no place for immoral persons in the spiritual paradise that Jehovah has established among his people today, nor will there be a place for any such in the Kingdom or in the Paradise earth, now so close at hand' (*WT* 1 January 1984, 30; italics in original).

'The *Youth* Book' (as *Your Youth: Getting the Best out of It* is referred to by the Witnesses) devotes a whole chapter to 'Masturbation and Homosexuality': 'From a physical standpoint,' the chapter begins, 'the majority of doctors say that occasional masturbation is harmless. Like most psychiatrists, they say that damage comes only if the practicer has feelings of guilt that cause mental and emotional disturbance, these, in turn, producing physical upset. But doctors and psychiatrists are imperfect humans, subject to error, and their views change' (36). Masturbation, the society states, is 'giving in to, and being dominated by, "sexual appetite,"' and is therefore 'loose conduct,' 'uncleanness,' 'covetousness,' and 'greediness': 'How? Well, it is an expression of desiring something that does not rightly belong to one. God has provided marriage as the arrangement in which to satisfy sexual desires. But the person who practices masturbation is, in effect, trying to obtain that satisfaction without pay-ing the price' (37; see also *WT* 1 June 1983, 23–8). The chapter concludes with the ambiguous exhortation:

If you are now fighting the practice of masturbation, remember: You are certainly not the first or the only one who has faced this problem. Even though you find yourself having a hard struggle to break a masturbation habit, never feel that Jehovah God and his Son Jesus Christ have given up on you. If you sincerely keep working to overcome it, they will kindly and patiently help you to build up the needed strength so that you come off victorious. (43)

Masturbation is 'self-abuse,' and a masturbator 'needs to deaden his sexual appetite in order to please God. He needs to cultivate the self-control that is necessary to de-emphasize sex in his life and to leave his sexual organs to adjust to any pressures in the normal way.' How? 'He must keep busy in theocratic pursuits, in meeting attendance, field service, making return visits, conducting Bible studies, helping others spiritually, and he will receive the strength to control his sexual appetite' (*WT* 1 June 1983, 27–8).

In 1978, the society, determined to make the Bible more palatable to Witness children, released *My Book of Bible Stories*, which followed the format of standard secular books of Bible stories. Of much more significance was the release at 'Kingdom Truth' district assemblies in 1982 of the 256-page, copiously illustrated book *You Can Live Forever in Paradise on Earth*. Clearly the Watch Tower Bible and Tract Society regards this book – which is largely directed at contemporary youth – as a blockbuster among its publications. The society has said, 'It is expected to play a major part in stepping up the Witnesses' global work of encouraging the study of the Bible in the home' (*WT* 1 January 1983, 25). Initial reaction to the new book was positive among Witnesses: 'It is simple enough for the children to grasp the truth and intelligent enough for the parent to make their decision ... This new publication is like putting all the Society's literature in one small volume' (32). By the end of 1983, more than 15,000,000 copies had been printed in fifty-five languages (*WT* 1 January 1984, 28).

So concerned is the society to speak to youth directly that in 1982 it began publishing a series in *Awake!* called 'Young People Ask':

This feature tries to imitate Jehovah God who stated: 'I will give [you] advice *with my eye upon you.*' (Psalm 32:8) ...

It is hoped that *parents especially* will use this series to increase the dialogue with their teenage children. A practical format is provided for a balanced conversation. Many parents already are using each issue as a part of a weekly family Bible discussion ...

The feature's value is not limited to teenagers or those in their twenties ... The articles ... are intended to help you to understand yourself and others better, as well as to see the wisdom of Bible counsel.

BE SURE TO READ THEM! They will help you to deal with your unique pressures. (8 January 1983, 23; italics in original)

Thus, the society keeps its eye on youth but enlists the assistance of parents to apply Bible counsel to their children as well. In this way, it seeks to keep youth under control spiritually and ideologically for as long as it can – at least until 'teenagers and those in their twenties' have made their personal decision to become, through dedication and baptism, full-fledged Jehovah's Witnesses.

CHAPTER SEVEN

The Seeds of Dissension

From the point of view of our present rulers, therefore, the only genuine dangers are the splitting-off of a new group of able, under-employed, power-hungry people, and the growth of liberalism and scepticism in their own ranks. (*1984*, 208–9) 54)

Like other sectarian groups, Jehovah's Witnesses must depend heavily upon ongoing conversion to sustain the levels of fervour and commitment necessary to keep the group vital. The demand for continued proselytizing does serve to provide a stream of converts entering the mainstream of the Witness community and helps to maintain the sectarian quality of the group; but the major source of membership growth is the children born to members. The problems occasioned by this phenomenon within sectarian movements was explained by Richard Niebuhr:

By its very nature the sectarian type of organization is valid for only one generation. The children born to the voluntary members of the first generation begin to make the sect a church long before they have arrived at the age of discretion. For with their coming the sect must take on the character of an educational and disciplinary institution, with the purpose of bringing the new generation into conformity with ideas and customs which have become traditional. (Niebuhr [1929] 1957, 19–20)

The need for strong internal indoctrinational and disciplinary programs for children born into the movement results largely from the nature of the child's experience, which stands in marked contrast to that which brought his parents into the group. The element of 'choice' that was present during his parents' conversion is denied the 'native' child. Like Barbara Harrison, children born into the society pass through childhood 'drenched in the dark blood-poetry of a religion whose adherents [draw] joy from the prospect of the imminent end of the world' (Harrison 1978, 14). In order to maintain the child's adherence through to adulthood, the society must attempt to restrict the world accessible to the child to that world which conforms to the society's vision: the child must be discouraged from exploring other 'truths.'

As discussed in chapter 6, parents have traditionally been the primary agents of the society in the child's indoctrination process. Parents are expected to bring up their children in the 'discipline and mental-regulating of Jehovah' to ensure that their offspring will remain faithful members of the community. They work hard at it, for the cost of failure is high; the parents' own salvation can be jeopardized if their children stray and bring their own blood-guilt upon their parents' heads. Total rejection of the organization on the part of the child as he matures towards adulthood involves the parent in a situation of having to choose between the child and the organization in accordance with the group's strict principles of ostracism, principles which are more rigorously enforced as the years pass. Charles Taze Russell's attitude towards the management of disfellowshipped individuals is noteworthy:

Such an excluded brother or sister should not be treated as an enemy nor thought of as such; but as an erring brother, as the Apostle says ...'If any man obey not our word by this epistle [if he be disorderly, unwilling to submit himself to sound reasoning and loving generous rules of order] note that man, and have no company with him, to the end that he may not be ashamed; yet count him not as an enemy, but admonish him to a brother.' ... He should not be passed by on the street unnoticed by the brethren, but be treated courteously. The exclusion should be merely from the privileges of the assembly and from any special brotherly associations, etc. peculiar to the faithful ... He is a brother still, but not in the best of standing. (*The Watchtower and Herald of Christ's Presence* 1 March 1912, 82–3)

By contrast, the 15 September 1981 *Watchtower* stated, with explicit reference to the Apostle Paul's words in 1 Corinthians 5:11, 'But now I am writing you to *quit mixing in company* ['not associate,' TEV] [*sic*] with anyone called a brother that is a fornicator or a greedy person or an idolater or a reviler or a drunkard or an extortioner, *not even eating with such a man*' (22; italics in original). Five months after the publication of this passage the society demonstrated its intention to follow the letter of the law to its logical extreme when, after the Governing Body failed to gain consensus on the disfellowshipping of Raymond Franz for alleged apostasy, a local congregation in Gadsden, Alabama, disfellowshipped him for 'eating a meal with his benefactor Gregerson' (Ostling 1982, 41). The punitive measures have become refined to the point where one might ask whether many elders delight as much in the process of keeping the organization clean as in the cleanliness itself. Morality, as suggested by P.D. Ouspensky, is a hallmark of humanity – a definitive distinction between the works of apes and man:

But at the same time delusions are nowhere more easily created than in the region of morality. Allured by *his own particular morality* and moral gospel, a man forgets the *aim* of moral perfection ... He begins to see an aim in *morality itself*. Man is charmed with his 'niceness.' He desires that everyone else should be just as nice as he ... Then appears delight in morality for morality's sake, a sort of moral sport ... (Ouspensky [1920] 1970, 206; italics in original)

When other men fail to measure up to a given set of standards, fear begins to develop. Even thought must be censured with a form of Orwellian *crimestop* to prevent the contamination of such high ideals. From the depths of moral paranoia comes the expression of moral tyranny. Morality in its most debased form – unyielding convention, rule, and LAW – has pervaded the consciousness of the adult population of the Witnesses with increasing intensity during the last few years and has devolved with equivalent force upon the children of the membership.

In the case of a family member's being disfellowshipped, the same stringent regulations of moral censure apply. If the offender is a minor child parents are told to care only for his *physical needs* and *discipline*; in other areas of family interaction the wrongdoer must remain silent and refrain from participation. If the disfellowshipped individual is a marriage partner, all interaction must be reduced to a bare minimum and all religious discussion is expected to terminate (*WT* 15 December 1981, 27–8). That such rules of conduct effectively terminate all normal family relationships is of no concern to the society in its quest to maintain 'unity at all costs.' It argues that 'the conduct of the wrongdoer has changed his relationship with Jehovah and therefore with his family who are Jehovah's Witnesses' (*WT* 15 September 1981, 17). Furthermore,

If someone is disfellowshipped, he must at the time have had a truly bad heart and/or been determined to pursue a God-dishonoring course. Peter said that the condition of such a person is worse than before he became a Christian; he is like 'a sow that was bathed but has gone back to the mire.' (2 Peter 2:20–22) This should help Christian relatives and others to have God's view of a disfellowshipped person. (WT 1 January 1983, 31)

Therefore, one should not feel sympathy for a disfellowshipped person. The relationship between a disfellowshipped husband and his wife will naturally be strained, for 'it will not be possible to have spiritual fellowship with him, sharing in Bible discussions and prayer with him as she once did ... She will certainly feel this loss.'

Another sort of loss may be felt by loyal Christian grandparents whose children have been disfellowshipped. They may have been accustomed to visiting regularly with their children, giving them occasion to enjoy their grandchildren. Now the parents are disfellowshipped because of rejecting Jehovah's standards and ways. So things are not the same in the family. Of course, the grandparents have to determine if some necessary family matters require limited contact with the disfellowshipped children. And they might sometimes have the grandchildren visit them. How sad, though, that by their unchristian course the children interfere with the normal pleasure that such grandparents enjoyed! (WT 1 January 1983, 31)

The disfellowshipped person rather than the congregation must bear full responsibility for the anguish created – 'We may not be able to undo all the hurt or make up for all the loss that the disfellowshipped person has caused his Christian relatives' – but the fact remains that 'the expelled mate is not the sort of person that we want to be around. And we need to be careful not to get involved in fellowshipping with him' (31). The society quotes Matthew 10:34–8 to support its position: 'Jesus said: "*I came to put, not peace, but a sword. For I came to cause division, with a man against his father, and a daughter against her mother, and a young wife against her mother-in-law. Indeed, a man's enemies will be persons of his own household. He that has greater affection for father or mother than for me is not worthy of me*"' (WT 15 September 1981, 27; italics in original).

The synchronized manipulation of the carrot of approbation with the big stick of divine retribution is extremely effective in controlling the behaviour of the adult convert who has chosen to relinquish his ties with the world and to obey the organization in all things in order to experience the spiritual paradise now and the earthly paradise in the future. The organization increases over time its elaborations on the wretchedness of the world outside the Witnesses' own community. If the group were composed strictly of converts, there would be limited need for such an extensive boundary mechanism since converts in the very act of conversion reject the world of their own accord. The external world must be regarded as inimical, hostile, and ugly, as a primary 'enemy,' and this 'enemy' becomes an integral asset to the entire group to be expounded upon by the members in attempting to steer the community's children well away from contact with that world.

'The enemy' is, in fact, a category endemic to all human communities because it is a part of the definition of the parameters which establish the 'I' and 'Thou,' the 'Self' and 'Other,' the 'Friend' and 'Foe.' Such designations can be used to denote those who share a true communication in their mutual acceptance of one symbolic system and to separate them from those who do not. Thus, to Jehovah's Witnesses, all fellow Witnesses are referred to as 'The Friends'; there is no room for 'enemies' within their community. The 'friend' is one with whom the individual can communicate about mutual concerns within a common framework for understanding his universe – that is, within the framework of an 'institutionalized set of beliefs' (Rokeach 1960, 35). However, since there is no room within their community for 'the enemy,' the Witnesses are unable to accommodate heterodoxy of any kind; thus, the community itself tends to stagnate. As Rollo May remarked: 'I need my enemy *in* my community. He keeps me alert, vital. I need his criticism. Strange to say, I need him to posit myself against ... Our enemy is as necessary for us as our friends. Both together are part of authentic community' (1972, 428). In keeping with this idea is Orwell's presentation of Emmanuel Goldstein and his heretical '*book*' as a creation of the Party: 'The heretic, the enemy of society, will always be here, so that he can be defeated and humiliated over again ... Goldstein and his heresies will live for ever. Every day, at every moment, they will be defeated, discredited, ridiculed, spat upon – and yet they will always survive' (*1984*, 271).

Within the relatively strict boundaries of the Witness community, one would expect to discover that its members grow within that community's shared universe in such a way as to feel at home in it. The defection rate, however, does not support such a proposition. While the appeal of the world beyond the parameters of the community could be put forward to explain the high defection rate, the experiences of individuals such as Barbara Harrison indicate that a move into that alien world is often a painful and terrifying experience. Many of those who leave give clear indication that they were 'driven' rather than 'seduced' away. Certainly the punitive internal discipline must be considered as a fractious element in itself.

As the organization increases the social and doctrinal pressures that contribute to the isolation of the group, a concomitant pressure builds from within the membership itself. Like a giant pressure-cooker, this cultural container must let off steam and does so by forcibly ejecting elements of dissension from within; the process must be regulated in such a way as to sustain optimum pressure on the membership without occasioning a major explosion – a difficult task indeed in an 'hermetically sealed community' (Ostling 1982, 36). That internal problems would eventually prove more disruptive to the Witnesses than any overt failure of prophecy was suggested by Alan Rogerson, who, in 1969, in a prophetic moment of his own, wrote: 'It is, I believe, a superficial judgement to claim that 1975 will be the making or breaking of the Witnesses; they are already prepared to survive that date and it is more likely that changing social conditions will take the greatest toll of their members' (19). Trying social conditions, created by a reconsideration of the entire thematic universe within which the Witnesses live, have taken their toll. The internal social repression of people already disillusioned by the failure of Armageddon to arrive on schedule – however the society may choose to rationalize its further delay – has in itself created a divisive atmosphere within the organization. Within this atmosphere, dissident members now struggle to break the hermetic seal and allow fresh air to fill the vacuum that they perceive exists at the centre of the organization. The Witnesses' cauldron of transformation and liberation has thus become, for many, the crucible of oppression from which they in turn must seek, through reflection, redefinition, and reaction, yet another 'truth.'

Jehovah's Witnesses are reminded constantly that the omniscient Jehovah is able to 'read the heart' and 'read the thoughts' of any individual. Although they have often been accused of spying on one another ('Jehovah's Witnesses have a spy network that would "make the KGB and the CIA look like amateurs,"' one disgruntled member was quoted as saying in the *Melbourne Sunday Press* 5 February 1978), human monitoring pales into insignificance when compared to the 'mental-regulating of Jehovah' that good Witnesses believe in as a literal reality. In Orwell's Oceania, thought control has not yet been perfected. Although one of the main two aims of the Party is 'to extinguish once and for all the possibility of independent thought,' a corollary problem is 'how to discover, against his will, what another human being is thinking' (194). For Jehovah's Witnesses, this isn't a problem: Jehovah is capable of determining that for himself – or so the faithful Witness is required to *believe*. Whether the individual Witness is actually observed doing something 'untheo-cratic' is irrelevant; eventually the sin will out, and the sinner will be exposed. Furthermore, nonconformists are 'marked' by the elders in the expectation that eventually they will do something deemed to warrant disfellowshipping: 'Even though no name has been mentioned, individual members of the con-gregation would then be obliged to "mark" a person, or persons, of that kind, just as Paul advised the brothers in Thessalonica. If the disorderly one should still persist in his wayward course of conduct, he remains in grave danger of eventually committing a serious sin that could lead to his being disfellow-shipped' (*oaom*, 152–3).

The belief in constant observation by God – as well as monitoring by elders, parents, and peers – creates among Jehovah's Witnesses a situation not unlike that in *Nineteen Eighty-Four*:

A Party member lives from birth to death under the eye of the Thought Police. Even when he is alone he can never be sure that he is alone. Wherever he may be, asleep or awake, working or resting, in his bath or in bed, he can be in-spected without warning and without knowing that he is being inspected. Noth-ing that he does is indifferent. His friendships, his relaxations, his behaviour towards his wife and children, the expression of his face when he is alone, the words he mutters in his sleep, even the characteristic movements of his body, are all jealously scrutinized. Not only any actual misdemeanour, but any eccen-tricity, however small, any change of habits, any nervous mannerism that could possibly be the symptom of an inner struggle, is certain to be detected. (211–12)

The *Melbourne Sunday Press* article cited above carried the headline 'SECT SPLIT ON SPY CLAIMS: REBELS HIT "BIG BROTHER" SOCIETY' and contained inter-views with members who said:

'it was not uncommon for church "spies" to watch members' homes, interrogate neighbours, or follow them in their cars to see if they were breaking any "rules."'

'The church has even been known to keep tabs on members' sexual habits,' said one member this week.

The members declined to be named for 'fear of reprisals.'

'Sometimes they go to incredible lengths to find out about members' personal lives.'

'It's a big brother society.'

In Oceania, if the Party says that 'two plus two make five,' then so be it (*1984*, 261, 293). Continued membership in the Party – continued *life* – depends on the individual's not merely accepting but *believing* what the Party tells him to believe. 'The Truth' is determined by the Party. An identical dynamic works within the Organization of Jehovah's Witnesses where, 'unity at all costs' and the avoidance of 'independent thinking' force the membership into 'rejecting the evidence of their own eyes.'

Many Witness doctrines seem to some members to be challengeable on purely mathematical grounds. The logistics of the resurrection expressed by the Witnesses ('Even allowing half of [the land surface of the earth] to be set aside for other uses, there would be more than half an acre [c. 0.2 hectare] for each person. As to earth's potential food production, one-half acre [c. 0.2 hectare] will actually provide much more than enough food for one person' [*ABU*, 1400]) seem at least naive insofar as no account is taken of vast stretches of infertile land, including deserts, mountains, and tundra, that have virtually no arable soil. Indeed, their images of paradise invariably contain vast snow-capped mountain ranges (see figure 41). The Witnesses concede that other animal life is one of the important motifs of the earthly paradise, and they believe that carnivores will become herbivorous ('The lion will eat straw just like the bull' – Isa. 65:25). Yet a recent *Awake!* article unwittingly pointed to some of the logistical difficulties of this belief:

In order to protect some of the threatened animals from the hunter, governments set up hunting restrictions outlawing the killing of these animals. In the
United States, for example, a herd of 3,000 Rocky Mountain mule deer in Ari-
zona was protected. The result? With thousands of its natural predators being
trapped, shot or poisoned by government hunters, the mule deer increased its
population within 10 years to about 40,000 animals.

A happy result? In a way, yes. But, alas, the deer began to die en masse.
What was wrong? Their habitat became overpopulated. Dead deer were found
with stomachs full of pine needles, certainly not on the menu of deer unless they
are on the verge of starvation. (22 May 1983, 11)

Complete protection is in store for citizens of God's crime-free world. The Bible assurance is: "God . . . will wipe out every tear from their eyes, and death will be no more, neither will mourning nor outcry nor pain be anymore." —Rev. 21:3, 4

Figure 41 *Awake!* 22 November 1975, 16

If, as the Witnesses are required to believe, all mammals are to become herbivores in the New World, the starvation problem is likely to be exacerbated.

More serious challenges to Witness doctrine by those who insist that two plus two make four have arisen from Watch Tower Society calculations of chronology, as we have seen; all the archaeological evidence amassed during this century from Babylonia indicates that the Witnesses are twenty years out in their calculations. More centrally, the arbitrary mixing of literal and figurative interpretations of biblical numbers and dates has fuelled criticism by dissidents. David Reed asked rhetorically in the March 1982 issue of *Comments from the Friends*, 'What happens to Witnesses who read Revelation 7:4–8 and conclude that twelve symbolic numbers add up to a total that is also symbolic?' (3) The answer, of course, is that they could be disfellowshipped since the assumption that 144,000 is a literal number is a critical tenet of belief.

A more complex logistical problem surrounds speculation as to how various species of animals and plants got here in the first place. The Witnesses quote Genesis 1:12, 21, 25, stressing that God made each creature 'according to its kind,' although, in terms of contemporary biology, they admit that it is not clear whether 'kind' refers to genus or family. 'When the Bible speaks of God as creating various kinds of life on earth, it does not mean every single species known to man ... The kind to which it refers is large enough to allow for great variety within but not for interbreeding with other kinds' (*DMGHE*, 51). Since no terrestrial animal survived the flood without the direct assistance of Noah and the ark (a boat built by four inexperienced carpenters), all 3,000 species of land mammals classified so far must have descended from the basic 'kinds' that Noah gathered together two by two:

Since the Bible says that Noah brought some of all the various kinds of land animals and flying creatures into the ark, some persons have asked, 'How could there possibly have been room for all those animals?'

... If we allow 100,000 cubic feet of space for deck floors and other inside parts, there still remain nearly 1,300,000 cubic feet of usable space. This is equal to the carrying capacity of ten freight trains of about forty-eight American stockcars each!

Also, investigation reveals that, of some 3,000 'species' of land mammals classified by zoologists, only about 300 include any that are larger than a horse, whereas some 2,200 are no larger than a rabbit. Marine mammals such as the huge whales and dolphins would be no problem, as they would have remained outside the ark ... (*IBRWG*, 42)

The Witnesses pay little attention to the thousands of species of birds, reptiles, insects, and other terrestrial animal life, although birds and reptiles are depicted on or about the ark.

Since 'species' is not synonymous with 'kind' in Witness etymology, all 3,000 species of mammals apparently developed from a cluster of 'family kinds.' Adam, for example, 'may have had to deal only with basic family kinds rather than all the varieties of creatures that have developed out of those family kinds' when he named them in the Garden of Eden (*WT* 15 July 1976, 437). Still, all species extant today 'developed' from those fundamental family kinds – in a matter of 4,354 years! The Witnesses do not attempt to explain Australia, with its isolated species (although they show two kangaroos hopping towards the ark [*MBBS*, 18]) but they do believe that mammoths and dinosaurs perished at the time of the flood when extant 'families' survived by seeking refuge on the ark (see Story 10 in *My Book of Bible Stories* 18–21). Very few scientists would suggest that such rapid speciation as that described by the Witnesses would be possible. Otherwise, that kind of development within family and generic 'kinds' is exactly the process that most biologists would call 'evolution.'

The average educated adult obviously has difficulty, not with the basic biblical concepts of creation and the flood, but with the arguments advanced to defend them. Young Witness students have a particularly difficult time reconciling logical thought acquired at school with Witness literature read at home. Just as logic is inimical to Ingsoc, so it is inimical to Jehovah's Witnesses. Faith rather than logic and common sense is the required motivating factor.

The inability to accept the anomalies of Witness doctrine is not the only cause of defection. Some people leave the organization out of simple boredom. Until 1977, at the Book Study as well as the *Watchtower* Study, the conductor asked the questions printed at the bottom of each page, and the other members of the group would raise their hands to answer. If called upon to answer a question, members would read one or two sentences out of the paragraph numbered to match the question. Then the paragraph was read in its entirety. This process resulted in slow, boring meetings. Procedural changes were announced in the 1 February 1977 *Watchtower*: '1) Read the paragraph in *The Watchtower* (or other publication); 2) Read the question thereon; 3) Call on those raising their hands for answers, discussing fully the paragraph and supporting scriptures' (96). The society's expectation of intelligence does not seem to be very high; nor do they expect 'homework' to be done:

There should be a number of advantages in reading the paragraphs before they are discussed. This will quickly refresh the minds of all who have studied over the lesson in advance, and in the event some have not been able to do this previous to the meeting, the reading will at least familiarize them with the material before it is discussed. Everyone will be encouraged to concentrate on the reading, rather than look ahead for the answer in the next paragraph. Those who are shy, or who are slow in organizing their thoughts, will be able to prepare better to put their words together and so gain confidence to raise their hands. There should be freer participation and fuller discussion of the finer details of the study, with emphasis on the application of key scriptures before passing on to the reading of the next paragraph.

This new arrangement should be a blessing to all of God's people, as they seek to be filled with the accurate knowledge of his will in order to walk worthily of Jehovah. – Col. 1:9, 10. (96)

Under this format, studying a book may take up to a year of weekly, one-hour meetings. Most of the books range in length from 180 to 300 pages and could be read and understood by the average undergraduate student in a matter of hours. As a result of this prolonged examination of Jehovah's 'progressive light,' the Witnesses are left with the impression that Jehovah's 'Truth' is very profound indeed, an impression that stems more from the approach than from the theology. Despite the organization's attempts at sparking enthusiasm and promoting fuller participation in the meetings, the situation has continued to deteriorate, resulting in adjustments to the format of study material itself. It would appear that the organization concluded that the paragraph-by-paragraph and sentence-by-sentence dissection of their material was too challenging for the masses to grasp. In 1979 they released *Commentary on the Letter of James* – a work subsequently used as material for the short talks of the Ministry School – in which they examine the book of James, not a verse at a time, but a word or phrase at a time.

Such a piecemeal treatment of Watch Tower publications ensures that any internal contradictions within the literature will not be detected – especially by the initiate or the new convert. One of the most common means the dissidents use to convince borderline Witnesses to leave the organization is to have them read Witness publications from cover to cover, allowing the literature to stand or fall on its own merit. Often Witnesses who do this – and comment on new releases in public meetings before they have been formally discussed in traditional question-and-answer format – are accused of being 'presumptuous' and of 'running ahead of the organization.' Any suggestion that the society encourages genuine open debate, or even discussion, not contained by the strictures of a given answer to a given question must be rejected. Indeed, the enthusiasm for alleged 'apostasy' endemic in the Brooklyn headquarters in 1980 was a direct result of individuals reading the Bible without reference to Watch Tower Bible study aids, as we shall see.

TABLE 9

Year	Remnant of 144,000
1970	10,526
1971	10,384
1972	10,350
1973	10,523
1974	10,723
1975	10,550
1976	10,187
1977	10,080
1978	9,762
1979	9,727
1980	9,564
1981	9,601
1982	9,529
1983	9,292

The exploration of the entire issue of disaffection is made problematic by Memorial records for the period from 1970 to 1982 as set out in table 9. The individuals represented in this table are those who believe themselves to be of the Remnant of 144,000 chosen ones destined to rule in heaven. Membership in the Remnant was basically limited to Jehovah's Witnesses who were baptized by 1935 when it was announced that a Great Crowd of Other Sheep would remain on earth throughout eternity (*LEFSG*, 148 and *UWTG*, 112). Therefore, the number of the Remnant should decline at an ever-increasing rate with each passing year as its geriatric membership dies off. However, as table 9 shows, there was an increase in partakers in 1973, 1974, and 1981. The society has always allowed for the possibility that on rare occasions one of this select group could become unsuitable to serve with Christ as a 'king.' If a member of the Remnant is disfellowshipped, for example, he is usually considered to be part of the 'Evil Slave' Class rather than of the 'Faithful and Discreet Slave' Class, and hence would be replaced by a member from the ranks of the Great Crowd in a process not unlike a worker bee's taking on the qualities of a queen. The highly speculative book *Life Everlasting in Freedom of the Sons of God* explains:

It is possible that some baptized Christians were added to the anointed remnant, not to increase the number, but to replace any of them who had proved unfaithful to the heavenly calling and who would therefore leave a vacancy to be filled. But despite the bringing in of such ones as replacements, the number of the anointed remnant kept decreasing because more of these died faithful and were taken into the heavenly kingdom than the number of replacements brought in. (149)

In the 1 February 1975 *Watchtower*, the society offered an explanation for a rise in the number partaking: 'In fact, for the past 1,900 years Jehovah has been selecting these, for a total of 144,000 members. By now that number appears to be *nearly complete*' (84; italics added). This statement was intended as a broad hint to the membership that they should not presume to join the ranks of the Anointed. But it backfired. If the number was *nearly* complete, many of the older 'Other Sheep' reasoned, perhaps there was a chance to become a member of the Anointed. Many, upon reassessing their 'calling,' found a heavenly destiny to be an appealing idea.

The early increases – those in 1973 and 1974 – occurred for several reasons. Overtly, many Witnesses, having reread integral passages from Revelation, had sincerely determined to their own satisfaction that the intention of the Bible was clearly that they too were destined for heaven. Especially was this so among the older Witnesses, those whose friends had been members of the Remnant before their death. Covertly, some older people who had been unsure of their status began to focus on more spiritual destinies as death approached; when one is physically tired with the onset of old age, the prospect of gradual recuperation to physical exuberance over a period of ten centuries may seem more of a punishment than a reward. Others may have sought to avoid the trauma of Armageddon by joining the Remnant at the eleventh hour. Still others may have become inactive by the 1970s due to infirmity or forgetfulness, but were reactivated by the prospect of an impending holocaust. If they were members of the Remnant when they became inactive, they could legitimately partake of the emblems when they returned to the fold.

Still, in 1975 the society clearly feared a continuation of the upward trend in Memorial partakers, and in an article entitled 'Anointing to a Heavenly Hope – How Is It Manifest?' (*wT* 15 February 1975, 105–11) the Governing Body warned readers against mistakenly presuming a heavenly calling. The writers clearly blamed the increase on the ignorance of the membership as to the nature of the calling: 'What might cause some to assume mistakenly that they are of the anointed ones who should partake of the Memorial emblems? Lack of knowledge could be responsible for someone assuming wrongly that he or she was thus anointed. One may fail to realize that, as with other favors of God, receiving such anointing depends, not upon the one wishing nor upon the one running, but upon God' (107). The article warned against self-aggrandisement and pride. When blacks in Africa began to partake of the 'emblems' in the 1970s the Governing Body attributed the influx of partakers in part at least to the tribal roots of 'unruly' ones who allegedly exhibited unbecoming fetishist behaviour after partaking of the 'blood of Christ' (105). Others who made the mistake of partaking of the emblems had reportedly experienced 'spiritual enlightenment' through drug abuse or simple fantasizing (107–8). All of these partakers were duly reprimanded, and some were disfellowshipped.

The problem is much more widespread than meets the eye, because most members of the Remnant are by now exceedingly old, and the death rate theoretically should increase from year to year. The society claims that it expects a death rate of 1 per cent per year for *all* of its membership (*Yearbook* 1974, 254), although this estimate is obviously artificially high. Yet between 1970 and 1975, the number claiming to be members of the Remnant went *up* from 10,526 to 10,550, implying that none of the Remnant had died during that time. Between 1973 and 1982 the number went down by only 10 per cent despite the fact that almost all of those recognized as being legitimately of the remnant are currently seventy or older.

The increase from 1980 to 1981 was not so much the result of ignorance or self-aggrandisement, as an indication of dissent, for the easiest way to give a protest vote that the Governing Body will have to reckon with is to partake of the emblems; indeed, some dissenters readily admit not only to partaking of the emblems but to organized infiltration of certain Kingdom Halls at Memorial time. Younger witnesses who partake are often questioned immediately afterwards, and if they clearly made a mistake out of ignorance of the law they are reprimanded and not counted in with the figures sent to Brooklyn. But to knowingly partake of the emblems without absolute assurance that one is a member of the 144,000 is a disfellowshippable offence. To use the Memorial as a form of protest is, therefore, usually a final act of desperation before one leaves the fold.

Walter Szykitka noted in regard to his abandoning the Witnesses' vision and the Brooklyn Bethel:

The Witnesses tied up the whole history of the world in one knot. They explained everything.

I had lived my life until the age of twenty-five or -six believing that I was never going to die, or that if I did die in a car crash or something, God would resurrect me and I'd live forever in the New World. I can remember the exact moment when I realized I was not going to live forever. The physical moment: I was working in my office at Bethel and I got up from my desk to go into the file cabinet; I was bending down to get a file, and – it came out of nowhere – I said, Hey, you're going to die one day. And in that one second the knot unraveled. (Harrison 1978, 97)

World order, world meaning, and self within the world all dissolve in the critical unravelling of human history and the death of personal ontogeny. To define man and his relationship with his world is the primary function of symbolic structure in the mythic sense, as Paul Ricoeur noted: 'The first function of the myths of evil is to embrace mankind as a whole in one ideal history. By means of a time that represents all times, "man" is manifested as a concrete universal' 1967, 162). As their ideal history unravels, the disaffected are often caught in existential crises. In their search for new meaning and order they often begin a quest for a new standard of 'Truth' and, like Harrison and Szykitka, begin to frequent libraries and bookstores. Dora Dorset, a school-teacher who "drifted away" from the Witnesses after attending university, recalled in an interview:

I bought the most ridiculous books – ridiculous in terms of my total lack of background for understanding them. I started with the Roman philosophers. That really scared me. Maybe I was too dumb to learn anything! By the time I got to university I was so scared of being incapable of learning I worked day and night hoping for a bare pass in each subject. I was utterly astonished when I graduated with an 'A' average. I didn't realize until then that maybe – just maybe – the world which had been so incomprehensible just four or five years before was beginning to make sense. And *I* was capable of understanding it.

The phenomenon of over-achieving after leaving the Witnesses is not peculiar to Dora. According to Dr James Penton, who has himself helped many Witness youths into university, a pattern of high academic achievement is common among them. This pattern is understandable in that these young people are not in university or college primarily to learn a specific job skill; but rather they are there as part of the quest for a meaningful world and the creation of an informed self to inhabit that 'new world.'

In assessing the role of the believer in the process of religious abuse, Harvey Cox noted: 'The seduction of the spirit ... is the twisting of people's natural and healthy religious instincts for the purposes of control and domination. It is the cruelest abuse of religion because it slyly enlists people in their own manipulation' (1973, 16). Against these words we must weigh Nietzsche's comment that 'the herd animal' (i.e., the grass-roots believer) is incapable of leading itself, and therefore not only desires a leader, but seeks one. According to Nietzsche, the 'priests understood that ... Again it is the priests who exploit this condition and win the "people over"' (1968, 157–62). Although one tends to sympathize with Cox's estimation of the inhumanity which can ultimately result from the abuse of the believers' trust and veneration, the culpability of both the 'priests' and the 'people' suggested by Nietzsche must be considered. In what ways do people become enlisted in their own manipulation? Simone de Beauvoir wrote in *The Ethics of Ambiguity* that mystification of his own position leads the committed believer – the 'slave' – to see his role as an exalted one, in which he can experience a sense of pride and of 'getting somewhere' (1948, 85). This feeling arises as a result of membership – a sense of 'being in' or 'belonging to' an organization the power of which is used for the eventual advantage of the constituent members. In a form of social contract, the members abrogate responsibility for decision-making to the authority of the church in exchange for the security that the doctrinal assumptions of the church provides. In the very act of investing their trust and their commitment in the organization, they divest themselves of their power – except in the sense that their power has been invested in a larger pool which is expected to expand. In Orwellian terms, 'if he can make complete, utter submission, if he can escape from his identity, if he can merge himself in the Party so that he *is* the Party, then he is all-powerful and immortal' (*1984*, 267). The organization, in effect, comes to serve as an exclusive catalyst in the affirmation of the individual before self and cosmos. Eventually, the paracletism of the organization and the mystification of the believer create a tight, hermetically sealed thematic unity from which none may withdraw readily.

But how *does* one come to withdraw? When the weight of contradiction and doubt or the enforced ostracism from a closed system results in the withdrawal of an individual from his community and the abandonment of his symbols of significance, the individual is left in a state of existential crisis. If the disaffected member has long pondered the perceived disharmonies of his thematic universe (as has Winston Smith, for example), and has laid the ground-work for an alternative perception of self and world, he is prepared for the actual break – whether that break is of his own accord or has been forced on him by the community. But for those who are forced to abandon their symbols of significance suddenly, as happens when one is summarily disfellow-shipped or when a friend or relative opts to abandon rather than follow the community, the lack of an alternative can be psychologically disruptive. In either case, the establishment of meaning becomes for the individual an all-consuming struggle to extricate himself from the symbolically defined purposes and destiny of the organization man mentality imposed by the former system as he begins to reassert himself in the larger world as a person in his own right. This is no mean feat. One recalls Tillich's words: 'A self which has become a matter of calculation and management has ceased to be a self. It has become a thing' ([1952] 1962, 124). In short, such an individual must create for himself, not only a new world, but a new 'self' to live within that world. Herein lies the potential of human free will, creativity, and responsibility, in which that energy or commitment which has long been vested or invested in an institution is reassumed by the individual, who thereby obtains freedom to renew the search for meaning and the struggle to exist more humanly.

After the failure of Armageddon to arrive on schedule as suggested by the oracular voice of Brooklyn, more and more Witnesses began to search for the significance of their past and to re-evaluate their dreams for the future. 'Life Everlasting in Freedom of the Sons of God' had proven to be chimerical indeed, and freedom within the organization that had moulded their lives non-existent. This search for freedom produced increased oppression from Brooklyn. Symptomatic of this situation was a spreading air of discontent expressed in protests and public interviews starting in 1978 in the wake of mass disfellowshippings and continuing to this day. Protests in which Witnesses claiming to be in good standing with their congregations wore paper bags over their heads to protect their identity became commonplace across the North American continent. Pickets marched outside Kingdom Halls and Bethel offices in numerous cities, often before television cameras and the press. Intellectuals were reprimanded for expressing their views, and inactive publishers were tracked down and pressured to write letters of disassociation. For an ever-increasing number of dissenters, the challenge is to build other, more meaningful 'new worlds' out of the wreckage and disillusionment of an optimistic vision turned nightmare. The current crisis is of particular interest because there is a movement afoot to re-order Brooklyn's empire as well.

Unlike the disaffected of earlier generations, the current dissidents appear prepared to wheel on the oppressor in their struggle for liberation.

Whereas the Witnesses curb any enthusiasm for reading material counter to their beliefs, the dissidents encourage the reading of Watch Tower literature in the assumption that the society's 'contradictions' will reveal themselves in due course. Many dissidents monitor every word and image that the Watch Tower Bible and Tract Society publishes. In the view of such dissenters, the society has become its own worst enemy. Note this description of 'Bethel' taken from the pages of the Watch Tower publication *Aid to Bible Understanding* and reprinted in *The Bible Examiner*:

Bethel became a symbol of rank apostasy from true worship (1 Ki. 12:31–3). Jehovah God did not delay in expressing his disapproval through 'a man of God' sent to Bethel to foretell its future desolation, and by ripping Bethel's altar apart ... Despite these warnings, Bethel continued as an idolatrous sanctuary ... Thus Jeremiah, over a century later, 'could' refer to it as a warning example to those trusting in false gods to their eventual shame. (*TBE* 1, no. 4 [October 1981]: 12–13; compare *ABU*, 220)

Jerry Bergman remarked, 'Many Jehovah's Witnesses now see a very real parallel between the typical Bethel and the antitypical Bethel, the Bethel of old and the present Bethel ... Has Bethel lost God's favour? Many of the 1,000,000 ex-Jehovah's Witnesses who have abandoned allegiance to the Watch Tower Society since 1970 would say, YES!' (*TBE* 1, no. 4:13)

CHAPTER EIGHT

Crisis at 'The Top'

He is too intelligent. He sees too clearly and speaks too plainly. The Party does not like such people. (*1984*, 54)

Dissident members of the Jehovah's Witnesses are at present undergoing a renewed search for freedom – freedom of thought, speech, action, and worship. Supposedly, 'freedom' was one major factor in their original association with the Witnesses, or at least in that of their parents. As George Richardson noted: 'New sects all start with profuse professions of LIBERTY, because usually their members are excluded by someone else. But they, too, end up the most full-blown bigots because they do not really determine what true freedom means and, therefore, do not hold to it' (*TBE* 1; no. 4 [October 1981]:4). The fall from liberty into slavery is endemic in political institutions as well as religious ones, and warrants careful examination. For dissident Witnesses today, the search for their perceived loss of freedom has taken them back to the works of their charismatic founder, Charles Taze Russell. Many who have experienced oppressiveness within the contemporary society are shocked to discover that Russell himself warned against the danger of transforming the loosely knit collection of 'ecclesias' of his day into an 'organization.' In fact, Russell was a vocal advocate of liberty and despised denominational and sectarian boundaries which served to divide the Christian community rather than to unite it. As he wrote in *Studies in the Scriptures*:

The real need of the Church of Christ is still more liberty – until each individual member shall stand free and independent of all human bonds, creeds, confessions, etc. With each individual Christian standing fast in the liberty wherewith he was made free by the Lord (Galations 5:1; John 8:32), and each individual Christian united in loyalty to his Word, very quickly the original unity which the Scriptures inculcated would be discerned and all true children of God, all members of the New Creation, would find themselves drawn to each other by the cords of love far more strongly than are men bound in earthly systems and societies. (Vol 6 [1904], 242)

While the above passage might lead some to accuse Russell of wild-eyed idealism, his vision of the organization as a potential oppressor was explicit and he argued his point at length:

We belong to NO *earthly organization* – We adhere only to that *heavenly organization* – 'whose names are written in heaven.' (Hebrews 12:23; Luke 10:20). All the saints now living, or that have lived during this age, belonged to OUR CHURCH ORGANIZATION: such are all ONE Church and there is NO OTHER recognized by the Lord. Hence any earthly organization which in the least interferes with this union of saints is contrary to the teachings of Scripture and opposed to the Lord's will – 'that they may be ONE.' (*Zion's Watch Tower and Herald of Christ's Presence* February 1884: 1, 2)

The propensity for factionalism within the Christian community was a major concern for Russell and he took care in his Last Will and Testament to safeguard the International Bible Students' Association from the threat of sectarianism. In 1915, just months before his death, he pleaded his case one last time:

I think that if the International Bible Students' Association can be shown to be a section of Babylon we all ought to get out of it ... If anyone can tell me how he got into the Babylon by getting interested in the affairs of the Watch Tower Bible and Tract Society, let him show me how he will jump and I will jump with him. (*The Watchtower and Herald of Christ's Presence* 15 July 1915, 218, 219)

One million dissident Witnesses have already left the organization, and in an attempt to stem the tide, the contemporary leadership has sought to justify alterations made over the years:

Things published were not perfect in the days of Charles Taze Russell, first president of the Watch Tower Bible and Tract Society; nor were they perfect in the days of J.F. Rutherford, the succeeding president. The increasing light on God's Word as well as facts of history have repeatedly required that adjustments of one kind or another be made down to the very present time. But let us never forget that the motives of this 'slave' were always pure, unselfish; at all times it has been well-meaning. (*WT* 1 March 1979, 23–4)

The interface between the social and symbolic forces operating in the Watchtower Bible and Tract Society is reflected in its publications and is an important factor in understanding the compelling dynamic which moves the mass of Jehovah's Witnesses along predictable courses of action consonant with the undulating world view of the Governing Body in Brooklyn. The extent to which the Witnesses *do* share a consistent mass world view is a measure of the power and persuasiveness of the corporate structure of the Watch Tower Bible and Tract Society, acquired through the careful manipulation of symbols which serve to legitimize its position. Jehovah's Witnesses will brook no criticism from within, as many concerned members who have attempted to voice alternative opinions regarding the basic doctrine or application of social pressure have discovered to their chagrin. Individualism is not tolerated, especially where criticism of the power structures of the society itself is concerned. Obedience is the key to successful retention of power by the Governing Body; whenever there is a shift in the doctrinal base, a purge of dissident members can be expected as a matter of course (*1984*, 212).

Behind the power of this organization to dominate the lives of so many people is the acceptance of the Watch Tower Bible and Tract Society quite literally as the voice of Jehovah – God's 'mouthpiece.' From this carefully cultivated perspective, the Governing Body is seen in much the same way as Moses saw the Burning Bush – as an unapproachable, unchallengeable, inexplicable symbol of the power of Jehovah himself. The Governing Body is composed of flesh-and-blood men, just as Moses' Bush was comprised of leaves and twigs; however, the power and glory with which the ruling few are invested by the multitudes of Witnesses – the esteem that these few men in New York receive collectively from over two million participating Witnesses world wide – cannot be explained merely in terms of the sum of the parts. The Witnesses themselves would immediately explain this phenomenon in terms of God's channelling 'new' or 'progressive light' through his organization.

Whenever one approaches an alien power system such as that represented by the Witnesses, it is always tempting to dismiss the whole process as one terrific scam – to regard the leaders with the jaundiced eye of scepticism as if they were racketeers deliberately leading the multitudes down the proverbial garden path. But this assessment would be totally unfair. There is little doubt that all members of the Governing Body are absolutely sincere in the belief that they collectively are the ones who have been chosen by God to direct the operation of Jehovah's organization on earth. All have been tried and tested many times over and not one of them became a member of the Governing Body by luck of the draw or by force. Since 1975 decisions made by the Governing Body are arrived at by two-thirds majority vote rather than by consensus (Franz 1983, 40–94, 283).

When Winston is confronted by O'Brien, he expects to detect in the Inner Party member a sense of *stance*, but it simply isn't there: 'He is not pretending, thought Winston; he is not a hypocrite; he believes every word he says' (*1984*, 259). The six members of the Governing Body that we have talked to all conveyed exactly the same kind of sincerity. Several of the members have been on the Board of Directors of the Watch Tower Bible and Tract Society for decades; the current president, F.W. Franz, worked with both Russell and Rutherford, and not only preceded Knorr in terms of conversion, but sat on the Governing Body long before Knorr's arrival (*Yearbook* 1975, 195–6). Others are comparative newcomers, having worked their way up the ranks from the local level. Leo K. Greenlees, for example, began pioneering in Canada in 1931, and subsequently was given difficult pioneering assignments in Montreal and the Maritimes. In 1936, he was invited to join the Bethel staff in Toronto, where years later he became the treasurer for the branch office. In 1964, he was invited to Brooklyn, and subsequently was appointed to a position on the Governing Body. While in Toronto, Greenlees conducted wedding ceremonies for hundreds of young couples who remember him fondly as sincere, amiable, and avuncular.

By whatever process they arrived 'at the top,' members of the Governing Body have been thoroughly tested for faith and sincerity every step of the way. Such a responsibility is a full-time job:

The Governing Body of Jehovah's Witnesses has continued to give a good lead during the service year in caring for the interests of Jehovah's Kingdom earth wide. The Governing Body holds weekly meetings, with all the committees represented, to discuss matters presented to it by the various Branch Committees and to consider recommendations for appointment of branch personnel and traveling overseers, as well as other business coming before it ...

Jehovah's favour has been manifest on the Kingdom-preaching and disciple-making work of his name-people during the past service year and all of us are determined to hold 'firmly to the faithful word.'* (*Yearbook* 1978, 259)

However outsiders may regard the corporate structure in political or business terms, the Witnesses themselves believe – and have it constantly re-affirmed for them – that the Watch Tower Bible and Tract Society is a theo-cracy; God rules through the Governing Body by divine inspiration: 'The various corporate religious societies (associated with the principal one, Watch Tower Bible and Tract Society of Pennsylvania) that have been formed by Jehovah's Witnesses throughout the earth in compliance with the laws of vari-ous governments cooperate with the Governing Body in carrying on the evan-gelizing work commanded by Jesus' (*Yearbook* 1978, 258). In keeping with the design of the organization, the word 'theocratic' is used frequently to describe the mind-set and social deportment of 'good' Witnesses. As we have seen, to be theocratic is to be 'good'; to be untheocratic is to be 'bad.' Although the average Witness does not consciously tie being 'theocratic' to its implicit root, 'theo-cracy,' the assumption is made that those who are good are ruled by God, or more specifically live their lives in accordance with the will and rules of God, as determined by the Governing Body. In short, anyone who conforms his will to that of the Governing Body is theocratic, good, and shares the hope of salvation in paradise. The anticipated paradise is the terrestrial, physical extension of the heavenly Kingdom of God, and the society is perceived to be at the vanguard of that kingdom. Indeed, Jehovah's Witnesses believe that the nucleus of the Governing Body, all of whom are anointed members of the Remnant of the 144,000 chosen ones, will survive Armageddon to supervise the establishment of God's 'nation' on earth as an extension of the heavenly kingdom, prior to their resurrection 'in the twinkling of an eye' to rule with Christ for a thou-

---

* Very few Witnesses can name all members of the Governing Body at any given time. As in *Nineteen Eighty-Four*, '*Who* wields power is not important, provided that the hier-archical structure remains always the same' (211). In January 1984 the fourteen surviv-ing members were Carey Barbour, Jack Barr, Lloyd Barry, John Booth, Fred Franz, George Gangas, Leo Greenlees, Milton Henschel, Ted Jaracz, Karl Klein, Martin Poet-zinger, Albert Schroeder, Lyman Swingle, and Dan Sydlik.

sand years in heaven. Theocracy, then, is already well established as the *modus operandi* of Jehovah's Witnesses (*OAOM*, 22, 204).

Once that fact is understood, we can gain some insight into the corporate dynamic that provides the Watch Tower Society with its power – and its problems. If, as all Witnesses claim, the Governing Body, as part of the 'Faithful and Discreet Slave' class, is the *only* voice of God on earth, then its decisions are by definition theocratic, which is to say, 'wise and good' or 'discreet.' Since one of the major functions of the Governing Body (besides writing and editing *The Watchtower* and other publications) is to select individuals who will represent the interests of the Watch Tower Society (and, by implication, God) as 'travelling overseers' – that is, men who will communicate directly with the congregations and individual publishers in the circuits or districts assigned to them – such individuals are, it can be argued, appointed by God's inspiration. The hierarchy of the church is thus exceedingly strong, and the power structure clear: no minor publisher or servant is in a position to challenge the views or opinions of a man higher up the hierarchical ladder; for to challenge someone appointed by the Governing Body is tantamount to challenging God himself. And the masses *do* believe that the Governing Body represents Jehovah and provides the keys to the realization of his promises of a New World. It is credited with 'perfection' (*UWTG*, 115).

Absolute obedience to or belief in the suggestions of the Governing Body is a central element of the power the organization has acquired over the years, so much so that the 1966 'suggestion' concerning Armageddon's possible arrival on or before October 1975 immediately took on the quality of 'truth.' The practical aspects of this manipulation of the symbolic system against the background of absolute belief and social obedience have already been discussed. The major growth of the organization from 1,058,675 members in 1966 to 2,138,537 members in 1976 is directly attributable to this suggestion; in fact, considering that the growth rate generally is from 2 per cent to 4 per cent per year, it is highly unlikely that rates of up to 13.5 per cent per year would have occurred without the boost injected by the society's manoeuvre. This in itself was a major demonstration of the organization's ability to influence its membership through symbol manipulation, mirroring precisely the methods used fifty years earlier.

Once such growth had been achieved, the emphasis shifted to consolidation of gains by stemming the tide of dissension which swelled within the contemporary organization and threatened to disintegrate the group from within. In the last five years, the Governing Body has exercised its discretionary power in increasingly totalitarian fashion. Especially is this so in the Brooklyn head-quarters, where members of the Bethel family are expected to obey '1,177 policies and regulations' or leave (Watters 1981, 4).

The epitome of self-actualization for the Witnesses is Bethel Service, which is described as 'whole-souled service' to God and the organization (OKPD, 145). But for many within Bethel – and to any objective observer from outside the organization – Bethel Service is intolerably demanding, by any contemporary standard:

Bethel family members start their day's activity early. Gathered at the breakfast table, they enjoy a thorough discussion of the day's Scripture text and comments. After breakfast they go to their assigned work, at which they spend at least 8 hours and 40 minutes a day for five days of the week, and four hours on Saturdays. Monday evenings the members of the family study the *Watchtower* lesson for the week and attend the family's Theocratic Ministry School. Other evenings as well as Saturday afternoon and Sunday are used for attending congregation meetings, sharing in the field ministry and attending to personal matters. Those who have been appointed as elders at Bethel also have the privilege of giving public talks in nearby congregations. The schedule is a full one. (OKPD, 146)

Once again, one is reminded of Oceania:

In principle a Party member had no spare time, and was never alone except in bed. It was assumed that when he was not working, eating, or sleeping he would be taking part in some kind of communal recreation: to do anything that suggested a taste for solitude, even to go for a walk by yourself, was always slightly dangerous. There was a word for it in Newspeak: *ownlife*, it was called, meaning individualism and eccentricity. (*1984*, 81–2)

The usual term for Bethel Service before 1980 was 'at least four years' but since 1980 only one-year contracts are signed. However, 'Any who can do so are encouraged to stay beyond that and make Bethel their life's work' (OKPD, 146). Besides a two-week vacation, the only fringe benefits that the Bethel workers receive are 'spiritual': 'Bethel is a marvelous place to serve. In such a theocratic atmosphere as exists at Bethel homes there is excellent opportunity for spiritual growth. It is richly rewarding to work all day in association with others who love Jehovah and to know that one's work benefits so many of

Jehovah's people (*OKPD*, 147). As Jerry Bergman remarked in *The Bible Examiner*, Bethel workers receive a certain amount of social prestige as well: 'Even if a Witness swept Bethel's floors ten years ago, he is still a Bethelite and that is seen as somehow more righteous, holy and knowledgeable of God's laws than a non-Bethelite' (1, no. 4 [October 1981]: 12).

Despite the society's claim that Bethel is 'a marvelous place to serve,' many volunteer workers have left the ranks in disillusionment and, occasionally, disgrace, bringing with them tales of witch hunts conducted within the Brooklyn Bethel. Among these, Randy Watters and Robert Sullivan were the most outspoken; they prepared cassette tapes and brochures outlining salient details of their voluntarily quitting Bethel and eventually quitting the organization altogether. The society has neither acknowledged nor denied Watters' allegations, which were outlined in an eight-page brochure entitled *What Happened at the World Headquarters of Jehovah's Witnesses in the Spring of 1980?* and which were confirmed more recently by Raymond Franz in *Crisis of Conscience* (1983).

According to Watters and Sullivan, the trouble began in the late sixties when an editorial committee of three researchers, led by Raymond Franz, was commissioned by Nathan Knorr, president of the Watch Tower Bible and Tract Society, to compile *Aid to Bible Understanding* (1969; 1971). Knorr gave the committee a free hand to read the Bible without reference to Watch Tower publications; if they came up with any 'new light' – acceptable deviations from established Watch Tower doctrine – they were to inform the Governing Body. One area that gave the committee difficulty was Bible chronology. Upon re-examination of the calculations of 1966, they came to realize, privately – perhaps with the help of the convincing documentation of Carl Olof Jonsson, who had written to the society by this time to share his findings – that the date 607 BC was of questionable significance and was probably historically inaccurate (Watters and Sullivan 1981, taped interview). But most of the Bible chronology accepted by the Witnesses hinges on this date, including the all-important 1914. Furthermore, the society was already committed to the notion that Armageddon was coming by 1975. Rather than accept any expressed reservations concerning the 607 BC date, the Governing Body chose to retrench; to challenge Watch Tower belief that Christ returned in 1914 to set up his kingdom in heaven was to challenge the entire framework of Witness doctrine. As *The Watchtower* repeatedly emphasizes, 'The ending of the Gentile Times in the latter half of 1914 still stands on a historical basis as one of the fundamental Kingdom truths to which we must hold today' (1 January 1983,

11). Raymond Franz and the other members of the Writing Committee kept their counsel.

When 1975 came and went without major incident, and pressure mounted on the Governing Body to provide a public and formal explanation, Raymond Franz and the other members of the committee came to the conclusion, privately, that *several* aspects of Witness doctrine needed review since they did not seem supportable from a scriptural standpoint. However, from the standpoint of the Watch Tower Society, this fact in itself was a form of *thoughtcrime*, 'the essential crime that contained all others in itself.' But they were not discovered, and the process of personal doctrinal re-examination continued for many months. Still, 'thoughtcrime was not a thing that could be concealed for ever. You might dodge successfully for a while, even for years, but sooner or later they were bound to get you' (*1984*, 20; cf OAOM, 152).

In 1980, Raymond Franz took a leave of absence from Bethel – certainly not a common course of action for a member of the Governing Body – ostensibly to rest and 'ease his internal strain.' *Time* magazine reported:

On May 21, Franz was summoned to Brooklyn for a fateful grilling by his Governing Body colleagues. Did he doubt that Jehovah had only one chosen organization? Did he question the official End-times chronology? Franz sought to avoid confrontation but could 'only bend so far.' It was not enough. Opponents were unable to get a two-thirds majority for his disfellowshipping on the spot, but he was forced to resign from Bethel. In all, about a dozen officials were purged, almost certainly the worst doctrinal crisis Watch Tower headquarters has ever faced. (Ostling 1982, 40)

Watters explained the sequence of events which led up to Franz's departure:

While one member of the Governing Body [i.e., Raymond Franz] was away on leave of absence, a special committee was established to extract confessions of all of his close friends and acquaintances, in order to determine everything he had ever said in private that could be used against him. For two weeks these committees intimidated members of the Bethel family and recorded their confessions. Then the unfortunate fellow was suddenly called back to Bethel and made to listen to these tapes ... Then he was cast out and stripped of his privileges.

Several others were subjected to long hours of intense interrogation as the 'Watchtower committees' set up series of 'special questions' to ask any person suspected of talking about what was going on in the Governing Body. (1981, 4; cf *1984*, 245–6, 249)

Addressing the elders of the Bethel family on 29 May 1980 – a week after the interrogation of Franz – Lloyd Barry, now vice-president of the Watch Tower Bible and Tract Society, was very explicit about the application of 'Law' to the 'mother organization,' suggesting that the Governing Body is not merely an *advocate* of the Law but a *lawmaker* in its own right:

When we talk about law, we talk about organization. With all our hearts we need to search after that law. Jehovah doesn't give individuals interpretation. We need a guide, and that is the 'faithful and discreet slave.' We should not be getting together in a clique to discuss views contrary to the 'faithful and discreet slave.' We must recognize the source of our instruction. We must be like an ass, be humble, and stay in the manger; and we won't get any poison. (Watters 1981, 5; cf *1984*, 252)

At the same meeting, Albert Schroeder, another member of the Governing Body, said that 'some have fallen away from the Organization – not from the Bible – saying there is no need for coming under law.' He elaborated:

We serve not only Jehovah God but we are under our 'mother.' Our 'mother' has the right to make rules and regulations for us ... This book, entitled *Branch Office Procedure*, contains 28 subjects; and its sub-sections involve regulations and administration. In it there are 1,177 policies and regulations ... This is an improved, fine-tuned organization; and we are expected to follow its policies. If there are some who feel that they cannot subject themselves to the rules and regulations now in operation, such ones ought to be leaving and not be involved here in the further progressive work. (Watters 1981, 4)

Raymond Franz alluded to the tactics used to force his resignation in a letter dated 23 December 1981 to the Gadsden congregation:

Finally, I now know that effort is being made, by phone, even by long distance, to try to find something to use against me in an effort to incriminate me ... Even though the person contacted has never made any complaint about me, the request is made to see if they can remember anything I said that might be viewed as improper.

... For the past eight weeks my wife and I have been subjected to much mental anguish ... Now there is added to all this the knowledge that a surreptitious inquiry is being carried on that is clearly adverse to my rightful interests. I experienced similar treatment last year in New York, where similar efforts were made for one month – and not one word was said to me during that time to indicate to me that my conduct was in any way under accusation ... (Franz 1983, 325–6)

Several Watch Tower officials were treated with even less dignity than Franz in the initial purge, according to Watters and Sullivan. Two husband-and-wife teams were disfellowshipped (Rene and Elsie Vasquez and Cristobal and Norma Sanchez), and Nestor Kuilan was denied an appeal after being disfellowshipped 'for covering an apostasy' (Watters and Sullivan 1981, taped interview) as was seventy-year-old Ed Dunlap. Watters wrote:

In the following weeks and months I noticed that the members of the Governing Body minced no words in slandering and name-calling such individuals, and being careful not to mention their names for legal reasons. They were called 'spiritual fornicators,' 'mentally diseased' and 'insane'; they were said to be following the 'teaching of demons' and that they were 'adding to the scriptures.' One poor fellow had his phone calls redirected through the 'service department' to check up on outside connections. 'Spies' were everywhere, and many members of the family would turn in even their own friends for suspicion of 'apostacy.' (1981, 4; cf Franz 1983, 247–88)

Raymond Franz was forced to resign from the Governing Body subsequent to the 21 May 1980 hearing. Later, he was to write in a letter to the Gadsden congregation, 'I have no desire to undergo similar mistreatment again, particularly since there is nothing to indicate that the truth of the matter can be made known in such a way as to remove the unwarranted stain produced' (23 December 1981). Although the society gave Franz a lump sum of $10,000 to help him relocate, Franz found himself out on the street at fifty-eight years of age with a potential heart problem, no job, and no accommodation. He and his wife were invited by a long-time acquaintance, Peter Gregerson, to move to East Gadsden, Alabama, where they purchased a mobile home and parked it on Gregerson's property. Since their friend was chairman of the board of a grocery chain (Warehouse Groceries), he was in a position to offer Franz employment. As it turned out, Gadsden was an unfortunate choice of locale; the congregations there had been in turmoil prior to 1980 – as Franz well knew: 'I was serving on the Service Committee of the Governing Body at the time that Gadsden experienced a very disturbing period for many families, one involving a large number of the young people in the area. By way of the Service Department I was made aware of serious mishandling of matters by the local committee, requiring the sending in of a special committee to straighten things out' (Letter, 20 December 1981, 2 [Franz 1983, 372]).

The person who had initiated the request for a review of the errant committee and who had 'thus contributed substantially to the bringing in of the outside committee assigned by the society' was none other than Peter Gregerson. Understandably some elements within the Gadsden congregation were displeased with Gregerson – especially those elders who had been embarrassed by the reprimand 'from the top.' These elders complained bitterly that Gregerson had 'caused many brothers throughout Gadsden and our circuit to be disturbed.' Gregerson, who had hired some thirty-five Jehovah's Witnesses for his grocery chain, was asked to submit a 'letter of disassociation' that was to have far-reaching implications. He knew that if he failed to write such a letter, the elders would probe deeply into his personal affairs and conversations in order to 'dig up' any offence that could be considered 'disfellowshippable' – they would likely do the same thing that the Governing Body had done to Raymond Franz, searching for evidence of thoughtcrime.

In his letter, Gregerson admitted that he had been 'experiencing serious doubts regarding certain teachings of the Watchtower Society,' but he added that he had kept such doubts to himself: 'I have not even discussed them with the Body of Elders for fear of accidentally causing conversation within the congregation.' But thoughtcrime is thoughtcrime, and 'the Party is not interested in the overt act: the thought is all we care about' (*1984*, 256). For the society, too, it is the thought that counts. 'I have had "confidential talks" with very few people, almost all in my own family,' Gregerson protested. Ironically, one of the major attacks against Franz was to come from within Peter Gregerson's family (Franz 1983, 309–27, 360–75).

In his letter of disassociation, Gregerson stressed that his views 'have not changed regarding Jehovah God, Jesus Christ and the plain teachings of the Bible such as resurrection. As Jehovah God is my judge, I am conscious of no conduct unbecoming a Christian. For almost 50 years, since the winter of 1931–1932, when my dad started taking me to meetings, I have been a regular and hard working Jehovah's Witness. My good name and reputation is of great value to me, both among you and in the community at large.' Clearly, Gregerson could not have predicted the long-term effects of his disassociation; but he understood that further monitoring of his private conversations would not only be annoying, it would lead to automatic stigmatization by the local congregation, whether or not he was found guilty of any offence such as apostasy:

So that my 'good name' can be preserved, and so that there will be no further trouble and disturbance within and among you, I hereby resign from association with the organization.

This does not change my respect for the good done by the Watchtower Society. It does not change my friendship and love for you as individuals. Of course, I will accept whatever attitude you choose to show me. (Franz 1983, 366–7)

On the basis of this letter, Gregerson was declared 'disassociated' in March 1981. (This correspondence is reproduced in Franz 1983, 314–75.)

That summer, Gregerson's youngest brother, an elder in the Gadsden congregation, happened to see Raymond Franz, Peter Gregerson, and their wives eating together in a Gadsden restaurant. Ordinarily, nothing more would have been said, but the Governing Body had been watching Franz from a distance, and the local body of elders kept in touch with Brooklyn. It became plain that Franz and Gregerson had become fast friends. In the 15 September 1981 *Watchtower*, the society made plain a tightening of the rules with respect to treatment of disassociated individuals: 'Persons who make themselves "not of our sort" by deliberately rejecting the faiths and beliefs of Jehovah's Witnesses should appropriately be viewed and treated as those who are disfellowshipped for wrongdoing' (23). The *Watchtower* article 'Disfellowshipping – How to View It' reiterated Paul's words, 'Quit mixing in company ... *not even eating with such a man*': 'A meal is a time of relaxation and socializing. Hence the Bible here rules out social fellowship, too, such as joining an expelled person in a picnic or party, ball game, trip to the beach or theater, or sitting down to a meal with him' (24). A footnote immediately following this admonition specified that 'much clearer separation should exist in the cases of disfellowshipped or disassociated wrongdoers.' Specifically mentioning problems 'that arise in connection with business or employment,' the article continued:

What if you were employed by a man who was now expelled by the congregation, or you employed a person to whom that happened? What then? If you were contractually or financially obligated to continue the business relationship for the present, you certainly would now have a different attitude toward the disfellowshiped individual. Discussion of business matters with him or contact on the job might be necessary, but spiritual discussions and social fellowship would be things of the past. (24)

The magazine article might have been written specifically for Franz.

The 15 September 1981 shift from convention to 'Law' was just the impetus needed for the Gadsden congregation to accomplish what the Governing Body in Brooklyn had failed to achieve. The article was discussed formally at the *Watchtower* Study on 25 October 1981, and it became clear to the elders of East Gadsden that action could be taken against Franz in accordance with the 'New Light' that had just been revealed to them. The elders had the blessing of a circuit overseer, Wesley Benner, who had been assigned to question Franz. Following normal Witness procedure, on 5 November 1981 Benner accompanied Dan Gregerson on a visit to Raymond Franz, during which Dan Gregerson laid a formal complaint. Franz wrote: 'Dan presented himself as the accuser in the matter, stating at the beginning of the coversation that he had seen me eat with Peter Gregerson (the occasion being some months ago, previous to the publication of the September 15, 1981 *Watchtower*)' (Letter, 12 November 1981, 1). In response to the accusation, Franz told the men that the attitude of the society towards socializing with the disassociated was a new policy, and should not be applied retroactively 'unless one believes in ex post facto laws' (Letter, 8 December 1981, 2). He also informed his visitors of his intention to write to the Governing Body to seek clarification of the matter, and that day (5 November) he sent a letter to the Governing Body that was never answered. On 6 November 1981, the Body of Elders of East Gadsden congregation sent Franz the first of two formal letters. To his horror, Franz noted that he was scheduled to be judged by his own accuser, Dan Gregerson. Under these circumstances, he questioned the possibility of his obtaining a fair trial and asked for an expanded judicial committee. In their response of 19 November the elders wrote that they had replaced Dan Gregerson with Larry Johnson and further indicated that they were acting without consulting with the Governing Body, although the chairman of the judicial committee, Theotis French, later admitted to calling Brooklyn more than once.

The disfellowshipping hearing on 25 November 1981 – less than three weeks after the initial accusation was levelled – heard Dan Gregerson's testimony and that of another witness who claimed to have seen Franz and Peter Gregerson entering a restaurant separately on a day not long after the 15 September article became law. Two weeks later, Franz wrote a long, well-reasoned, and eloquent letter of appeal to the elders, with copies to the Governing Body, who still did not intervene. He also warned the society of a possible snowballing effect if the tendency towards local dogmatic stances were not reversed (Franz 1983, 371).

The appeal committee, named by Wesley Benner, was composed of Willie Anderson, who had been a central figure in the initial Gadsden scandal that had caused the Service Committee of the Governing Body to intervene in the first place; Earl Parnell, who like Anderson had had strained relations with Gregerson – but in his case because Peter Gregerson's daughter had divorced Parnell's son; and Ron Dibble, Parnell's son-in-law. 'With perhaps one exception,' wrote Franz, 'I cannot conceive of a committee of three individuals that would have less to recommend itself for an objective, unbiased hearing of my appeal than the one that has been selected' (Letter, 20 December 1982, 3). Subsequently, Franz sent another letter to the Brooklyn headquarters – to no avail. The appeal committee postponed their 21 December meeting to Christmas Eve and then shifted it again to 28 December (Franz 1983, 324).

Franz formally withdrew his appeal in a letter dated 23 December 1981, noting that seven weeks had passed since he had asked the Governing Body for clarification, without an answer. 'That forty years of full-time service could be discounted on such a petty basis indicates to me that there is no concern to take into account my conscientious feelings ... nor concern to show me from Scripture wherein I have erred,' he wrote. The Governing Body did not intervene in the committee hearings. In fact, the Governing Body subsequently encouraged a crackdown on dissension and apostasy with a vengeance, especially within the Brooklyn headquarters itself (Franz 1983, 325–6).

According to Watters, Albert Schroeder 'decreed that no more than two persons at a time could in future meet for private study at Bethel.' Both Watters and Sullivan declared that most of the Bethelites were ruled by fear during the period of inquisition – a view supported by Raymond Franz, who in an interview with Bob MacEwan on CBC's public affairs program *Fifth Estate* (16 March 1982) said of the Brooklyn headquarters, 'In my mind, only one motive, only one emotion could create such an atmosphere, and that is fear.' He elaborated in a personal letter to us:

The 'fear' within the Bethel family was of a kind probably not felt by those of the majority who had no questions, or if felt, felt subconsciously; it did undoubtedly affect those with questions or who had vague feelings that all was not well in the spiritual paradise. My reference to fear on the Fifth Estate program was the fear of the administration, I should say *within* the administration, not fear felt generally within the family. I believe that fear of truth motivated the authoritarian approach taken. (Letter, 15 December 1982)

CHAPTER NINE

Nineteen Eighty-Four

All members of the Inner Party believe in this coming conquest as an article of faith. (*1984*, 194)

According to the chronological calculations of Jehovah's Witnesses, the world as we know it should end by the autumn of 1984. Every recent publication of the Witnesses' official corporate mouthpiece, the Watch Tower Bible and Tract Society, has pointed to 1914 as marking the end of the 'Gentile Times' or the 'Appointed Times of the Nations' when Christ returned to heavenly power, casting Satan to the earth, where the Devil began misleading the entire inhabited earth' and causing global grief as described in Matthew 24. In 1958, the Witnesses' main doctrinal primer, *From Paradise Lost to Paradise Regained*, emphasized that 'Jehovah the great Timekeeper has scheduled Armageddon to come at the close of the "time of the end." That time is near':

We know Armageddon is near for another reason. Jesus said that the generation of people living when the 'time of the end' began would not pass away before Armageddon breaks out. When did Jesus say this? When he told us about the many parts of the sign of the 'time of the end.' That sign is made up of many different happenings. All these happenings must come upon one generation to make up the sign. Since 1914 they have come. What does this mean? Jesus answers: 'When you see all these things, know that he is near at the doors. Truly I say to you that this generation will by no means pass away until all these things occur' (Matthew 24:33, 34). (*PLPR*, 205)

Watch Tower publications have consistently stated that Armageddon will come within the life-span of those Witnesses who in 1914 were aware of the Watch Tower prophecy that the Gentile Times would end that year. The 8 October 1966 issue of *Awake!* suggested that the 'generation' of Matthew 24:34 was the adult generation alive in 1914: 'It is to be carefully noted that the youngest of those who saw *with understanding* the developing sign of the end of this system of things from its start in 1914 are now well over sixty years of age! In fact, the greater part of *the adult generation* that experienced the start of the "last days" has already passed away in death. The generation to which they belonged is now well along toward its complete passing away' (18; italics added). Two years later, the Watch Tower Society released a special issue of *Awake!* with striking headlines: 'IS IT LATER THAN YOU THINK? IS TIME RUNNING OUT FOR THIS GENERATION? WHAT WILL THE 1970'S BRING?' (8 October 1968, cover). Regarding the meaning of 'generation' at Matthew 24:34, the Watch Tower writers announced, 'Jesus was obviously speaking about those who were old enough to witness *with understanding* what took place when the "last days" began' (13; italics in original); in other words, the scripture referred to the generation of active publishers or preachers who knew what they were doing and why. The article elaborated: 'Even if we presume that youngsters 15 years of age would be perceptive enough to realize the import of what happened in 1914, it would still make the youngest of "this generation" nearly 70 years old today' (8 October 1968, 13–14). This argument was reiterated in *The Watchtower* of 15 February 1969:

However, there are people still living who were alive in 1914 and saw what was happening then and were old enough that they still remember those events. This generation is getting up in years now. A great many of them have already passed away in death. Yet Jesus very pointedly said: 'This generation will *by no means* pass away until all these things occur.' Some of them will still be alive to see the end of the wicked system. (101; italics in original)

The same belief was reinforced in *Man's Salvation out of World Distress at Hand* (1975) with touching personal poignancy: 'We older folks of "this generation" in our seventies or in our eighties have seen the present "world" change for the worse, steadily deteriorating since that epoch-making year of 1914 C.E.' (283). There is a sense of nostalgia here but also a sense of 'faith beyond all understanding.' (It must be remembered that the Watch Tower Society's current president, F.W. Franz, is already well into his nineties.) The statement mirrors one of Orwell's: 'The world of to-day is a bare, hungry, dilapidated place compared with the world that existed before 1914, and still more so if compared with the imaginary future to which the people of that period looked forward' (*1984*, 189).

The Witnesses have consistently linked 'generation' with 'life expectancy' (*ABU*, 1066) and believe that the length of the 'generation' alluded to by Jesus at Matthew 24 was literally the life-span of seventy years indicated at Psalm 90:10 (*ABU*, 642). But as *Awake!* has stressed, this is an *absolute* deadline: 'Even if we were to use seventy or eighty years as the length of a generation, this would not enable us to determine the time for Armageddon's commencement. Why? Because this war of God is not scheduled to occur exactly at the end of this generation. It comes *within* the generation' (22 September 1962, 28; italics in original).

Without making reference to the actual year 1984, the Witness publications have for decades been counting down the years from 1914 to the present. For example, the 8 October 1968 issue of *Awake!* stated, 'The fact that *fifty-four years* of the period called the "last days" have already gone by is highly significant' (13; italics in original). *The Watchtower* of 1 January, 1983 (released in December 1982) was more emphatic:

Since most of mankind today pays no attention to that calculation of God's time, and since Christendom with its hundreds of sects and denominations dispute its correctness, have those opposers who far outnumber Jehovah's Witnesses won the hot dispute concerning the setting up of God's Kingdom by Christ in the heavens in 1914 C.E.? The fulfillment of Jesus' prophecy concerning what would mark 'the end of the world' (*AV*), or 'the conclusion of the system of things' (*NW*), thunders back to us the answer No! *Sixty-eight years* after 1914 we see in existence the state of affairs foretold by Jesus. (11; italics in original)

More recently, the 15 May 1983 *Watchtower* declared that Jesus Christ 'has been present in his God-given Kingdom since the end of "the times of the Gentiles" in the year 1914, *69 years ago*' (21). The year 1984 marks the *seventieth* year since 1914, and it is a widespread belief among the Witnesses that Armageddon must come some time before the autumn of 1984. Hence the literature is becoming increasingly suggestive (see figure 42) and increasingly entrenched: 'It will come exactly on time, according to God's schedule. It will not be late. (Hab. 2:3) Remember, the destruction of Jerusalem in 70 C.E. came quickly, when the Jews did not expect it' (*UWTG*, 183). The implied

Figure 42 *WT* 15 July 1983, cover

parallel between the destruction of Jerusalem seventy years after Christ's *first* coming, and the destruction of the world seventy years after his *second* coming is obvious to any thinking Witness.

What happened in early autumn of 1914 to make the Witnesses believe that their calculations regarding the Gentile Times were correct? *The Watchtower* of 15 May 1983 elucidated:

It was Friday, the second day of the month of October of the year 1914. Into the dining room of the headquarters staff of the Watch Tower Bible and Tract Society at 124 Columbia Heights, Brooklyn, New York, U.S.A., stepped the president of the Society. It was just about seven o'clock in the morning. Before going to his place at the head of the dining-room table, he paused. To get the undivided attention of the Bethel family members seated at the dining tables, he clapped his hands. Then, with a positive voice, he made reference to the opening words of verse 3 of the song entitled 'Our King Is Marching On!' as found on pages 162, 163 of the songbook *Hymns of Millennial Dawn*, saying, 'The Gentile Times have ended, for their kings have had their day.' First then he took his regular seat, to preside over the daily religious program of the Bethel family breakfast. (16)

That, then, was *that* – the official announcement that God's kingdom had been established in heaven. As A.H. Macmillan, one of the 'principal servants at Bethel headquarters' at the time, remarked, the moment was decidedly anti-climactic:

'We were highly excited and I would not have been surprised if at that moment we had just started up, that becoming the signal to begin ascending heavenward – but of course there was nothing like that, really.' Sister Merrill adds: 'After a brief pause he [Russell] said: "Anyone disappointed? I'm not. Everything is moving right on schedule!"' (*Yearbook* 1975, 73).

Across the Atlantic, the same date that for the Witnesses came to mark the beginning of Christ's kingdom – 2 October* 1914 – also marked the begin-

---

* October 2 has also been posited by the Witnesses as the anniversary date of Christ's birth (in the month of Ethanium a literal 33½ years before his death on 14 Nisan AD 33 – hence, in 2 BC) and of Adam's creation 'in the early autumn.' This association of dates would appear to be another example of the mystification and legitimization process described in chapter 3 above.

ning of the career of one of the most controversial writers and 'prophets' of the twentieth century – George Orwell, at that time known as Eric Blair: 'On 2 October 1914 Eric Blair made his first appearance in print when a local newspaper, the *Henley and South Oxfordshire Standard*, published his short patriotic poem, "Awake! Young Men of England"' (*CEJL* 1:595). The date – and Orwell's first published word with its familiar punctuation – are, of course, matters of coincidence, but uncannily so. And so is the title of his final novel – *Nineteen Eighty-Four.* The world outside the domain of the Watch Tower Bible and Tract Society has ascribed to '1984' a peculiar significance deriving almost exclusively from Orwell's prophetic political treatise *cum* novel. As William Steinhoff has written, 'Whether or not *1984* is an ideological superweapon, one can say that it changed the world by representing the past and present so as to modify people's expectations of the future' (1975, 222). David Kubal was more explicit: 'That art creates culture is nowhere more evident than in the case of *Nineteen Eighty-Four.* The date itself has definite relevance in Western civilization and not merely to those who have read the novel. It has become a general metaphor suggesting a certain kind of political state while calling up an emotion of apprehension about the future' (1972, 132). What much of the world has come to think of as an Orwellian metaphor, the Jehovah's Witnesses have come to think of in quite literal terms as the postulated end of the corrupt world.

Orwell was familiar with Jehovah's Witnesses, and defended their right to freedom of speech, although he does not seem to have been overly enamoured with what they had to say. In an article entitled 'Freedom of the Park' in the *Tribune* of 7 December 1945, Orwell objected to the arrest of pamphleteers outside Hyde Park:

A few weeks ago, five people who were selling papers outside Hyde Park were arrested by the police for obstruction. When taken before the magistrates they were all found guilty, four of them being bound over for six months and the other sentenced to forty shillings' fine or a month's imprisonment. He preferred to serve his term, so I suppose he is still in jail at this moment.

... The main point of this episode is that the sellers of newspapers and pamphlets should be interfered with at all. Which particular minority is singled out – whether Pacifists, Communists, Anarchists, Jehovah's Witnesses or the Legion of Christian Reformers who recently declared Hitler to be Jesus Christ – is a secondary matter. It is of symptomatic importance that these people should have been arrested at that particular spot. (*CEJL* 4:57–9)

With his interest in civil rights, as well as his prominent position as an editor of the *Tribune*, Orwell would have been very much aware of the existence of Jehovah's Witnesses and possibly of their beliefs, if not their organizational structure. Certainly what the Witnesses said about 1914 being a turning point in history paralleled his own view that man somehow lost his innocence with the advent of the First World War: 'Among people now alive there are two very sharp dividing lines. One is between those who can and those who can't remember the period before 1914; the other is between those who were adult before 1933 and those who were not' (*CEJL* 4:72). The significance of 1914 to world history is explored in his novel *Coming Up for Air* (1939). Orwell alludes again and again to such concepts as 'the Kingdom of Heaven on Earth,' 'the much-derided "Kingdom of Earth",' and the idea that 'the Kingdom of Heaven has somehow got to be brought on to the surface of the earth' (*CEJL* 2:32–3; 4:193). He also had a curious interest in Bible chronology, and briefly reviewed *Chronological Tablets, Exhibiting Every Remarkable Occurrence from the Creation of the World down to the Present Time* (1801):

With some interest I looked up the date of the creation of the world, and found it was in 4004 B.C. and 'is supposed to have taken place in the autumn'. Later in the book it is given more exactly as September 4004.

At the end there are a number of blank sheets in which the reader can carry on the chronicles for himself. Whoever possessed this book did not carry it very far, but one of the last entries is: 'Tuesday 4 May. Peace proclaimed here. General Illumination.' That was the Peace of Amiens. This might warn us not to be too previous with our own illuminations when the armistice comes. (*Tribune* 31 December 1943)

William Steinhoff has presented a convincing argument to show that Orwell modelled the Party in *Nineteen Eighty-Four* on the early Roman Catholic Church (1975, 184–5). The structure of the Watch Tower Bible and Tract Society is also modelled after the early 'congregation'; indeed, Clifford Forward, formerly a Jehovah's Witness missionary in Laos and a graduate of the Watch Tower Bible School of Gilead, has been quoted as saying, 'The Watch Tower Society is a clone of the Catholic Church in medieval times' (*Seattle Post-Intelligencer* 28 May 1983). Although each 'church' would deny any connection with the other, they do have at least one assumption in common: both claim to be theocracies.

In 'The Prevention of Literature' (1946), Orwell wrote that 'a totalitarian state is in effect a theocracy, and its ruling caste, in order to keep its position, has to be thought of as infallible' (*CEJL* 4:86). This sentiment is echoed in the novel by O'Brien, the 'Grand Inquisitor' of Ingsoc who is also Winston's Saviour: '"You are in my keeping ... I shall save you. I shall make you perfect"' (*1984*, 247).

Nineteen Eighty-Four presents the projected extension of totalitarian oligarchical collectivism into the futuristic 'dark ages' that Orwell saw must follow if totalitarianism was allowed to take its course. O'Brien calls Winston Smith 'the last man' (273), and Orwell contemplated calling the novel 'The Last Man in Europe' (*CEJL* 4:507) – Smith is the last enduring specimen of Renaissance Man, the final living example of the Renaissance Heresy.

And what is the Renaissance Heresy? Simply the rise of humanistic and rationalistic thought or 'independent thinking' that, over the past four centuries, has attempted to elevate man above God. The Witnesses extend the same heresy back to Adam (*YCLF*, 101). The Ingsoc Party and the Watch Tower Society both seek to reassert theocracy by reversing the heresy of the assumed supremacy of man. Goldstein himself is merely a chimera, an invention of the Party designed to trap the would-be heretic or *thoughtcriminal*, and '*the book*' that Goldstein is supposed to have written is the bait:

'... You have read *the book*, Goldstein's book, or parts of it, at least. Did it tell you anything that you did not know already?'

'You have read it?' said Winston.

'I wrote it. That is to say, I collaborated in writing it. No book is produced individually, as you know.' (*1984*, 210)

Once Winston has been exposed as a heretic, O'Brien's task is to reprogram him; one of the aims of the Party is 'to extinguish once and for all the possibility of independent thought' (194). O'Brien admits that the description of the Party given in *the book* is true, from an objective standpoint; but 'reality is not external':

'... Reality exists in the human mind, and nowhere else. Not in the individual mind, which can make mistakes, and in any case soon perishes: only in the mind of the Party, which is collective and immortal. Whatever the Party holds to be truth, *is* truth. It is impossible to see reality except by looking through the eyes of the Party. That is the fact that you have got to relearn, Winston. It needs an act of self-destruction, an effort of the will. You must humble yourself before you can become sane.' (252)

According to O'Brien,

'... The first thing you must realize is that power is collective. The individual only has power in so far as he ceases to be an individual ... Alone – free – the human being is always defeated ... The second thing for you to realize is that power is power over human beings. Over the body – but, above all, over the mind. Power over matter – external reality, as you would call it – is not important. Already our control over matter is absolute.' (267)

When Winston protests the apparent ridiculousness of this statement, O'Brien explains: '"We control matter because we control the mind. Reality is inside the skull ... You must get rid of those nineteenth-century ideas about the laws of Nature. We make the laws of Nature"' (268). Since the Party determines what is truth, and since 'nothing exists except through (collective) human consciousness,' the Party can determine that evolution did not happen (for example) and that the universe is geocentric (268–9).

The reprogramming of Winston Smith starts with his acceptance of the premise that 'God is power' a premise similar to that posited by Jehovah's Witnesses in *You Can Live Forever in Paradise on Earth* (1982): 'We can believe because a Supreme Power, Almighty God, prepared the earth with everything needed to satisfy what we want' (7). O'Brien describes for Winston the visionary millennium in which, under Ingsoc, '"... There will be no loyalty, except loyalty toward the Party. There will be no love, except the love of Big Brother"' (270); later, he adds '"... You must love Big Brother. It is not enough to obey him: you must love him"' (285). As the symbol of Power, Big Brother represents God, and only with the acceptance of God will Winston be able to achieve a spiritual paradise 'with everything forgiven, his soul white as snow.' He experiences 'the feeling of walking in sunlight' as he strides down the white-tiled corridor of the Ministry of Love. But it is only later in the Chestnut Tree Café with its paradoxical background Musak singing '"Under the spreading chestnut tree/ I sold you and you sold me"' that Winston achieves his final affirmation. Years before, in this same café, he had seen the three 'untouchable' dissidents, Jones, Aaronson, and Rutherford (coincidentally, the names of three prominent Witnesses during the Second World War). being shunned: 'There was no one at any of the tables nearest to them. It was not wise even to be seen in the neighbourhood of such people. They were sitting in silence before glasses of the gin flavoured with cloves which was the speciality of the café. Of the three, it was Rutherford whose appearance had most impressed Winston' (64). On that occasion, too, the same song was sung from the telescreen and 'when Winston glanced again at Rutherford's ruinous face, he saw that his eyes were full of tears' (76). Winston, too, sheds a tear when he hears the song (296); but when he hears the trumpet-call of 'Victory – greatest victory in human history – victory, victory, victory!' his conversion is complete: 'He had won the victory over himself. He loved Big Brother' (300). As O'Brien had said,

'... We are not content with negative obedience, nor even with the most abject submission. When finally you surrender to us, it must be of your own free will. We do not destroy the heretic because he resists us: so long as he resists us we never destroy him. We convert him, we capture his inner mind, we reshape him. We burn all evil and all illusion out of him; we bring him over to our side, not in appearance, but genuinely, heart and soul.' (258)

Jehovah's Witnesses use 'free will' and 'freedom' in a similar way. In the preaching handbook *Make Sure of All Things* (1953), the notion of relative freedom was introduced as a cardinal principle: 'The subject of freedom involves the faculty of "free will", which God as Creator Superior has given to angels and men so that they can conduct themselves voluntarily in a way pleasing to their Maker. It is this field of "free will" action wherein governments, both theocratic and man-made, grant controlled liberties and freedoms' (122). The Witnesses' *Aid to Bible Understanding* (1971) emphasized that only Jehovah God has absolute, unlimited freedom; that of the individual is 'relative freedom':

There is a distinction between limited freedom and bondage. Freedom within God-given limitations brings happiness; bondage to creatures or to imperfection, weaknesses or wrong ideologies brings oppression and unhappiness. Freedom is also to be differentiated from self-determination, that is, ignoring God's laws and determining what is right and what is wrong for oneself ... True freedom is freedom bounded by law, God's law (608).

Relative freedom is thus bound up with the notion of relative subjection, for 'As Supreme Authority, Jehovah God is the source of all delegated rightful authority' (*TMEL*, 198).

For Jehovah's Witnesses, as for Ingsoc, 'God is Power': 'Throughout the Scriptures God's power and "dynamic energy" as the Maker of heaven and earth are repeatedly highlighted. (Isa. 40:25, 26; Jer. 10:12; 32:17) The very term of "God" in Hebrew (*'El*) is believed to have the root meaning of "mighty" or "powerful." (Compare the use of the term at Genesis 31:29 in the expression the "power [*'el*] of my hand.")' (*ABU*, 1324). Jehovah is 'Almighty in power'; 'he is all-powerful, being the Almighty God ... His power and knowledge extend everywhere, reaching every part of the universe' (*ABU*, 665). He is 'the Source of all energy': 'All the things of the universe are bundles of particles of energy from him. These have been brought together into masses large and small. The twentieth-century scientist Albert Einstein worked out this formula for it: energy equals mass times the speed of light squared (or, $E = mc^2$). Little wonder, then, that this Source of all energy finds nothing impossible for him ...' (*ABU* 666). Despite his awesome power, Jehovah's ultimate purpose is essentially geocentric, the Witnesses believe: 'God has a purpose that he will work out and that cannot be thwarted. (Isa. 46:10; 55:8–11). His purpose, expressed at Ephesians 1:9, 10, is to establish 'an administration at the full limit of the appointed times' (*ABU*, 666; *MSWD* 330–1). God's primary purpose (according to the Witnesses) is the establishment of a class system not unlike that described in *Nineteen Eighty-Four*: a special 'priestly' or 'Kingdom' Class (O'Brien: 'We are the priests of power') of an elite 144,000 rulers (*TMEL*, 226); and the 'Great Crowd' or 'Other Sheep' Class who, although they were to do the bulk of the work, were 'not of the Kingdom fold' and thus would 'attain to eternal life on earth' (O'Brien: 'And remember that it is for ever') (*TMEL*, 238; *1984*, 267, 271). In both theocracies, 'If the Inner Party is described as the brain of the State, [the Outer Party] may justly be likened to the hands' (*1984*, 209).

Jehovah's Witnesses – like the Oceanians – are kept constantly in a psychological state of war (see figure 43). Hence, people who 'fall away from the Truth' are called 'battle casualties' or 'prisoners of war,' the world is called 'the enemy' against which the Witnesses must 'fight the good fight' and 'gird their armour on' (see, for example, *WT* 1 January 1983, 23). This state of preparedness is essential if oligarchical collectivism, *qua* theocracy, is to work, according to Goldstein's '*book.*' But 'the essence of oligarchical rule' that is enunciated there is 'the persistence of a certain way of life, imposed by the dead upon the

Figure 43 *Awake!* 8 June 1981, cover

living' (*1984*, 211). In the sense that about 135,000 members of the 'Spiritual Nation' are already dead, this can be said to be true of Jehovah's Witnesses as well.

The proles are equivalent to non-Witnesses, with whom Jehovah's Witnesses are discouraged from associating, but whom the Witnesses try to recruit into their ranks by their preaching activity. Jehovah's Witnesses are not in the least interested in changing the world or the people in it; but by contrast they are intensely interested in regulating 'all the beliefs, habits, tastes, emotions, mental attitudes' etc., of their members, among whom 'not even the smallest deviation of opinion on the most unimportant subject can be tolerated' (211) when it comes to matters of doctrine, as we have seen.

The fourteen members of the Governing Body of Jehovah's Witnesses were chosen from the 'Kingdom' Class to direct the work of the Witnesses on earth. Among the members of the Governing Body are the executive of the Watch Tower Bible and Tract Society, whose board of directors is also comprised of members of the Remnant. Despite the fact that the number of the nation's representatives on earth must ever decline as its aging members die, the nation is nevertheless regarded as expanding as the ranks of the 'great crowd of companion worshippers' increase. The size and scope of the 'nation' is measured by its capacity to achieve increased productivity in terms of publishing and preaching activity.

Members of the Great Crowd do not have access to the halls of government, now or ever. They were born at the wrong time in history to be allowed to partake of the blood and body of Christ, however symbolically; for only those who had knowledge of Jehovah's Witnesses prior to 1935 – when it became clear that the organization would swell to more than a literal 144,000 – are considered eligible for membership in the 'Anointed' class. Any member of the Great Crowd who suddenly declares himself a member of the Remnant is regarded with grave suspicion. Still, as in Ingsoc, despite the fact that 'there is far less to-and-fro movement between the different groups than formerly,' there is a certain amount of interchange between the two branches of the 'Party' (*1984*, 210; cf *UWTG*, 112).

It can be seen, then, that Jehovah's Witnesses have a carefully stratified society with a select class in control of the visible organization. Within this anointed group there is a secondary gubernatorial stratification. Most of the 9,300 Anointed left on earth, being very old, have no positions of responsibility. They are treated with great respect by the ordinary members of the Great Crowd, especially on Memorial Day (14 Nisan of the Jewish calendar), when the members of the Remnant partake of the bread and wine. But only a few of the members of the 'nation' serve in actual administrative positions of any significance in the organization on earth. They patiently await death – which for them will mean becoming kings with Christ in heaven as part of the Kingdom Government.

Just as Ingsoc is divided into the ministries of Peace, Truth, Love and Plenty and various departments (the Records Department, the Fiction Department), so the Watch Tower Society is divided into departments – the Writing Department, the Service Department, the Teaching Department, the Publishing Department, and the Personnel Department – each of which reports to Governing Body committees of the same names: the Writing Committee, the Service Committee, the Teaching Committee, the Publishing Committee, and the Personnel Committee (WT 1 January 1977, 16). Most of these departments conduct their work entirely within the walls of the Brooklyn headquarters; but the Teaching and Service committees constantly send directives out into the field – to the various congregations – through an elaborate administrative network starting at the Brooklyn headquarters and descending through various branch offices to districts, circuits, and eventually to congregations. Below the inner sanctum of Brooklyn, few of the appointed overseers or administrators are members of the Remnant.

These 'theocratic arrangements' established by and through the Watch Tower Bible and Tract Society come, the Witnesses believe, from Jehovah himself, 'the great Organizer of theocratic government.' They were first described in detail in *'This Means Everlasting Life'*, a Watch Tower publication that was released in 1950 – not long after *Nineteen Eighty-Four*:

The organization of the Christian congregation is Theocratic, because God is its organizer and is its top director at all times. It operates Theocratically, because it functions by taking orders from God down through his Son Jesus Christ, and not up from the organization members below ...

... When a justified believer is baptized into the 'body of Christ' and so becomes a member of the Theocratic organization, he comes under Christ Jesus the Head and so comes under certain responsibilities and cannot act independently to direct it. He must submit himself to organization instructions. (TMEL, 125–6)

If Jehovah God is the 'Great Theocrat' (TMEL, 126), Jesus Christ is the 'Theocratic liaison officer between all members and all local groups of the congregation all over the earth' (*TMEL*, 129). Through this liaison, official servants in the congregation are 'put in position under the guiding influence of God's spirit of holiness': 'So the appointments are not by a democratic or popular election, as when the people of Rome used to vote to elect a pope, nor by a political government of this world. But appointments are through the Theocratic organization from the Top down' (*TMEL*, 129). Those who are appointed in this manner have 'divine authority' like that of the apostles (*TMEL*, 198, 203). Beneath God and Christ, they are heads of the 'visible Theocratic organization,' and as such must be obeyed – in fact, feared:

We are to have a proper fear toward the Superior Authorities in the sense of not wanting to displease them. If we do good by carrying out the divine will we have no need to be afraid, because the Superior Authorities are against only the evildoers ... But if we do wrong by acting against the divine will, then we have reason to fear punishment, for the Superior Authorities have the power to execute judgment upon wrongdoers. This power of execution is symbolized by the sword ...

People of this world often conform outwardly to the laws of the land simply for the sake of escaping legal punishment. But a lover of righteousness does not subject himself to the Superior Authorities just to spare himself the divine wrath and execution of judgment. He does it because it is right and it gives him peace of heart. One's own conscience, says the apostle, should be a force stronger than fear to move Christians to do right. (*TMEL*, 199–200)

The structure of authority and the nature of one's subjection to those in the visible organization who have authority are almost identical in principle to the rules laid down by O'Brien in *Nineteen Eighty-Four* (267–70).

The dictatorial nature of Jehovah and therefore of His organization is not disputed by the Witnesses:

The Theocratic Creator has the right to do with his own creatures and organization what his perfect will dictates, and no creature has the right to complain and say: 'Why did you make me this way and put me here or there?' It is a great privilege and honor to serve the Most High God in any position high or low and under subjection to any other or all other servants appointed by God ... All through the Theocratic organization, from Jesus on down, the principle of subjection is in evidence. (*TMEL*, 156–7)

Goldstein's *The Theory and Practice of Oligarchical Collectivism* describes the structure of Oceanic society as having at the apex of power the elusive and perhaps illusionary Big Brother. Like Jehovah, 'Big Brother is infallible and all-powerful':

Every success, every achievement, every victory, every scientific discovery, all knowledge, all wisdom, all happiness, all virtue, are held to issue directly from his leadership and inspiration. Nobody has ever seen Big Brother ... We may be reasonably sure that he will never die, and there is already considerable uncertainty as to when he was born. Big Brother is the guise in which the Party chooses to exhibit itself to the world. His function is to act as a focusing point for love, fear, and reverence, emotions which are more easily felt towards an individual than towards an organization. (*1984*, 209)

Goldstein's 'heresy' here is that of looking at theocracy objectively and analytically, of focusing on the 'how' rather than on the 'why.' As Winston writes in his pathetic diary: '*I understand* HOW: *I do not understand* WHY' (67). The HOW is explicable in terms of the empirical method of thought that is inimical to Ingsoc. The WHY can be explained only in terms of faith, which is inimical to logic. Somewhere in between these two realities lies common sense – for Orwell (and for Winston Smith) a cardinal principle of survival.

Each Jehovah's Witness, as an individual, chose at some point in his life to come out of 'this world,' opting instead for the world view offered by the Watch Tower Bible and Tract Society in which the ultimate concern is identified as Jehovah. But in the view of the dissidents, the original theocracy whose divine king was Jehovah became over the years a closed system in which the organization itself became the ultimate concern of many, if not most, Jehovah's Witnesses. Individual Witnesses came to be not so much concerned with divine retribution as with the threat of social ostracism enforced often arbitrarily by the organization through its congregations. For them, the liberator had become the oppressor, and they found it necessary to search once again for yet another new and liberating 'truth.' Some find such a truth in the world of business and commerce; others find it in colleges and universities; still others find it by abandoning the proscriptions of Jehovah for the prescriptions of Jesus Christ. Whatever 'truth' the disaffected Witness searches for, he can at least be assured that he is not alone in his quest. Now, more than ever before, groups of dissidents try to provide a comforting buffer for the outcast Witness, and have formed a complex network – a safety net, if you will – to protect those who slip off the tightrope.

None the less, ultimately the struggle to re-evaluate one's life and reassert oneself in the world is an individual one. Nor is it peculiar to Jehovah's Witnesses or members of other sects who find that they must abandon – or be abandoned by – the organization that has provided for their spiritual needs. The intertwined social and symbolic dynamic of the process of opting for or opting out of a system of belief, of a society, of a way of life, obviously has broad application in a contemporary world in which there has evolved a proliferation of closed systems and closed societies within which individuals respond, either voluntarily or by coercion, to voices of power and authority in the expectation of achieving a significant destiny consonant with the promises and expectations of one's ultimate concern. But when that ultimate concern changes so that it is no longer in harmony with the stated values and goals of the system or society, one reaches a state of crisis. If enough people within the society come to doubt the value or veracity of the collective vision, the constituent membership can either change the vision, or opt for a different system or society. To change the vision implies the existence of a system of democracy – or revolution. Either way, it assumes the predominant position of the constituent membership in matters of 'the collective concern.'

But when power has been granted to a specialized priesthood or 'Faithful and Discreet Slave' class – a collective oligarchy set apart from the membership by aloofness and visions of a different destiny – the membership at large is powerless to effect change. Accordingly, the spiritual aristocracy, manipulating its armies in the name of God, is in a position to make demands which, if not met, lead the unthinking faithful to castigate, punish, and eventually abandon those individuals who fail to conform to shifting doctrinal imperatives. The society is thus kept pure, but only in a superficial sense; since the demands of the aristocracy are constantly shifting, purity can never be more than a relative term. The membership is trained, but never educated. It is destined never to be capable of independent thought or even independent feeling. If, in a meeting of Jehovah's Witnesses, the congregation is asked, 'What are your feelings on this particular belief?' the answer will be read from a Watch Tower publication; the conforming multitudes are *told* what they shall think and feel. For many dissidents, the mass manipulation of brain and heart that the administration of the Watch Tower Society requires of Jehovah's Witnesses is the ultimate tragic apostasy.

Assuming that the world and Jehovah's Witnesses survive 1984 (Armageddon *could*, of course, come at almost any time), what will happen to the organization? We can only speculate and let history judge us right or wrong; but our guess is an educated one. The Witnesses have already been through a 'dry run,' so to speak, as recently as 1975. In that year, the society announced expansion plans for its factories as if it expected nothing to happen. In 1984, it will again undertake a major expansion – this time in terms of technological development. Its immense printing plant in Brooklyn is already using helium-neon and argon-ion laser-beam reprographic equipment in its printing process – the most up-to-date 'state-of-the-art' technology. The computer facilities are likely to expand, as are facilities for word processing; efficient use of time and space in the printing and distribution of more than a billion pieces of literature per year remains the society's greatest challenge. The Watch Tower Society recently acquired another block of factories and homes in Brooklyn Heights in New York; it now virtually owns the district. Its factory has nineteen converted M.A.N. presses and eight high-speed offset presses, with another five offset presses constantly in use at Watchtower Farms in upstate New York. By 1984, the society had acquired forty multi-language electronic photo-typesetting systems capable of handling up to 240 languages. Branch offices have also been expanding their printing facilities, and new branch offices opened recently in more than thirty countries, including Australia, Britain, Canada, India, New Zealand, and South Africa. Although the society produced some four million cassette tapes in 1983 alone, the Witnesses are not likely to expand into television or other electronic and audio-visual mass media, since they remain more committed to the notion of the printed word personally distributed by an actively involved membership: 'Even as early Christians used the then new codex system of bookmaking for spreading the good news, so modern-day Christians are using the marvel of electronic printing tools' (*Awake!* 22 June 1983, 20). The 1983 *Yearbook* adds that the presses and computers are a gift of God: 'To assist his dedicated people to accomplish this two-fold publishing work, Jehovah has provided his forward-moving organization with many high-speed offset printing presses as well as modern bookbinding equipment. He has also equipped his people with the latest technology in the field of computer phototypesetting' (258).

Statistics for 1983 listed in the 1984 *Yearbook* and the 1 January 1984 *Watchtower* indicate that Jehovah's Witnesses have weathered the recent storm of dissent and crisis quite handily, achieving a 6.8 per cent increase in publishers world wide – an increase of 159,088 over 1982; 161,896 were baptized, indicating an attrition of only 2,808, almost all of which can be attributed to deaths. As 1984 approached, the Witnesses showed a more united front than ever before. The economic climate of the early eighties is a major positive factor in their growth; confronted by unemployment and potential economic ruin, many people opt for millenarian solutions, such as those the Witnesses provide, as part of a 'disaster syndrome' (Rhodes 1980, 30–49). As international tensions increase, individuals seek solace in the sects. As Michael Barkun remarked in *Disaster and the Millennium* (1974), 'Millenarian beliefs are a form of explanation: they tell us why we are in the dreadful circumstances of the present. They also respond to the failure of a disintegrating society: they tell us that problems that appeared insoluble will be dealt with totally, favourably, and summarily, "in the twinkling of an eye"' (56). Ultimately, 'There is one kind of prediction which remains quite congenial to the growth of millenarianism, and that is a generalized, nonspecific sense of dread' (59; see figure 44).

Like most such sects, Jehovah's Witnesses offer a final solution to the world's woes. Any who seek solace are particularly susceptible to the promises held out to them and often overlook the other side of the balance sheet – the side that includes the total abrogation of the right to think for oneself. For many, of course, this abrogation of responsibility to an external body that promises in return to take care of all one's spiritual needs is a great solace in itself.

As far as organizational growth is concerned, there is likely to be a fairly major increase in 1984 as inactive Witnesses hedge their bets and become active again; the number of publishers could possibly pass the 2,750,000 mark in 1984, but may then level out in subsequent years. If the current leadership stays in power and does not alter its doctrinal directives, the organization is likely to stall in growth. But the chances of the current geriatric leadership clinging to power for long is very remote indeed; many are in frail health, including F.W. Franz.

If a new, dynamic leader is appointed – one who has the courage or temerity to shelve or 'adjust' current assumptions about end-times chronology – then the organization could conceivably pass the four million mark by the end of the century. The expanded building program around the world is clear evidence that at least some elements within the Governing Body see the possibility of the 'last days' lasting a lot longer than the current official end-times doctrine would indicate. Nor do the bulk of the grass-roots membership regard 1984 as being particularly significant itself; for the most part they

Figure 44 *Awake!* 8 June 1980, cover

simply haven't thought about it – nor are they encouraged to do so. The 1984 deadline is one that the upper echelon of the current leadership – in particular President Franz – has held for many years; but, fearing repetition of the 1975 fiasco, the Governing Body has been reluctant to emphasize this belief in any overt way to a membership that is waiting to seize any hint as to when Armageddon may come and to blow it out of all proportion.

Increasingly, the Watch Tower Bible and Tract Society and the Organization of Jehovah's Witnesses it represents refer to themselves as a 'nation' and see themselves as leaping into the breach to govern the world (under the heavenly direction of Christ, of course) after Armageddon has flattened and subdued the nations of the world. At the 1983 Kingdom Unity district conventions, for example, mention was made of the 6.8 million people who attended Memorial celebrations in 1983. The speakers compared this 'population' of potential Witnesses with the populations of recognized sovereign countries, some two hundred of which have fewer than six million citizens. The Witnesses see themselves, not only as a theocracy, but as a global nation that some day will be a force to reckon with.

One thing is clear: the Organization of Jehovah's Witnesses will not lie down and die, no matter how much dissension might be generated from within, and no matter how much persecution is generated from without. As long as its members believe that Jehovah is with them, as long as they assume that anything the Governing Body does is in perfect accordance with His will, they will support the organization to the end of the century and beyond. Individuals may come and individuals may go, but the society will continue; like Orwell's Ingsoc Party, it is 'immortal.' It may be a classic example of Orwellian oligarchical collectivism, but as long as committed Jehovah's Witnesses are prepared to accept their organization as a theocracy, that is what it shall remain.

Glossary of Terms Used by Jehovah's Witnesses

Anointed, The   The 144,000 'chosen ones' of Revelation 14:1–3 who are 'redeemed from the Earth' to reign with Christ for the duration of the millennium. Among the 9,300 members of the Anointed remaining on earth are the leaders of Jehovah's Witnesses, including the fourteen-man Governing Body. Synonymous with 'Little Flock,' 'Bride of Christ,' 'Kingdom,' and 'Faithful and Discreet Slave' classes.

Apostasy   The sin of rejecting one or more of the published beliefs of the Watch Tower Bible and Tract Society for some alternative doctrine. Also, the sin of attending a rival church.

Armageddon   The imminent 'holy war' between Christ and his forces and Satan and his forces. During Armageddon (or Har-Magedon) the world as we know it will be destroyed.

Assembly   A gathering of Jehovah's Witnesses from several congregations or circuits. Circuit assemblies are held semi-annually and district assemblies annually.

Baptism   Water immersion symbolizing 'dedication' or commitment to the teachings of the Watch Tower Bible and Tract Society.

Bethel   The residence and factory of any major branch office of Jehovah's Witnesses. In Brooklyn, specifically the residences.

Bethel Family   Residents of Bethel, who live and work in the home and factories.

Bible Study, A   A person who has agreed to a prolonged examination of Watch Tower literature under the guidance of a Jehovah's Witness, usually conducted weekly, but at least monthly.

Body of Elders   The appointed leaders of a congregation.

Book Study   A weekly gathering of Jehovah's Witnesses to read and discuss Watch Tower publications a paragraph at a time.

Branch Committee   A group of three pre-eminent Jehovah's Witnesses who represent the interests of the Watch Tower Bible and Tract Society in a given country.

Branch Office   The national office or centre of the Watch Tower Bible and Tract Society. There are currently ninety-five such offices around the world.

Bride of Christ   See 'The Anointed' above.

Brooklyn   In Witness parlance, the headquarters of the Watch Tower Bible and Tract Society.

Brother   A male, baptized Jehovah's Witness; also the title used to address same (as 'Brother Smith').

Christendom   The collectivized 'Christian' churches other than Jehovah's Witnesses.

Christianity   Jehovah's Witnesses.

Christ's Return   The Second Coming of Jesus Christ as the enthroned king – which the Witnesses believe happened in 1914.

Circuit   A group of about twenty congregations geographically close to one another and led by a 'circuit overseer.' Several circuits comprise a 'district.'

Convention   A large assembly. 'Convention' usually refers to the process of conducting an assembly – hence a 'convention overseer' is the prime convener of an assembly. Most Witnesses use the terms interchangeably.

Dedication   The spiritual commitment to Jehovah and the Organization of Jehovah's Witnesses, which precedes public baptism.

Disassociation   The voluntary removal of oneself from membership in a congregation of Jehovah's Witnesses and more broadly from the Watch Tower Bible and Tract Society.

Disfellowshipping   The most serious punishment of Jehovah's Witnesses, characterized by social ostracism.

District   A geographical area incorporating several 'circuits.' A 'district overseer' reports to the 'branch committee' in a given country.

Elder   A person appointed to a position of leadership or responsibility in a congregation.

Emblems, The   The bread and wine circulated at the time of Memorial

(14 Nisan of the Jewish calendar) symbolizing the body and blood of Christ. Only members of the Remnant of the Anointed partake. All other Witnesses watch.

Evil Slave Class   Disfellowshipped or disassociated members of the Anointed Remnant who unrepentantly oppose the Watch Tower Bible and Tract Society.

Faithful and Discreet Slave Class   See 'The Anointed' above.

Falling away   The process of decreasing activity and interest in the preaching activity of Jehovah's Witnesses.

Field service   The house-to-house preaching activity of Jehovah's Witnesses, including back calls and home Bible studies. In the parlance of the Bethel staff, 'The Field' refers to the congregations.

Gentile Times   The period of time from 607 BC (the postulated date of the fall of Jerusalem) to Christ's return in 1914. The seven 'gentile times' totalled 2,520 years, according to Witness calculations.

Gilead   The missionary school of the Watch Tower Society.

Goat   One who is opposed to Jehovah's Witnesses.

God   The non-trinitarian Jehovah, creator of Christ and the rest of the universe and therefore omniscient, omnipresent, omnipotent – the Father of all things.

Governing Body   The fourteen-man ruling committee of the Watch Tower Bible and Tract Society. All claim to be members of the Anointed Remnant.

Great Crowd   The vast majority of Jehovah's Witnesses whose ultimate hope is for everlasting life on Paradise Earth. Also 'Other Sheep.'

Har-Magedon   See 'Armageddon' above. The Witnesses use 'Armageddon' in speech, but most Witness literature uses 'Har-Magedon.'

Hell   Hades or Sheol: The Grave. The Witnesses do not believe in hell fire.

Holy Spirit   God's 'active force'; the energy used by God to create the universe and to monitor and bless his creation.

Irregular Publisher   A Jehovah's Witness who preaches only spasmodically.

Jehovah   See 'God' above. The name is of obvious importance to 'Jehovah's Witnesses,' who claim to be God's chosen servants on earth.

Jehovah's Witnesses   Dedicated, baptized publishers of the presence of God's Kingdom, whose legal agency is the Watch Tower Bible and Tract Society. The name is used generically to refer to the children of baptized publishers, and to any who associate with the organization by attending meetings or assemblies regularly.

Jesus Christ   The first-born Son and Heir of God, formally an archangel, who came to earth for 33½ years before being resurrected to heaven to await his enthronement in 1914. He will shortly extend his kingdom to the earth after Armageddon.

Judgement Day   The thousand-year period of reconstruction of paradise on earth beginning at Armageddon and culminating in a final test of the perfected race of mankind after Christ hands the keys to the kingdom over to Jehovah. Also, the time of testing up to the culmination of Armageddon itself.

Judicial Committee   The tribunal of congregational elders appointed to conduct hearings into a complaint or accusation of wrongdoing on the part of a Jehovah's Witness.

'Kinds'   Divisions of animal life, especially mammals, but by extrapolation birds, insects, etc., approximating *genera*. The Witnesses believe that further speciation occurred through adaptation in the centuries following the global flood of Noah's day, but they do not accept the possibility of evolution.

Kingdom, The   The heavenly government of the enthroned Jesus Christ and the 144,000 Anointed, established in 1914 and to be extended to the earth after Armageddon. Often used colloquially to refer to paradise itself.

Kingdom Hall   The central meeting place of one or more congregations of Jehovah's Witnesses.

Last Days   The period of time between the return of Christ in 1914 and Armageddon.

Mark, to   To note and observe the behaviour of a 'disorderly' Witness.

Memorial   The celebration of Christ's death on 14 Nisan of the Jewish calendar, on which day each year all Jehovah's Witnesses gather to watch as the members of the Anointed Remnant partake of the emblems of bread and wine. In 1983, memorial attendance reached a peak of 6,767,707 in 46,235 congregations; only 9,292 partook.

Millennium   The thousand-year period of Christ's rule over the earth, beginning after Armageddon, during which time paradise will be restored, the dead will be resurrected, and humankind will attain perfection.

Minister   A baptized publisher of Jehovah's Witnesses.

Missionary A graduate of Gilead missionary school who is a full-time
  minister of Jehovah's Witnesses, usually serving in a foreign assignment.

Named, to be The process of publicly declaring that an unbaptized
  member of the congregation (usually a child) has sinned or erred in
  some way. Such 'named' ones are usually ostracized by their peers, on
  pain of parental punishment.

New Light; New Understanding Information released through the publications of the Watch Tower Bible and Tract Society that indicate a doctrinal shift or insight slightly different from previously published beliefs;
  also the doctrinal shift itself.

New Order; New System; New World The anticipated paradise to be
  established on earth after Armageddon and extending interminably at
  the end of the millennium; the process of governance postulated for the
  New World. The terms are used interchangeably.

New World Society Jehovah's Witnesses as an organization; more specifically, the Watch Tower Bible and Tract Society.

1914 The date of Christ's invisible return or Second Coming, when he
  cast Satan to the vicinity of the earth and set up his kingdom; the end
  of the Gentile Times.

Old World The current world we live in prior to Armageddon, the ruler
  of which is Satan the Devil.

144,000 See 'The Anointed' above. The number is regarded as a literal
  one by the Witnesses.

Organization, The A synonym for the Watch Tower Bible and Tract
  Society of Jehovah's Witnesses.

Other Sheep See 'Great Crowd' above.

Overseer One in a position of prime leadership in a congregation,
  circuit, district, or branch.

Paradise Eden, or Edenic conditions expected to blanket the earth by
  the end of the millennium and last thereafter 'to time indefinite.' After
  Armageddon, the paradise will be achieved by hard manual labour on
  the part of the surviving Jehovah's Witnesses.

Partake, to The process of sipping the wine and eating the unleavened
  bread at Memorial. Only members of the Anointed Remnant partake,
  or are considered 'partakers.'

Person of Good Will A member of the public who has shown an interest
  in Jehovah's Witnesses, usually by purchasing Witness literature.

Pioneer A full-time volunteer minister of Jehovah's Witnesses who must put in at least ninety hours of preaching per month.

Presumptuousness The sin of 'running ahead' of the organization by trying to anticipate the meaning of prophecy or Scripture before the society has made its opinions known.

Probation Punishment whereby a person who has erred is required to report his activities to an elder on a regular basis for a period of one or two years.

Progressive Light See 'New Light' above.

Public Talk A weekly meeting in which a mature, male Jehovah's Witness discusses a specific topic of belief, usually based on Witness literature in accordance with an outline circulated by the society. Also, the main Sunday address at an assembly.

Publisher A Jehovah's Witness who 'preaches the good news of the kingdom' on a voluntary basis, usually part time.

Regular Publisher A person who engages in preaching activity for at least an hour per month for a period of a year (from September to August).

Reinstatement The process of allowing a repentant disfellowshipped person back into the congregation 'in good standing.' A reinstated publisher is not usually allowed to serve as an elder or overseer.

Remnant The 9,500 members of the Anointed 'Bride' Class who are still alive on earth, some of whom currently lead the activities of Jehovah's Witnesses through the agency of the Governing Body of the Watch Tower Bible and Tract Society. Only the Remnant may partake of the emblems at Memorial. Upon death, members of the Remnant are resurrected instantly to rule with Christ in heaven.

Resurrection The process of being brought back to life either in the spirit (as in the case of the 144,000) or in the flesh (after Armageddon). The Witnesses believe that Jehovah remembers all personality traits and will imbue the resurrected with the personalities they had at the time of death.

Satan the Devil The adversary of God, once the archangel Lucifer, who rebelled against God. He was cast out of heaven in 1914 and since then has been 'misleading the entire inhabited earth.' He will be tortured during the millennium, released briefly at the end of it, and then destroyed forever.

Second Coming; Second Presence See 'Christ's Return' above. The Witnesses prefer to use the term 'second presence' (*parousia*).

Secretary   In a congregation, the liaison officer between the body of elders and the circuit overseer or branch.

Servant   A Witness in a minor position of responsibility in the congregation.

Service   See 'Field Service' above.

Service Meeting   A weekly meeting characterized by pep talks and demonstrations designed to assist Jehovah's Witnesses in their ministry and keep them abreast of developments in the congregation.

Sheep; Sheeplike Ones   Jehovah's Witnesses and their potential converts.

Sister   A female baptized Jehovah's Witness; the title used to address same (as 'Sister Jones').

Society, The   Abbreviation of the Watch Tower Bible and Tract Society.

Soul   The living body of animals and man. *Not* 'spirit.'

Special Pioneer   A full-time minister of Jehovah's Witnesses who must preach at least 140 hours per month for a small stipend.

Spirit   1 / Breath of life; 2 / an invisible being (angel, demon or 'active force').

Spiritual Food   The outpouring of information from the Watch Tower Bible and Tract Society through its literature.

Theocratic   Literally, 'ruled by God,' but used colloquially to mean 'good,' 'holy,' or 'faithful.'

Theocratic Ministry School   A weekly meeting designed to train publishers in preaching activity and public speaking.

Truth, The   The collection of beliefs of Jehovah's Witnesses, but more specifically the organization defined by those beliefs: Jehovah's Witnesses themselves. Hence, one is 'in the Truth,' or one 'came into the Truth,' or one 'found the Truth.'

Watch Tower Bible and Tract Society   The corporation that claims to be the official legal voice and spiritually directed agency of Jehovah's Witnesses on earth, based internationally in New York and Pennsylvania, but with ninety-five branch offices around the world.

Watchtower Study   The most important meeting of Jehovah's Witnesses, featuring the synchronized weekly formal question-and-answer coverage of *The Watchtower*'s feature articles, held in every congregation, usually on Sundays.

Witnessing; Witness Work   The process of distributing or studying Watch Tower literature with the public.

Worldly   Of the 'Old World.' Hence, a 'worldly boy' is a young, male non-Jehovah's Witness.

Zone Overseer   The representative of the Watch Tower Society responsible for supervising the activities of the branch offices in a given major geographic area.

Significant Dates

Creation of Adam	'in the fall' 4026 BC
Start of the Flood	2370
First 'Jubilee Year'	1424
Desolation of Judea (Watch Tower calculation)	607
Desolation of Judea (secular calculation)	587–6
Birth of Christ	c 2 October 2
Death of Christ	14 Nisan AD 33
Fall of Jerusalem	70
Birth of Charles Taze Russell	16 February 1852
66th 'Jubilee Year'	1877
Russell establishes his own group of Bible Students	1877
1914 first established as 'end of the Gentile Times'	1877
Zion's Watch Tower and Herald of Christ's Presence first published	July 1879
Watch Tower Tract Society established	1884
End of 'Times of the Gentiles'	1914
Heavenly 'Second Presence' of Christ begins	c 2 October 1914
Death of Charles Taze Russell	31 October 1916
1925 established as a 'significant date'	17 July 1917
Purge of Bethel headquarters	Late July 1917
Major rift causes 25 per cent decline	1918
Armageddon, expected by many, fails to materialize	1925
67th 'Jubilee Year'	1927

Establishment of 'Other Sheep' Class	1934–5
Death of J.F. 'Judge' Rutherford	8 January 1942
International assembly draws 165,829 people	26 July 1953
International assembly draws 253,922 people	3 August 1958
1975 first established as a significant date	25 June 1966
Armageddon, expected by many, fails to materialize	1975
68th 'Jubilee Year'	1977
Death of Nathan H. Knorr	7 June 1977
Some 30,000 disfellowshipped in major purge	1978
Major purge of Brooklyn headquarters	May 1980
End of seventy-year 'generation' from 1914	1984

Bibliography

GENERAL WORKS

Aberle, David F. 'The Influence of Linguistics on Early Culture and Personality Theory.' In *Theory in Anthropology*, ed Robert O. Manners and David Kaplan, 303–17. Chicago: Aldine Publishing 1968
Assagioli, Roberto. *The Act of Will.* Baltimore: Penguin Books 1973
Barkun, Michael. *Disaster and the Millennium.* New Haven: Yale University Press 1974
Becker, H.S. *Outsiders: Studies in the Sociology of Deviance.* New York: Free Press of Glencoe 1963
Beckford, J.A. 'Religious Organization.' *Current Sociology* 21, no. 2 (1975)
Brinsmead, Robert D. 'The Gospel Versus the Sectarian Spirit.' *The Bible Examiner* 1, no. 3 (1980): 5–18
Buber, Martin, *Between Man and Man,* trans Ronald Gregor. London: Collins 1947
Campbell, Joseph, ed. *Myths, dreams and Religion.* New York: E.P. Dutton 1970
Cassirer, Ernst. *The Myth of State.* New Haven: Yale University Press [1946] 1967
Cavendish, Richard, ed. *Man, Myth and Magic: An Illustrated Encyclopedia of the Supernatural*, vol 3 ('Bran,' 324). New York: Marshall Cavendish 1970
Cohen, Abner, 'Political Anthropology: The Analysis of Symbols of Power Relations.' *Man* 4, no. 7 (June 1969): 215–35
– 'Political Symbolism.' *The Annual Review of Anthropology* 8 (1979): 87–113

Cox, Harvey. *The Seduction of the Spirit: The Use and Misuse of People's Religion.* New York: Simon and Schuster 1973

De Beauvoir, Simone. *The Ethics of Ambiguity*, trans Bernard Frechtman. Secaucus, NJ: Citadel Press 1948

Eliade, Mircea. *Myths, Dreams, and Mysteries: The Encounter between Contemporary Faiths and Archaic Realities*, trans Philip Mairet. New York: Harper and Row 1960

– *The Quest: History and Meaning in Religion.* Chicago: University of Chicago Press 1969

Festinger, Leon; J. Riecken; and S. Schochter. *When Prophecy Fails: A Social and Psychological Study of a Modern Group That Predicted the Destruction of the World.* New York: Harper & Row 1956

Freed, Josh. *Moonwebs: Journey into the Mind of a Cult.* Toronto: Dorset Publishing 1980

Freire, Paul. *Pedagogy of the Oppressed.* New York: Herder and Herder 1970

Jenkins, Iredell. 'Authority: Its Nature and Locus.' *In Authority: A Philosophical Analysis*, ed R. Baine Harris, 25–44. University, Ala: University of Alabama Press 1976

Kaplan, David. 'The Superorganic: Science or Metaphysics.' In *Anthropology: A Sourcebook*. Chicago: Aldine Publishing 1968

Keen, Samuel. 'The Golden Mean of Robert Assagioli.' *Psychology Today*, December 1974

Kuhn, Thomas A. *The Structure of Scientific Revolutions*. Chicago: University of Chicago Press 1970

Laternari, Vittorio. *The Religions of the Oppressed: A Study of Modern Messianic Cults*, trans Lisa Sergio. New York: New American Library 1963

May, Rollo. *Power and Innocence: A Search for the Sources of Violence*. New York: Norton 1972

Niebuhr, Richard H. *The Social Sources of Denominationalism*. New York: Meridian Books [1929] 1967

Nietzsche, Friedrich. *Will to Power*, trans Walter Kaufmann and R.J. Hollingdale New York: Vintage Books 1968

Ornstein, Robert E., ed. *The Nature of Human Consciousness: A Book of Readings.* San Francisco: W.H. Freeman 1973

– *The Psychology of Consciousness*. New York: Penguin Books 1972

Ouspensky, P.D. *Tertium Organum: A Key to the Enigmas of the World.* New York: Vintage Books [1920] 1970

Rahv, Philip. *The Myth and the Powerhouse.* New York: Farrar, Straus and Giroux [1954] 1964

Rhodes, James M. *The Hitler Movement: A Modern Millenarian Revolution*. Stanford: Hoover Institution Press 1980

Ricoeur, Paul. *The Symbolism of Evil*, trans Emerson Buchanan. Boston: Beacon Press 1967

Rokeach, Milton. *The Open and Closed Mind: Investigations into the Nature of Belief Systems*. New York: Basic Books 1960

Sebeok, Thomas A., ed. *Myth: A Symposium*. Bloomington: Indiana University Press 1972

Tillich, Paul. *The Courage to Be*. London: Collins [1952] 1962

– *Biblical Religion and the Search for Ultimate Reality*. Chicago: University of Chicago Press 1955

Watts, Alan W. 'Western Mythology: Its Dissolution and Transformation.' In *Myths, Dreams and Religion*, ed Joseph Campbell, 9–25, New York: E.P. Dutton 1970

Werkmeister, W.H. 'The Function and Limits of Political Authority.' In *Authority: A Philosophical Analysis*, ed R. Baine Harris, 94–100. University, Ala: University of Alabama Press 1976

Wittgenstein, Ludwig. *Philosophical Investigations*, trans G. Anscombe. Oxford: Blackwell [1953] 1968

WORKS ABOUT JEHOVAH'S WITNESSES

Alberta Report. 'A Heresy Trial in Lethbridge.' 27 February 1980: 22–6

– 'The JWs and the Sacred Blood.' 29 November 1982: 44

– 'Lethbridge's Leader of Dissent.' 8 February 1982: 41–2

– 'Suing Jehovah's Witnesses.' 21 November 1980: 24–6

Beckford, J.A. *The Trumpet of Prophecy: A Sociological Study of Jehovah's Witnesses*. New York: Wiley 1975

Botting, Heather D. 'The Power and the Glory: The Symbolic Vision and Social Dynamic of Jehovah's Witnesses.' Doctoral dissertation, University of Alberta 1982

Burganger, Karl (pseudonym for Carl Olof Jonsson). *The Watch Tower Society and Absolute Chronology: A Critique*. Lethbridge: Christian Fellowships International 1981

Clapp, Rodney. 'The Watchtower Cracks Again: Bible Study Led to the Ouster of a Top Jehovah's Witness.' *Christianity Today*, 19 February 1982: 32

Cohn, W. 'Jehovah's Witnesses as a Proletarian Movement.' *American Scholar* 24 (1955): 281–98

200 **Bibliography**

Czatt, Milton. *The International Bible Students: Jehovah's Witnesses*. New Haven: Yale University Press 1933

Franz, Raymond V. *Crisis of Conscience: The Struggle between Loyalty to God and Loyalty to One's Religion*. Atlanta: Commentary Press 1983

Gruss, Edmund C. *The Jehovah's Witnesses and Prophetic Speculation: An Examination and Refutation of the Witnesses' Position on the Second Coming of Christ, Armageddon, and the 'End of the World.'* Nutley, NJ: Presbyterian and Reformed Publishing Company 1972

Harrison, Barbara Grizzuti. *Visions of Glory: A History and a Memory of Jehovah's Witnesses*. New York: Simon and Schuster 1978

Henschel, Milton G. 'What Are Jehovah's Witnesses?' In *A Guide to the Religions of America*, ed Leo Rosten. New York: Simon and Schuster 1955

Hewitt, Joe. *I Was Raised a Jehovah's Witness: The True Story of a Former Jehovah's Witness*. Denver: Accent Books 1976

Hoekema, Anthony A. *The Four Major Cults: Christian Science, Jehovah's Witnesses, Mormonism, Seventh-Day Adventists*. Grand Rapids: Eerdmans 1963

– *Jehovah's Witnesses*. Grand Rapids: Eerdmans 1963

Jonsson, Carl Olof. *The Gentile Times Reconsidered*. Lethbridge: Hart 1983

Macmillan, A.H. *Faith on the March: My Life of Joyous Service with Jehovah's Witnesses*. Englewood Cliffs, NJ: Prentice-Hall 1957

Ostling, Richard N. 'Ostracized: A Sect Leader Falls.' *Time*, 22 February 1982: 36–41

Penton, M. James. *Jehovah's Witnesses in Canada: Champions of Freedom of Speech and Worship*. Toronto: Macmillan of Canada 1976

Penton, M.J., and Marilyn M. Penton, eds. *The Bible Examiner* 1, no. 1, through 3, no. 1. Lethbridge: Christian Fellowships International 1980–2

Reed, David. *Comments from the Friends* 1, no. 1, through 2, no. 4. Stoughton, ME: Radio Free Watchtower 1982–3

Rogerson, Alan. *Millions Now Living Will Never Die: A Study of Jehovah's Witnesses*. London: Constable 1969

Schnell, William J. *Thirty Years a Watchtower Slave*. Grand Rapids: Baker [1956] 1971

– *Into the Light of Christianity*. London: Marshall, Morgan and Scott 1960

Sheppard, John. 'Lethbridge's Leader of Dissent.' In *Alberta Report*, 8 February 1982: 41–2

Sprague, T.W. 'Some Problems in the Integration of Social Groups with Special Reference to Jehovah's Witnesses.' Doctoral dissertation, Harvard University 1942

Sterling, Chandler W. *The Witnesses: One God, One Victory.* Chicago: Regnery Press 1975

Stevenson, W.C. *Year of Doom, 1975: The Story of Jehovah's Witnesses.* London: Hutchinson 1967

Stroup, Herbert H. *The Jehovah's Witnesses.* New York: Columbia University Press 1945

– *The Jehovah's Witnesses.* New York: Russell and Russell 1967

Watters, Randall. 'What Happened at the World Headquarters of Jehovah's Witnesses in the Spring of 1980?' Manhattan Beach, CA: (privately published) 1981

Whalen, William Joseph. *Armageddon around the Corner: A Report on Jehovah's Witnesses.* New York: John Day Company 1962

White, Timothy. *A People for His Name.* New York: Vantage 1967

Zygmunt, Joseph F. 'Prophetic Failures and Chiliastic Identity.' In *Religion American Style*, ed Patrick H. McNamara. New York: Harper and Row 1974

Newspaper Articles Cited

The Birmingham News. 'When World Didn't End, Doubt Began.' 17 February 1982: 1A

The Calgary Sun. 'Couple Sue to Gain "Spiritual Paradise."' 22 January 1982: 36

The Melbourne Sunday Press. 'Sect Split on Spy Claims: Rebels Hit "Big Brother" Society.' 5 February 1978: 1

Seattle Post-Intelligencer. 'Ex-Jehovah's Witnesses Charge Church Repression.' 28 May 1983: 7

WORKS BY JEHOVAH'S WITNESSES

Authored titles published by International Bible Students Association and the Watch Tower Bible and Tract Society

Russell, Charles Taze. *The Object and Manner of Our Lord's Return.* Pittsburgh 1873

– *Food for Thinking Christians.* Pittsburgh 1881

– *Three Worlds or Plan of Redemption.* Pittsburgh 1887. Written in collaboration with N.H. Barbour

– *Millennial Dawn*. Pittsburgh 1886–1904. In 1904 the title of the series was changed to *Studies in the Scriptures*.

Vol 1: *The Divine Plan of the Ages* 1886

Vol 2: *The Time Is at Hand* 1889

Vol 3: *Thy Kingdom Come* 1891

Vol 4: *The Battle of Armageddon* 1897

Vol 5: *The Atonement between God and Man*

Vol 6: *The New Creation* 1904

Vol 7: *The Finished Mystery* 1917 (published posthumously with amendments)

Rutherford, Joseph Franklin. *'Millions Now Living Will Never Die'* 1920

– *The Harp of God: Proof Conclusive that Millions Now Living Will Never Die* 1921

– *Freedom for the People* 1924

– *Deliverance* 1926

– *Creation* 1927

– *Reconciliation* 1928

– *Government* 1928

– *Prophecy* 1929

– *Light* (2 vols) 1930

– *Preservation* 1932

– *Vindication* (vols 1, 2, and 3 published in 1931, 1932, and 1932 respectively)

– *Preparation* 1933

– *Jehovah* 1934

– *Riches* 1936

– *Enemies* 1937

– *Salvation* 1939

– *Religion* 1940

– *Children* 1941

Unauthored titles published by the Watch Tower Bible and Tract Society

Authorized King James Version of the Bible ('The Watch Tower Bible') 1942

The New World 1942

The Truth Shall Make You Free 1943

A Course in Theocratic Ministry 1943

The Kingdom Is at Hand 1944

Theocratic Aid to Kingdom Publishers 1945

'Let God Be True' 1946 (revised 1952)

Equipped for Every Good Word 1946

'This Means Everlasting Life' 1950

New World Translation of the Christian Greek Scriptures 1950

What Has Religion Done for Mankind? 1951

New Heavens and a New Earth 1953

'Make Sure of All Things' 1953 (revised 1957)

Qualified to be Ministers 1955

You May Survive Armageddon into God's New World 1955

From Paradise Lost to Paradise Regained 1958

Your Will be Done on Earth 1958

Jehovah's Witnesses in the Divine Purpose 1959

New World Translation of the Holy Scriptures 1961 (Revised 1981)

'Let Your Name be Sanctified' 1961

Watchtower Publications Index of Subjects Discussed and Scriptures Explained 1961 and 1966, with addenda for following years

All Scripture Is Inspired of God and Beneficial 1963

'Babylon the Great Has Fallen!' God's Kingdom Rules 1963

Make Sure of All Things; Hold Fast to What Is Fine 1965 (a revised version of *Make Sure of All Things*)

Things in Which It Is Impossible for God to Lie 1965

Life Everlasting in Freedom of the Sons of God 1966

Qualified to be Ministers (revised and expanded) 1967

Did Man Get Here by Evolution or by Creation? 1967

Your Word Is a Lamp to My Foot 1967

The Truth that Leads to Eternal Life 1968

Preaching and Teaching in Peace and Unity 1969

'Then Is Finished the Mystery of God' 1969

Is the Bible Really the Word of God? 1969

Your Word Is a Lamp to My Foot 1971

'The Nations Shall Know that I Am Jehovah'– How? 1971

Listening to the Great Teacher 1971

Theocratic Ministry School Guidebook 1971

Aid to Bible Understanding 1971

Paradise Restored to Mankind – By Theocracy! 1972

Organization for Kingdom-Preaching and Disciple-Making 1972

God's Kingdom of a Thousand Years Has Approached 1973

True Peace and Security – From What Source? 1973

Is This Life All There Is? 1974

God's 'Eternal Purpose' Now Triumphing for Man's Good 1974

Man's Salvation out of World Distress at Hand! 1975

Holy Spirit – The Force behind the Coming New Order! 1976

Good News to Make You Happy 1976
Your Youth: Getting the Best out Of It 1976
Our Incoming World Government – God's Kingdom 1977
One World, One Government, under God's Sovereignty 1975
Making Your Family Life Happy 1978
My Book of Bible Stories 1978
Jehovah's Witnesses in the Twentieth Century 1978
Choosing the Best Way of Life 1979
Commentary on the Letter of James 1979
Happiness – How to Find It 1980
'Let Your Kingdom Come' 1981
You Can Live Forever in Paradise on Earth 1982
Organized to Accomplish Our Ministry 1983
United in Worship of the Only True God 1983

Selected booklets published by the Watch Tower Bible and Tract Society

What Do the Scriptures Say about 'Survival after Death'? 1955
Christendom or Christianity – Which One is 'The Light of the World'? 1955
When God Speaks Peace to All Nations 1959
When All Nations Unite under God's Kingdom 1961
Blood, Medicine and the Law of God 1961
Take Courage God's Kingdom Is at Hand! 1962
When God Is King over All the Earth 1963
What Has God's Kingdom Been Doing since 1914? 1966
Divine Rulership – The Only Hope of All Mankind 1972
Human Plans Failing as God's Purpose Succeeds 1974
Is There a God Who Cares? If so – Why has he permitted wickedness? Will life ever be free of trouble? 1975
One World, One Government, under God's Sovereignty 1975
Unseen Spirits – Do They Help Us? Or Do They Harm Us? 1978
Enjoy Life on Earth Forever 1982
Good News for All Nations 1983
School and Jehovah's Witnesses 1983

Periodicals and Yearbooks published by the Watch Tower Bible and Tract Society

Zion's Watch Tower and Herald of Christ's Presence July 1879–December 1907
The Watch Tower and Herald of Christ's Presence January 1908–October 1931

The Watchtower and Herald of Christ's Presence October 1931–December 1938
The Watchtower and Herald of Christ's Kingdom January 1939–February 1939
The Watchtower Announcing Christ's Kingdom March 1939–
The Golden Age October 1919–September 1937
Consolation October 1937–July 1946
Awake! August 1946–
The Yearbook of the International Bible Students Association 1928–32
The Yearbook 1933
The Yearbook of Jehovah's Witnesses 1934–
Our Kingdom Ministry (a monthly news sheet with several regional editions distributed to publishers by major branch offices; originally called *The Informant*)

MISCELLANEOUS DOCUMENTS CONCERNING THE WITNESSES

'Facts for Shareholders of the Watch Tower Bible and Tract Society' (document prepared as background for the January 1918 internal elections). Brooklyn, NY, 15 November 1917
Transcript of Record: Pursuers Proof in the Case of Douglas Walsh *vs*. The Right Honourable James Latham Clyde, M.P., P.C. as representing the Minister of Labour and National Services [conscription case], in the Scottish Court of Sessions, November 1954
Cassette tape of interview with Randall Watters and Robert Sullivan, 1981

WORKS BY GEORGE ORWELL

'Awake! Young Men of England.' *Henley and South Oxfordshire Standard*, 2 October 1914
Down and Out in Paris and London. London: Gollancz 1933
Burmese Days. London: Gollancz 1934
A Clergyman's Daughter. London: Gollancz 1935
Keep the Aspidistra Flying. London: Gollancz 1936
The Road to Wigan Pier. London: Gollancz 1937
Homage to Catalonia. London: Secker and Warburg [1938] 1941
Coming Up for Air. London: Gollancz 1939
Animal Farm. London: Secker and Warburg [1945] 1949
Nineteen Eighty-Four. New York: Harcourt, Brace and World 1949
Decline of the English Murder and Other Essays. Harmondsworth: Penguin 1965

The Collected Essays, Journalism and Letters of George Orwell, eds Sonia Orwell and Ian Angus. Harmondsworth: Penguin 1970

SELECTED CRITICAL WORKS ON GEORGE ORWELL

Alldritt, Keith. *The Making of George Orwell: An Essay in Literary History*. London: Edward Arnold 1969

Bal, Sant Singh. *George Orwell: The Ethical Imagination*. Atlantic Highlands, NJ: Humanities Press 1981

Crick, Bernard. *George Orwell: A Life*. Harmondsworth: Penguin 1980

Hollis, Christopher. *A Study of George Orwell: The Man and His Works*. London: Hollis and Carter 1956

Kubal, David L. *Outside the Whale: George Orwell's Art and Politics*. Notre Dame, Ind.: University of Notre Dame Press 1972

Lee, Robert A. *Orwell's Fiction*. Notre Dame, Ind.: University of Notre Dame Press 1969

Sandison, Alan. *The Last Man in Europe: An Essay on George Orwell*. London: Macmillan 1974

Smyer, Richard I. *Primal Dream and Primal Scream: Orwell's Development as a Psychological Novelist*. Columbia: University of Missouri Press 1979

Stansky, Peter, and William Abrahams. *Orwell: The Transformation*. London: Granada 1981

– *The Unknown Orwell*. London: Constable 1972

Steinhoff, William. *George Orwell and the Origins of 1984*. Ann Arbor: University of Michigan Press 1976

Updike, John. 'Reflections: Kafka's Short Stories.' *The New Yorker*, 9 May 1983, 121–33 (allusion)

Woodcock, George. *The Crystal Spirit: A Study of George Orwell*. Toronto: Little, Brown 1966

Index